ALL THESE QUIET PLACES

Other Books by Christopher Krzeminski

What Are You Without God?: How to Discredit
Religious Thought and Rebuild Your Identity

I Am: Marco's Anthology

ALL THESE
QUIET PLACES

Written by
Christopher Krzeminski

&

Inspired by actual events recounted by
Jennifer August

CEK Books

Cover Art Direction by Jennifer August
Cover Art Design by Tess Welsh

ISBN-13: 978-0692422724
ISBN-10: 0692422722

For the valiant.

-Jennifer

Foreword
Jennifer August

For the last several years, I have come to understand that my experience with relationship violence is not unique in any way. What has been noteworthy is my response to it. Before I'd even met Victor, I was unwittingly nearing a full-on implosion of all I had believed to be true about myself. During our marriage however, I eventually felt my very essence being scrubbed away. I realized that the only way I would survive and assimilate back into society would be to take complete responsibility for having arrived in that position in the first place. This isn't a popular attitude at this point in time, but it's proven to be quite successful in capturing every goal that I could have possibly hoped. In heading toward a healthy self-concept and true empowerment, I came to understand that practicing accountability builds confidence. If a succession of choices could lead me to near disaster, then it was also true that a succession of different choices could lead me to productive and enjoyable circumstances. I was determined to find the groove that would afford me such an existence. This meant abandoning all of the coping skills I had created and used throughout my life.

First, I had to understand, examine, and finally release the reasons for the use of those skills. Therein lies the 'to blame or not to blame' option. I went with not blaming. Not anyone. Not my mother who has since become everything I ever imagined a mother could be. Not my father who tried to teach me that true strength comes in our moments of vulnerability. A powerful lesson indeed, one that I finally had the guts to learn. Not even Victor was to blame for my having shown up, ready to take whatever he dished out. It had to be me. I was going to own this chaos, and I was going to remove it and anything like it from my life for good. And so, the rigorous process of rebuilding began. I selected specific, healthy behavioral traits with the help of a few therapists and practiced them with vigilance until they became second nature. I held myself accountable for providing anything I needed, practical, emotional, whatever, all of which called for a great deal of perseverance and commitment. It was worth every moment of uncertainty, discomfort, and disorientation. Ever since, I have made decisions that benefit me first, knowing that whomever I choose to have around me will likewise benefit from my happiness.

Domestic violence in evolved societies isn't a gender issue from my perspective. It's a malfunction within the individual, whether focusing on the victim or the perpetrator. This view allows for each person involved to take responsibility for their contribution to the destructive dynamic between them, thus granting the opportunity for each to take full credit for their subsequent recoveries from such experiences should they choose that route. There's your confidence-maker. Empowered, confident individuals do not engage in degenerative behaviors, they contribute to the world around them with enthusiasm. They don't wait for someone to hand them the reins, they grab them and go. This is the philosophy that I landed on and it has served me well.

I've wanted to write this story for some time now and just couldn't seem to grab the right approach. After reading Christopher Krzeminski's first book and discussing pieces of my experience with him, it became obvious to me that he could very well be capable of tackling this messy but worthwhile story. Lucky for us, he agreed. The benefits of excavating this experience alongside Chris are many, and my comprehension of it has expanded beyond anything I could have imagined or expected. It's enough to feel adequate comfort in order to reveal such specific and intimate details, but to trust that my perspective on this piece of my life would be conveyed properly is a testament to the professionalism and true artistry displayed by this book's author. There are no words to which my brain has access that could possibly describe the level of gratitude I have for Chris' commitment to his interpretation of this story as well as his protection of my honor. I am proud of this work and relieved to have finally released this from my intensely guarded mental archives.

Jennifer August

Author's Note
Christopher Krzeminski

As an initial disclaimer, please note that, though this work is inspired by actual events, superficial aspects have been altered. In the interest of the privacy of those depicted as characters, everyone represented in this book has been given pseudonyms in place of their real names, and street and business names have likewise been fictionalized. For artistic purposes, some individuals in the story have been collapsed into one character.

Now, this was a book I never planned to write. In fact, I was preparing a wholly separate concept for book-length treatment when Jennifer and I had a conversation one night in October of 2013. We hadn't been discussing anything of particular consequence during the call, but for some reason, I was curious right then to know the end of a harrowing story in her life, a story that would eventually become the basis for All These Quiet Places. When she filled in the blanks and the complete chain of events washed over me, I said into the phone, "This is a story that writers dream about writing." Ultimately, she chose to give me just that opportunity, and when life hands you a chance like that, you don't question it, you don't second-guess, you don't even wonder how you got to be so lucky, you just get to work before life decides you're an ingrate or a coward or just gets plain sick of waiting on you.

When it came to giving the source material literary treatment, I had only one stipulation: I would not write characters that were pure monsters or angels, and the preservation of the complexity of people was a priority that Jennifer likewise shared. For her to have insisted this part of her life be told exclusively in pure dark or light would have been a readily granted social indulgence, I think, and I find it remarkable that she seemed incapable of accepting such an invitation. Instead, her insistence was on flying the project directly into uncomfortable places, and I fail to see how her wisdom in this regard could be impeached, mainly because I fail to see how it is anything but plain in the grandest of schemes that there are no heroes, no villains, no one so clean as to be above reproach, no one so bathed in filth as to be below empathy, and no final scene where everyone gets what they deserve. Life just does not offer such simplicity, no matter how appealing it may be.

I can look back and say with zero reservation that this project could not have worked without Jennifer's unflinching honesty and forthrightness in describing her life to me in our interviews. I'd like to think that I am capable of such candor, and I don't mean with others, rather myself. From what I witnessed with her driving through embarrassment, trepidation, trauma, anxiety, and whatever else just to accept the truth, honesty of that caliber yields boons of relief and peace, certainly enviable prizes. Such things are gifts we give ourselves, and watching Jennifer push through this process brought it home to me once again that relief and peace are always there waiting in the wings, waiting for us to come and take them, waiting to reward the honest and the bold.

As for my experience writing this book, I can say that I was often anxious, sometimes lost, and always uncomfortable, and with any luck, my disorientation meant that I was close to the heartbeats of the characters and the story. Simply to be given the opportunity to write this book in and of itself was a tremendous honor for me, not only because of my enthusiasm for the story but also because of the confidence it implied in my

ability, and at the absolute minimum, I take with me at the end
remarkable lessons in the emotional control and concentration
needed to delve into the minds of others and attempt to
understand how their behavior makes sense to them.

On that note, I've lived these characters' lives countless
times in the past year, running them through my head over and
over, and I wonder now what I would look like under someone
else's microscope. I wonder if I'd look the way I thought I did.
I wonder if I'd be mocked or condemned or pitied or beloved,
and if the judgments all landed against me, I wonder if I'd have
forfeited being understood by simple virtue of not having been
accepted. I wonder. Don't you?

Christopher Krzeminski

1.

Her eyes drifted over the art prints hanging along the walls. A low sun, hitting the side of a barn sitting in a rolling countryside of meadows and freckled patches of trees. A green and yellow post-impressionist house with cloudy swirls and smudges into an alternate reality. A rusty bicycle left upside-down on its handlebars with its front wheel missing. She felt nothing as she looked at the images, not even enough to be offended by their banality. She looked them over and felt nothing. The prints had just happened to come to rest in her line of sight.

The receptionist at the front desk feigned work with loud, shuffling paper, but Davi knew she was inspecting her on the sly, involuntarily mesmerized by her appearance. By now, she'd learned to recognize the searchlight heat on her skin wherever she went, and those who swept it over her always did the same things to pretend that they weren't. Then, the whispers would come, ranging in tone from titillated, soprano wonder to stormy, baritone disbelief, but what was being said between the hushes wasn't of any significance. No matter what other complaints she had, she had to admit that the meds always came through in that regard.

The door to the nearest office in the hall opened, and a man missing his suit jacket emerged and walked over to the receptionist. Davi tugged her baggy sweatshirt away from her stomach and edged off the seat. Her fingertips drifted up to her neck but fell back down to her lap when they grazed the hardened, raised scabs that had formed there, even though her nails ached to pry their way under them. Restraining the impulse was almost intolerable, leaving her with an itchy, bridled feeling just beneath the surface of her skin.

"Miss Wallace?" the man at the desk asked.

Davi nodded and got to her feet. The man turned to face her with a manila folder he'd collected from the front desk, lightly caressing his fingertips over the transparent, colored tabs that ran down its side. At the threshold to his office, she looked up into his round face and shook his hand.

"You look like you don't know shit. What the hell am I doing here?" she said.

The receptionist looked up from her work and whipped her head in their direction.

"I'm Doctor Mills. I'm a cognitive-behavioral psychologist. You were assigned to me by Doctor Goldstein a few days ago," he answered in overly enunciated words.

It was a rhetorical question, you idiot, she thought.

Mills retreated behind his desk and placed his manila folder on top of it before sitting down. She took a seat in the chair in front of him, dropping her purse and keys on the coffee table along the way. Her chair was facing the wall to his right, but she curled her leg under her and turned to look directly at him. There was nothing to look at on the wall anyway, and considering what the decorators had chosen for the waiting room, plain taupe slapped directly onto the drywall was probably for the best.

"Doctor Goldstein has informed me that you wish to be taken off your prescribed medications, and in order for him to proceed with your wishes, he requires you to have regular visits with me, according to the schedule to which we all agreed," he said, intently focused on the few papers in his folder.

"Yes," she said.

"What medications are you currently prescribed?"

"It's all there in the file."

While his focus was pointed down towards the desk, her eyes groped away at the top of his head, growing more brazen in their staring. She dipped her head to see if the motion in his periphery would draw his attention by reflex, but his fingers just plucked his ballpoint pen off the ink blotter and poised it over the open folder.

"I'd just like you to tell me. It is indeed here in the file."

"Prozac, Depakote, Xanax, Ambien, Risperdal, and Elavil," Davi recited with the ease of her ABC's.

"Why do you want to come off these medications?"

"Because I don't need them," she said.

"I'm sure Doctor Goldstein has explained to you, even if we were to have successful results in our visits, that some of these medications cannot simply be dropped just like that. There needs to be a gradual decrease in these chemicals in your system. Dropping them all at once is unsafe."

"I understand."

"Do these medications make you feel unwell? Any sort of nausea or malaise could—"

"I just don't need them," she said, keeping her monotone.

His pen went to work on his papers, and she began to think he might never look up from them. She'd sensed his tension in their initial handshake, all hurried and damp, but she hadn't expected him to be this different from Goldstein.

"I'd like to ask you some general background questions about yourself. Would that be alright?"

*   *   *

Davi folded her legs under her on the couch while the stereo on the kitchen table blared music through the house. She hugged her abdomen through her sweatshirt, feeling how sweaty her palms had gotten against the sleeves she'd pulled down over them.

Weeks ago, the party had sounded like fun, but sitting in the middle of it, she couldn't relax amidst the drunken hollers and carrying on. The house was dirtier than she was used to as well, the cat hairs all over the couch getting sucked onto her sleeves whenever they brushed against it. If someone hadn't just put The Talking Heads on the stereo, she would have considered trying to find a quiet room upstairs to sleep.

In the other room, a girl with lovely, dark-red hair was leaning against the wall and flirting with an older man in a flannel shirt with dashes of gray in his beard. The girl subtly twisted her hips at clever angles to get his eyes to tilt and tumble down the sides of her, all while smoking a cigarette out of one side of her mouth and grinning with the other half. The older man laughed and grazed his fingers against the red-haired girl's forearm. A small smile inched across Davi's lips, and she wondered if the coy, playful conversation their bodies were having was as obvious to them in the moment as it was to her from her seat on the couch.

Suddenly, the front door flung open with a bang, kicked back off the wall, and shuddered on its hinges. The flirting couple's shimmering hypnotism snapped in the clamor, and Victor flew through the doorway.

"You fucking whore!!"

He grabbed the collar of Davi's sweatshirt, pulling it backwards and down behind the back of the couch. Scraping away at her neck, her fingers fought to claw their way under the fabric to pull away enough space for her airway to draw a breath. Trapped blood throbbed inside her ears, and she began to miss whole frames of what her eyes recorded, splicing black slides into the reel. At a loss for how else to escape, her feet scrambled up onto the cushions to push her whole body over the back of the couch, but before they could find a hold, he grabbed a fistful of her hair and threw her down onto the floor. Her wooden barrette fell out as she tumbled, its metal clasp forking up in the carpet.

On the floor, she coughed and wheezed deeply, desperate to stay conscious, while someone threw himself onto Victor's back only to be bucked right off and sent crashing into a wall of rattling picture frames. She could hear his breath coming in hog snorts above her and kept her head down, going fetal to cover up as much as she could. The punches into her head and kicks planted in her back only registered a dulled, distant pain, but the girl with dark-red hair seemed to feel them. She dropped to her knees and was sick all over the carpeting. The music from the stereo on the kitchen table crept up in volume, the lyrics coming through much clearer without the din of crunching beer cans and laughter to muffle them.

Finally fatigued, Victor stopped the attack just as quickly as it had begun and looked around for the door. His Silverado's oversized engine was still rumbling on the lawn outside. Davi slowly parted her tortoise-shell hands to see if it had all ended, and seeing his back turned and walking away, she rolled over, attempting to get up and into the bathroom. Victor spotted something in the carpet near the door and picked it up. Back on her knees, Davi tried to stretch her back upright when he turned, fired, and struck her in the forehead with her wooden barrette. Half of her vision went black. Blood was pouring into her eye.

*   *   *

"I have six dogs and five cats," she said.

"Mm-hm."

Mills kept scribbling on his papers and shuffling them, just as the receptionist had done, but he didn't have much to say. Yes, she was married. No, she didn't have children. Answers like those needed a checked box or a quick stamp to be memorialized on paper, but he was writing sentences.

"I like cats myself," he said.

"I hate cats," Davi said calmly.

"But you have five of them?"

"My husband likes cats. I'm allergic to them."

"Having so many cats when you're allergic must be difficult. Do you have breathing problems around them?"

She didn't answer. The original agreement between her and Goldstein covered her timely appearance at sessions with Mills, but there were never any stipulations about what she had to say. Since Mills hadn't looked at her through fifteen minutes of background questionnaire, she decided to withhold her response and force his head up to see what she was doing. When he still didn't look up, she smirked, wagering that averting his eyes was no tactic that any university graduate program would have taught him.

"How do you feel about your dogs?"

"I like dogs," she said quickly.

"Mm-hm. But how do you feel about yours?"

She didn't answer and continued to stare, lacing the room with veins of contempt. His pen kept tapping on the paper, and he seemed resigned to silently moving on from the questions she refused to field. With her head turned to the side to stare at him, some of her hair had been brushing against her face. She grabbed a blue plastic clip out of her purse and curled the bothersome strands back over her ear. She clipped them in place on the white streak by her temple and smoothed her hands over the sides of her head, chafing at the waste of time these visits were going to be. While she wasn't foregoing spectacular opportunities for stimulation back at home, she might have at least been getting valuable sleep or taking care of the pets instead of adding a new chore to the lot, this time with some turnkey toting a tone-deaf bedside manner.

Eventually, his questions shifted into the subject of suicidal thoughts, and she made sure that none of those slid by with ambiguous silence. Those were the ones not to get wrong or ignore. One thing that Goldstein had made very clear was that the rules would change between them if they ever considered her to be a risk of harm to herself, and Mills seemed to notice her increased attentiveness to those questions, perking up a bit in his chair at the prospect of crisp cooperation. She wondered if he would wilt back down again once he realized that his next topic change had brought back the silence.

The clock ticks made everything drag, and the end of their first session couldn't come quickly enough. As she waited for the office door to spring open and turn her loose, Davi simply stared at him and answered when she felt like it. She stared and relished his avoidance. She stared and commanded his eyes to look away.

*   *   *

On her knees, Davi gripped onto a hardy weed and wrenched it back and forth until it finally broke free. Its roots brought a thick clump of earth with them that fell to pieces, cascading down the sides of the plastic bag as she stuffed it inside. To her delight, the weeding was churning up a rich topsoil smell alongside the deep, satisfying popping of the roots. She rubbed her sleeve across her nose to brush away a drop of sweat hanging on the end, and the musky scent of Calvin and Monty filled her nostrils. With the seasons changing, they needed to get baths and be groomed soon, before their shedding winter coats stuck to all of her clothes.

Shuffling over to the yellow squash, she smiled over her shoulder to see the Parsons from next door speaking with Victor and admiring the lawn from the driveway. Victor stood and nodded with each word, beaming with pride as though every comment wound up funneling into the same disbelief as to how he'd managed to get plain old grass to look so vibrant, uniform, and handsome. With a beer in hand, he squatted on the driveway in front of them and lightly patted the top of the lawn with his palm, demonstrating how none of the blades jabbed his hand on their own before they all did together.

The satisfaction he got from manicuring the lawn was beyond Davi. In her garden, eggplants, red onions, and pumpkins were all growing side by side, and each plant gave off its own unique aroma, had its own personality. In his lawn, the smell of the grass was hardly noticeable unless it had just been cut and even then only one-note. When the fruits of her labor were ready to be picked, they were fit to eat whereas Victor's immaculate lawn could only ever result in a showpiece. Still, she loved the fact that, between the two of them, the whole property looked wonderfully kept and downright alive by the middle of spring.

She shuffled to her left towards the zucchini and dropped the plastic bag. Leaning over the ring of marigolds surrounding the garden, she reached for a clump of weeds growing against the side of the house and felt a sensation of eyes on her as she grabbed them. She looked to the front yard. Victor and the Parsons were gone.

In the corner of her eye, she spotted a shadow on the ground by her side. Turning even more, she saw the front toe of Victor's boot and smiled up at him, but even though he was staring at her, he didn't acknowledge her seeing him. His lips were parted, and his eyes were somewhere else entirely, as though in a hypnotic state beyond conscious processing.

"Everything okay?" Davi asked.

Reflexively, he nodded, snapping back to the present by having to respond to the question. She nodded and chuckled to herself.

"The lawn really looks great, babe," she said.

"Damn right," he said, smiling.

Her hands reached out again for the clump of weeds growing against the side of the house, anxious to hear their roots sing their popping, percussive song. As she jerked her arm to pull them loose, the sensation of being watched dissipated. While she wasn't sure he had gone back inside, she didn't want to turn around to check.

*   *   *

Mills checked his watch and let out a long sigh. His scrawling notes poured onto several pages that he kept flipping between his fingers. Davi imagined that their general thrust was something along the lines of 'Patient overwhelming to practitioner, recommend removal from all medications without further visits.' The thought of his surrender made her squirm in her seat. She stuck a finger inside the collar of her sweatshirt to move the fabric off her throat.

"Well, that's about the full time for our first session," he said, still aimlessly flipping through the papers.

"Good."

"I will be conferring with Doctor Goldstein as we proceed, updating him on the progress that we make. As the psychiatrist on your case, he will be the one making determinations with respect to when and how to alter your medications."

"I know."

"Alright then," he said.

He closed his folder at last and dropped his pen on top of it with a thump. As he opened the door for her, his eyes finally reestablished contact with hers.

"I will see you in one week, yes?"

"Fine," she said, shaking his hand out of a kneejerk sense of civility.

"See you then, Miss Wallace. Please make an appointment with Janice before you leave."

Davi walked over to the front desk and carelessly swung her purse up onto it where it slid partway over the edge and hit the back of Janice's computer monitor. Janice looked up at her with a smile that crossed attempted graciousness with smelling a piece of rotten food.

"Same time next week?" Davi asked.

"That'll be fine," she said.

"Okay."

Davi swept her purse onto her shoulder and headed out the main doors. Pulling out a cigarette, she shaded her eyes with her hand and found her way to a bench under a tall elm in front of the office building where, even under its branches, the sun was too strong for her. If she wasn't worried about somehow missing her ride home, sitting and smoking with her eyes closed would have made the most sense, but she wanted to keep a lookout for Kerry's car. Besides, the faster she saw it, the faster she could get back.

Squinting was making her eyes water, and when she closed them completely for a break from the sunlight, tears released all down her face, frantic to relieve the itchy burning. Her nose started to run, and she wiped it across the underside of her sleeve. How ridiculous she would've looked had she worn mascara, but since she hadn't, she sat back on the bench, drew on her cigarette with her eyes closed, and let the tears stream down her cheeks in peace.

A purring engine turned into the spot right in front of her and idled. One of its automatic windows rolled down.

"Davi, it's me."

"Hey, Ker," Davi said, stubbing out her cigarette under the bench and blindly flinging it onto the grass.

"Didn't you see me pull in right in front of you? You didn't even react," Kerry asked once Davi had gotten into the car.

"I had my eyes closed."

"Hey, have you been crying?"

"No, it's just allergies," Davi said, sniffling. "Just didn't have a tissue on me."

"Well, here. For God's sake. How can you not carry a few tissues on you?" Kerry asked.

Davi blotted the streams of tears off her cheeks and blew her nose. She slid forward in the seat, and the car's leather beneath her resonated like a cello string.

"So, where's your car again?"

"Victor needed it today. His is in the shop," Davi said.

"Is it anything serious?"

"Just needs new shocks. His were worn out from driving into the woods so much over the years."

They came to a stop light, and Kerry dropped her visor to check her makeup in the mirror. After puckering her lips, she popped the lipstick tube out of her purse and reapplied. When the light turned green with her lips still unfinished, Kerry took her foot off the brake, and the car rolled forward into the intersection. Davi grabbed the side of the wheel and held it straight, until Kerry finally blotted and pushed the visor flat against the roof.

"Thanks. By the way, have I told you about Danny?"

"I don't think so," Davi said, inhaling another wet sniffle.

"When my mother passed away last year, I needed some questions answered about her will, and a friend of mine recommended this guy named Dan Eaton. He was a good lawyer, very impressive, but little do I suspect, the guy's like a dream. Fabulous hair and great teeth."

The car fell silent. Davi cracked open the corner of her eye and looked over at Kerry.

"Well, what about him?"

"Nothing really. Just sprang to mind," Kerry said.

*   *   *

Davi rubbed her eyes and yawned. The parts of her arms that she'd left above the covers as she slept were frigid to the touch. The morning temperature had to be way below freezing, considering how the crystalline frost in the corners of the window pane sparkled with only the streetlight hitting them.

Grumbling, she peeled the quilt back and kicked her feet over the side. For a second, she teetered backwards with her eyes half-closed as though to lie down again but then exploded forward, all the way onto her feet. Calvin was curled into a ball with his nose tucked under his tail at the end of the bed, and she leaned over and kissed him on the head as she passed.

In the hallway on the way to the bathroom, savory egg and coffee floated into her nose and lifted her eyes open. She turned back and dragged her feet to the kitchen where breakfast was nearly ready, waiting for her on the island. Victor must have just finished the eggs with the way the steam was barreling off the top of them, and the sausage smelled like it was ready to come off the range next. Her stomach growled lustfully, but she went over to his back to hug him from behind before she sat down to eat.

"Thanks, babe. Everything smells amazing," she said.

"You're welcome," he said, sliding the sausages out of the skillet and onto their plate on the island.

Back at the sink, Victor ran water over his used pans, hissing steam on contact. She sipped her coffee and looked over his broad frame, wondering how much extra time she could spare before her shower before realizing that he still had to do all the breakfast dishes before he went to work. He was never able to leave anything unwashed in the sink, and even if that habit was going to work against her this morning, Davi wasn't about to complain about his obsession with cleanliness. In terms of her dating history, he was a rare sort of man that way, often rumored to be extinct.

"I like the way your hair looks today," she blurted.

"Really? Thanks," he said with a chuckle.

With each sip, the coffee warmed her up a little more, and she noticed the clock on the wall read twenty after seven, a full half hour later than she expected. She gobbled down her pile of eggs, chewed through a sausage, and headed to brush her teeth. At this rate, there wasn't even time to shower.

"You have to leave soon, don't you?" Victor yelled from the kitchen.

"Yea, I'b ruddie lay," she yelled back with her toothbrush in her mouth.

The faucet in the kitchen sink turned off, and the front door opened and closed. Davi threw on the nearest warm clothes, scooped up her books and waitress uniform, and rushed to the door. Victor was at the sink, and Calvin was milling around the couch looking for a new spot to sleep.

"Hey, do you know where my keys are?" she asked, looking over at the rack by the door as she stuffed her arms into her coat.

"They're in the car. I just ran out and turned it on so it would heat up," he said.

He opened the door for her, and she yelped as a cold blast of air slammed into her face. At the car, he opened the door again, and she wrapped her arms around his waist and kissed him before jumping into the toasty Legacy. Her uniform and books bounced onto the passenger seat, and she slammed the door behind her as fast as she could to keep out the cold. Outside, he smiled and waved goodbye through the window. She kissed her fingertips and pushed them against the glass, and he did the same against the freezing exterior. The Legacy reversed down the icy driveway, and Victor jogged back into the house to finish cleaning the breakfast dishes before work.

2.

Davi tapped her foot up and down on the carpet, the soft sound of her sneaker cutting the waiting room's stagnancy just enough to bear. Janice had been curt with her when she'd checked in at the front desk and was now occasionally glaring at her across the room. Mills must have commiserated with her about how rude Davi had been in their first meeting, or perhaps Davi had been unwittingly short with her the previous week. Whatever Janice's problem was, she seemed deeply bothered. As far as Davi was concerned, Janice ought to be content to feel any emotion and leave it at that.

Mills opened his office door, and Davi shot to her feet before he could call her name. The precious seconds she spent walking into his office counted in the tally of how long she had to be in the setting altogether.

"How was your week, Miss Wallace?" Mills asked, closing the office door behind her.

"Hey, Mills," she said.

"I'd rather that you not call me by just my last name. 'Doctor' or 'Doctor Mills' is what I prefer."

She shrugged, content with the inevitability that she would continue to refer to him as 'Mills' and that he would continue to

15

put up with it. He took his spot behind the desk, and she sat in her same chair facing the wall, this time without turning around in it.

"So, I'd like you to tell me about your dogs," he said.

...

"Are you quite fond of them?"

"I already said I love dogs last time," she said.

"You have six?"

"Five."

He paused and flipped backwards through his notes.

"You told me last time that you had five cats but six dogs," he said.

"There was an incident recently, and one of them was killed," she said, her eyes canvassing the blank wall.

"I'm awfully sorry to hear that. Would you like to tell me what happened?"

"Sure, Mills. I'll tell you all about it."

He took a long breath, dripping in irritation. Davi shook around in the chair to settle in and get comfortable.

"I was walking out to the mailbox, sending a letter. We have this big bay window on the front of the house, and the dogs all line up there to watch me when I'm outside, one next to the other. I looked back as I was walking out, and they all were there in their usual place. Nothing unusual. But after I'd put the flag up on the mailbox and turned around, they were all gone. Just that fast."

Mills lips tightened as though he wanted to interject with a question but reconsidered, now having successfully gotten her to speak more than a few words at a time.

"I get back to the house, open the door, and I see this trail of blood all over. A few of them were sitting there looking at me, which was weird because they're always excited to see me.

They would never just sit and stare like that. So, I followed the trail to the other room, and there was Henry, dead on the floor. Torn to shreds. Blood everywhere."

Mills shifted in his seat and jotted something down.

"He was always aggressive with the other dogs. Dominant, I guess. He must have done something to make one of the others snap at him, which must have broken skin and drawn blood. A pack of dogs, the smell of blood, an unstable personality. From there, it's just straight biology, isn't it?"

"I see. How did you feel when you—"

"Henry was a Bichon Frisé, which are all white dogs, so I could see the blood all over his fur. He was torn wide open too. There were tendons and arteries hanging out of his throat, and he was all red. He was a white dog, but when I found him, he was all red with bits of his insides in his fur."

"You must have been devastated," he said.

She shrugged, and Mills nodded imperceptibly. Davi had recounted her story with her usual cyborg intonation, not bothering to look away from the wall even once, and only now that she had stopped talking could she feel Mills staring into her cheek with gull eyes, probing for that one right seam.

*   *   *

Her boots crunched through the underbrush without any trouble, but avoiding the invisible twigs that raked her across the face in the pitch black was slowing her down. On top of that, her hamstring was still throbbing from that misgauged step she'd trusted to land on solid ground but that had instead slid on a little stream of water running over mud.

By comparison, Victor and Hank moved effortlessly through the terrain, and the distance between them and her kept opening, in spite of her angry demands for them to slow up the pace. Ordinarily, they wouldn't have taken her out hunting with them and hadn't this time either. They had gone out of their way to leave their kill, pick her up at the house, and come all the way back.

Davi ducked under a branch thick enough to see coming in the black woods, and suddenly, silk strands pressed against her face with micro-tension. Little legs scurried across her neck, then down onto her hand, and the web's strength broke, collapsing onto her face and hair. She backpedaled and fell seated onto the rotting log she'd just climbed over.

"Son of a bitch!" she shouted, frantically slapping her clothes all over.

"Yep, here she is," Hank said to Victor, both of them in front of Davi by a good fifty feet.

"Davi, catch up already. It's just up here," Victor yelled back to her while sweeping his headlamp over the path they'd taken.

"I can't see a goddamn thing!" she shouted in frustration.

"Just follow where my lamp is pointed. It's right on where you need to go," he said.

"Absolutely ridiculous," she grumbled, hurrying to catch up while the little rays that made it through the overgrowth still lit the way.

Breaking into the tiny clearing where Hank and Victor were waiting, she caught her breath and pulled the last bits of web off her face. The doe seemed a decent size under the headlamps, even though Davi had never wrapped her mind around how deer could look so much smaller on their sides than standing up. Had she been there when they'd taken the shot, the doe probably would have looked like a record-breaker through the scope. Down on the ground now however, she seemed more like a crushed insect, her long, thin legs unnaturally curled and frozen.

Hank unsheathed the knife on his hip and slapped it into her hand while Victor lit a joint and puffed. Hank knelt down next to the doe and pulled its back legs away from its body.

"You're gonna stick her right through here and then cut all the way up through her belly. Keep your cut shallow at first, so you don't pop her bladder or cut through the intestines. Just break the hide," Hank said.

She considered asking why she was the one that had to do the cleaning but instead clenched the knife with purpose, opting to get the job done and get back to civilization as quickly as possible, but as soft as the white fur on the doe's belly looked, the hide was tough to cut without driving the knife deep into the body cavity. Frustrated, Davi shouldered Hank out of her way so she could get a better angle. Victor chuckled and passed Hank the joint.

"Okay, now you've got it started," Hank said. "Get your fingers inside that opening you made and pull the hide towards you. That'll give you some tension. Just watch your damn fingers."

Warm blood was spilling out all over her left hand while her right stayed pristine, safely away from the mess as it worked the knife handle. When she reached the sternum, the blade lodged in thick cartilage, and Hank knelt back down to hold the upper half of the doe steady.

"Really lean into it now. Saw it," he said.

For that kind of exertion, she liked her leverage better on her feet and began to throw her whole weight back and forth against her hands to make the blade move. Finally, the knife reached up into the doe's chest, and Hank gestured in a wave that that was good enough.

"Alright, good job," Hank said, ripping his knife out of the doe and wiping the blade on its back. "Now, get your hands in there and feel around for the heart and lungs."

"Just jam both my hands in there? I don't even know what they feel like."

Hank looked up from the doe and at Davi, his headlamp blinding her. She wiped the sweat off her face and squinted back at him.

"Well, you got a better plan?" he asked.

*   *   *

"Is it time to leave yet?"

"No, you still have twenty more minutes," Mills said.

"Well, I don't have anything else to say."

"Would you like to talk any more about Henry?"

"No."

She crossed her arms and rested them on her belly. Telling Mills anything of substance was already a departure from the blueprint, but she'd been feeling impulsive and antsy the last few days. Hearing her own voice speak was only meant to provide a break from the sterile vacuum of the office and its tedious trappings.

"I see. Well, this sort of therapy isn't for everyone, Miss Wallace. It's certainly not for the faint of heart."

Her ears pricked up at his tone, vaguely dismissive and condescending.

"We can sit here in silence and waste twenty minutes. That's no problem at all. Besides, I don't think you have what it takes to go as deep as we would need to in this process to get anything done. That's just my opinion. I suppose we'll never really know."

She smirked on the left side of her mouth, the side that Mills couldn't see from his desk. Trying to get a rise out of her might have worked had he not laid it on so thick, but with his ulterior motive telegraphed, she remained expressionless. She didn't have to say a word to achieve her goals. What she wanted out of the office complex was only a function of time, and while she sat and ran out the clock, he was the one who was going to have to take the risks.

"Twenty minutes. More like eighteen now. Do you know what time is, Miss Wallace?"

...

"Time is a collection of opportunities. And you just missed twenty of them," he said.

She sat stoically, restraining the urge to roll her eyes, which would surely only encourage him to keep speaking.

Mills dropped his gaze from her and began to scribble on his papers, his pen striking the page with a distant, little click whenever he began a new word or dotted an 'i'. With each new click, her fingers clenched deeper into the armrests. She knew he couldn't possibly be writing anything salient. Her brief story about poor Henry couldn't have made for more than a line or two of commentary. Yet there he was in the corner of her eye, clicking away, shuffling papers with his tie wobbling back and forth, getting by on appearances.

*   *   *

"I don't know if I want to see too much of this place," Davi said.

"We won't have to wander around anywhere. Max said they're keeping the ones they're looking to get rid of in the office," Victor replied.

The desolate country road was so pockmarked with potholes as to seem abandoned. Even the Silverado with its heavy-duty suspension had to slow down and swerve around some of the bigger ones.

"You can tell they put a lot of money into this place," he said, slowly dancing the truck through the moonscape.

Picking out their third dog had been on her mind for days, specifically what sort of personality would mesh with the established dynamic that she, Calvin, and Monty already had. Whichever one she chose needed to match the laidback attitudes of yellow Calvin and black Monty, Labs who both had their breed's characteristic heartwarming friendliness. She was confident in her ability to choose well and wisely, but the possibility of somehow making a mistake made her stomach shimmy. Returning a dog to these circumstances for any reason was too unsavory to contemplate.

The potholes lessened, and the trees gradually opened in front of them into a vast clearing where a sour, squashed office building sat at the beginning of a field, at the end of the road. With the truck back on reasonably flat track, Davi could finally release the crushing grip she'd had on the handle above her window. She took a deep breath and let it out slowly. Victor parked and turned off the engine, and her heart skipped a beat at the sound of unseen dogs, frantically yelping somewhere in the distance.

"Okay, I'll find someone at the office. You want to wait here?" he asked.

"No, I'll go in with you," she said, yanking her door handle open.

The barking was much louder outside where the echoes through the expanse were no longer scrubbed out by the Silverado's frame, and all the racket seemed to be coming from just behind a bend in the forest line. Davi cinched her jacket together around her neck and jogged towards the office to get out of the bitter cold. Victor reached the door first to hold it open for her and then followed her inside.

At the side of the counter, a husky woman with wind-whipped, tied-back hair and a dirty Redskins sweatshirt was clipping some papers together. From the clumps of dried mud on her boots and the deep red color in her cheeks, she looked to have just stopped into the office for a break from the cold herself.

"Hi, a friend of my husband's told us you guys were getting rid of some of your older dogs. We were looking to pick one up," Davi said.

"Yeah, just right in the next room there. There's about eight of them lined up against the wall. Let me know which one you pick," she answered, not looking up from what she was doing.

Plastic and metal started to click and clink as soon as Davi walked into the room the woman had indicated. The pet carriers shook on their long display tables, the dogs inside getting to their feet and pressing their noses against the grated doors. One Dachshund began screaming at them in piercing, high-pitched yelps and wouldn't stop, even when she came to put her hand in front of his nose. Victor covered his ears as he passed.

"Anyone but him," he said.

In the last crate, a Bichon Frisé wasn't making a sound, huddling himself into the back corner. His fur was oily and matted down, and a fresh scar wound its way through his whiskers on the right side of his face. Even though it looked to be completely healed, the fur there hadn't yet begun to grow back.

"What happened to the white one's face?" Davi yelled back into the main office.

The woman at the counter poked her head into the room to see which dog Davi meant.

"He started rubbing his face against the fencing all the time. Like a boredom thing or something," she said.

Davi held her palm up to the front of his cage, and although he looked over, he didn't get up. She popped open the lock and held her hand out for him to smell. His face reached towards it and licked once in its direction. When she reached in further and touched the back of his head to pet him, the muscles in his back tensed up visibly, and she lifted her hand off to let him calm down. On the side of his mouth, his scar made a jagged 'J' shape through his pink skin, and she wondered if it had been treated properly or just left to heal on its own. His dark black eyes looked over at hers, and slowly, he got to his feet and walked to the crate's threshold. Sniffing at her fingertips, he sat down, his front legs quivering under him. When her fingers softly slid back onto his head, he popped his head up to poke her under the forearm with his wet nose.

"This one," she said.

*   *   *

Pulling into the growing rush hour traffic ought to have been another rote task in a world stitched together by them, but she felt unsettled entering the flow of eager commuters, all pushing against one another to get home the fastest. Unsettled and hurried. Then again, those same two feelings had been chasing her around for days, inexplicably popping up at times when tension and anxiety didn't make any sense. No matter what she was doing, she just couldn't shake the feeling of a tailwind driving her along at a speed far faster than she herself would ever have chosen to go.

As uncomfortable as they made her, the sensations were still wholeheartedly welcome, delivering proof positive that the Novocain shroud that had settled over her for the last couple of years was cracking, and even if what seeped through was only darkness, at least it brought with it implications of motion. If nothing else, she could now look at the other commuters and feel how much she hated them being right on top of her instead of the horrendous distance that came from seeing only lifeless wooden blocks and mannequins where people like her were supposed to be.

But something was definitely wrong. Her mind was racing around like a bullet rattling inside her skull, and her jaws were locking up from her having clenched them without noticing. She was accustomed to never sleeping at night, but even her predictable drowsiness during the day no longer came, leaving her body feeling progressively more achy and exhausted as her mind buzzed along with irresistible impulses for more and more speed. Then, she remembered.

In the last week, Goldstein had lowered the dosages of the anti-psychotics. Whatever he'd done had to be the heart of the matter, not because she had the expertise to explain it but because the rest of the picture was so utterly static. Doubtlessly, Mills would have relished the thought of her acceleration, an opportunity to take credit for his having generated a reaction with his questions, but to her mind, this had to be about basic clockwork and how certain gears were now getting more grease than they knew what to do with. She decided to call Goldstein himself the next morning to let him know what was happening.

The light in front of her turned red for the third time since she'd been in line, and someone a few cars back honked his horn. Out her window, Davi spotted a placard in front of a medical office that read "Dr. Priya Holland, DDS" and "Cosmetic and Reconstructive Dental Care" in smaller lettering just beneath the name. She ran her tongue over the gap in her teeth on the right side and repeated the phone number over and over in her head until she could get home to a pen and paper.

*   *   *

On the kitchen island, the roast chicken was still emanating steamy puffs of savory lemon, a happy marriage of sweet and sour. Davi reached over her plate for another scoop of the green bean casserole in the heavy Pyrex dish. The casserole had turned out well, but she'd prepared far too much of it and made a mental note to halve the proportions next time. Victor stabbed his fork down into some green beans and shoveled them into his mouth. On the TV in the other room, an episode of Seinfeld covered their silence with background noise.

She took a sip of Diet Coke and looked around for her boys. Slick, her Doberman, was lying at her feet next to the island and occasionally looking up to gauge his chances of being fed some of the roast chicken. Her chocolate Lab, Zeke, was sitting on the couch getting playfully smacked on the nose by one of the cats. He opened and closed his mouth with deliberate futility, taking soft retaliatory bites in the direction of her swatting paw.

Suddenly, motion in her periphery made her grip the edge of the island out of reflex, and Victor's fist blitzed into her cheek, spraying everything with a fuzzy, black mist as her ears rang from the impact. Slick sat up on his hindquarters, confused as to what had just happened and inspecting her with concerned, protective eyes. A howl of pain trapped in her throat oozed out as a slow groan as she winced into her hand. A metallic taste flooded her mouth, and something hard was rattling around, blocking her jaws from closing together. She spit her bicuspid into her palm.

Victor's knife and fork continued to clink against the plate while Davi hurried to the bathroom. At the mirror, she pulled her lip back to see the gaping hole in her smile, her surrounding white teeth dipped in red watercolor.

"You're not your body. You're your mind," she whispered into the mirror as a rogue tear escaped down her cheek.

Tipping her hand, she watched her tooth fall into the waste basket with the tissue paper, and her tongue began to involuntarily explore its former place, finding sharp edges and unfamiliar sensations. In the other room, the studio audience on the TV laughed with delight as she turned the faucet and washed the blood out of her mouth. She resisted the urge to look back into the mirror.

Coming out of the bathroom, she pressed her hand against her throbbing cheek. Victor looked up at her and scoffed, dropping his utensils and retiring to the other room to smoke. She went over to the island and collected the used plates, placing them in the sink.

Victor sparked a lighter and drew deeply on his bong, making the water bubble down at the base. As Davi ran the water over the plates, he turned up the volume on the TV and the studio audience's laughter rose with it. She squirted a line of soap down the middle of the sponge and started to wipe away the leftover grease. If only she hadn't used the entire bag of frozen green beans for the casserole, she could've pushed the rest against her face now to keep down the swelling.

3.

"God, I hate that thing," he said.

Victor shrank away from the front of the terrarium. The ball python had been a gift from an ex-girlfriend years earlier, and he had never gotten rid of it. Once a month, he would throw a mouse or two into the glass case with it, immediately clapping the lid back on as quickly as he could. He certainly never touched the snake or took it out. He'd never even bothered to name it. The python just writhed around the twisted branch that kept it company and ate whatever it was given.

"Well, you'll be glad to be rid of it then, right?" Davi asked.

"Absolutely."

"Why did you keep it so long if you're afraid of it?"

"I don't know. I just never wanted to think about it at all, not even to give it away," he said, inching towards the doorway.

She wrapped tape from the lid of the terrarium all the way around the bottom and back up again to ease Victor's mind that the python wouldn't have a chance of getting loose during the car ride. She tested the lid in front of him to show that it had virtually no play to it and that the snake would be as secure and sealed away as it could be during the drive to the pet store.

"Okay, I'm going to pick it up once I get it covered," she said. "Make sure everyone's out of the way when I come through."

Victor left the room to corral the dogs, and she threw open a beach towel to drape over the terrarium. Before she covered the glass, she bent down to look at the python's face. The snake had curled into a knotted ball, agitated by the ripping tape and unusual attention. Surrounded by its coiled body, its head hid under the miniature shadow cast by the branch and flashed its forked tongue in rhythm with her breaths. Davi could see how scared and uncomfortable it was, but this was for the best. Surely, it both deserved and could have a better home.

"I'm coming out. Clear a path."

She walked into the living room with her arms under the terrarium, holding it up and against her chest. Overcome with curiosity, the dogs pressed against Victor's outstretched legs and arms to see what Davi was doing, but the extra weight she was carrying made her steps unusually heavy. As she passed in front of them and through the living room, the vibrations that her feet created as they thumped against the floor made them think twice and sit back.

Outside, she placed the box in the back seat of the Legacy and fastened a seat belt around it for Victor's sake. For any other trip, his truck would have been the natural choice, but without a back seat, the terrarium would have had to sit next to them up front, nearly guaranteeing that he would get into an accident at the sound of the first pop in the plastic lid or rattle in the glass. He closed the passenger door and took a deep, long breath as she started the car.

"You okay?"

"Let's just get to the store. I'll relax when it's all the way gone," he said, rubbing his palms on his jeans.

Davi looked over her shoulder as she backed out of the driveway and quietly shook her head at the package buckled in, shrouded, and taped shut, all to secure a python so accustomed to its box that it would have slithered around in its shattered glass before ever even considering leaving it behind.

*   *   *

"So, how was everything for you this week, Davi?"

...

Hopeful that she was getting comfortable with him and the office, Mills leaned onto his forearms and studied her in her chair, now turned to face his desk. The session had only just begun, but she was already tired of his doughy face.

Earlier in the week, she had met with Goldstein and Mills together to address her sleepless, draining hyperactivity, and Goldstein had taken it as a good sign that perhaps she was overmedicated or incorrectly diagnosed from the beginning. Considering the previous adjustment he'd made to her medications, Goldstein had determined that the relatively unaltered levels of antidepressants, which would have lifted a depressed person into a normal level of arousal, had been blasting her into a state of mania. With his latest correction to compensate, she had been calming down, and he'd assured her that that trend would only continue.

"I hope you understand that this office is a place where you can talk about anything that you like, Davi. Doctor Goldstein and I are in constant communication about what we would like to see for you, and legally and ethically speaking, you have privileges of confidentiality with us."

He was saying her first name in a way that made her bristle, and she noticed he was linking himself to Goldstein as he tried to convince her to speak. He must have noticed how much more open and compliant she'd been with Goldstein at their meeting and planned to siphon off some of that respect for the sake of his own rapport. She plucked a tissue out of the box and blew her nose to occupy herself. She wadded it up and dropped it on the table beside her.

"We can talk about anything you like. It doesn't have to be about you necessarily. I know that Henry was a big loss, and while I'd like to talk about that some more, I'll listen to anything under the sun that you'd like to say. Your favorite music? What are some of the things you enjoy?"

One downside of her increasing lucidity was that tuning him out was no longer so easy, and with as much as he'd been talking since she'd sat down, her patience was running low. Then, he had to go and bring up Henry again. As she suspected would happen, he had fashioned the only story she'd shared with him into a crowbar, prying away to see what other treasure chests of hers might have rusty, obsolete locks.

Mills adjusted his tie and combed his fingers back through his black hair, pushing it off his forehead.

"Listen, Davi. I think—"

Drawing a long breath, Davi spiked her elbow into the arm of the chair and raised her middle finger at him. He cut off his sentence with a double take, and his lips pressed together and flattened. She left her finger up, looking into his eyes with no-vacancy brusqueness, and Mills sat back a bit and picked up his pen. He dropped his other hand on the ink blotter, tumbling his fingers down onto it in a brief cascade of soft taps. Then, he was still, and they each sat and stared at the other, frozen for one perfect moment in time.

*   *   *

She took a huff on the inhaler and coughed, the airways in her chest tingling all the way back open to where she felt like she could even stand up straighter from the difference. Raking the cat litter in the laundry room had been kicking up a cloud of stench into her face that made her throat close, her breath thinner, and she could only deduce that the cats must have been especially busy that afternoon. She dropped the inhaler back in its junk drawer in the kitchen and headed back to the laundry room.

Through the glass in the back door, she studied her boys playfully chasing each other through the backyard in small, half-hearted bursts between breaks sniffing the grass and air. Slick seemed a good match for the other dogs, especially Smokey, her Chesapeake Bay Retriever, who was following him all around the yard and sniffing the places he sniffed. The others were content to ignore him, comfortable enough to flop onto the yard and roll around with him in their midst. By the far corner of the tall cedar fence, Zeke barked at Calvin who launched after him for a few yards only to stop, bark back once, and let his tongue hang out of his grinning mouth, dripping necklaces of saliva.

Pacing methodically amongst them, Victor was finishing his inspection of the lawn, canvassing the grass to see if there were any dog squats Davi might have missed. She looked down to knot the handles of the plastic bag she'd used to clean the cat litter, knowing that he wouldn't find a thing with how she'd scoured the yard, and just like that, the dogs' paws hurried onto the concrete patio alongside his boots. When she looked back through the door, Victor had an irritated look on his face as he approached, the dogs crowding around his legs and pressing against them for better position in the race to be the first one back inside.

Victor reached for the handle to the screen door but then instantly whipped around, shoving Slick away from his legs while Smokey raised his ears on his head. Seemingly without reason, he reached back and punched Slick straight in the chest, sending him reeling backwards, onto his side, into the grass. Whimpering and disoriented, Slick cowered on the ground as the other dogs dispersed away from Victor and the door.

Davi's eyes went liquid with rage, and before she knew what she was doing, she had thrown the door open, burst outside, and planted her fist in Victor's chest, knocking him onto his back on the concrete. Standing over him, she breathed in uncontrolled heaves, her heart slamming against its rib bars, demanding to be let out. She ran over to Slick and laid down in front of him, her hands probing his chest to see if anything hurt him. He rolled onto his side in front of her.

"Are you okay?" she whispered, cradling his head in her hands.

His shortened tail beat applause into the grass, and Victor clutched his chest, laid on the patio, and laughed.

*   *   *

The clock on the wall ticked away while Davi kept her posture petrified. Her arm propped up with middle finger extended, long streaks of white running through the sides of her dark hair, healing scabs on her cheek and neck that had turned brown, and eyes that burned laser trails over the desk into his. Twenty minutes of pressing her elbow into the armrest was the only thing that made her move an inch and even then just enough to relieve the numbness.

Mills drummed his fingers on the edge of his desk and mindlessly stared off into his calendar. Watching his eyes lose their appetite for anything in the present made her blood seethe. The more he looked away, the more alien the sensation of respect became, the more she stared at how his jugular throbbed in his neck, the more she noticed how exposed it was, the more she could tell he was overwhelmed and weak and pathetic and incompetent and deserving of being attacked.

Mills coughed and calmly leaned forward, adjusting his seat in the chair. He reached into his desk drawer and pulled out a thick, bound packet of paper. He placed it down in front of him and began to leaf through the pages.

"What's that there, Mills? Some—"

"How would you feel about taking a psychological test?" he interrupted. "It's very thorough."

Her eyes softened.

"It takes about three to four hours to complete the whole thing, but the results could help you understand yourself better," he said.

Slowly, she lowered her middle finger and reached over his desk for the packet. He looked up and handed it to her, and she plopped it onto her lap and peeled back the cover page.

"If you'd like to try it, just take it home with you, and when you're done, drop your answers off with Janice as soon as you can. If you bring it back soon enough, I'll have the results ready to review in our next session."

The questions were all simple, some verging on total transparency as to what attitudes the test writers were looking to isolate and examine. Davi picked the whole packet up and quickly flipped through the pages, riffling her thumb over the edges.

"The results will take about an hour for me to go over with you, and so, we'll need to meet for two hours next time if you are in fact interested," he said.

She turned to the cover page and ran her palm over it, smoothing it back down.

"Okay, Millsy," she said. "Sounds like fun."

*   *   *

Davi leaned over to sip her soda while she wiped her hands on her apron and felt the wads of tips billowing up out of the front pocket. She stuffed the loose dollars down deeper, deciding to wait on organizing them into a roll until the lunch crowd was gone and her last three tables were cleared.

In the dining room, the two cops seated at the counter were gone from their stools, already paying their bill at the register.

"Bye, guys. See you later," she said, waving to them.

"Thanks, Carla," the one with short blond hair replied.

She didn't know those two, but they clearly knew her, calling her by the nickname that her customers from the department used. The other cops from the police station down the block must have told them to get her as their waitress, but with the especially busy lunchtime rush, she hadn't had time to linger for any chitchat. If any of the regulars came in tomorrow to give her a hard time and ask why she'd been cold with the rookies, she'd just place her hands on the table, lean down into their faces, and tell them overly seriously that there was something about them that she didn't like. Then, she'd wait to see if they'd bought it.

"Everything okay over here?" she asked, passing by the couple still eating at her other table. "Would you like me to refill that for you?"

The middle-aged man nodded with a mouthful of pastrami and horseradish, edging his empty glass towards her with the back of his hand. They were eating calmly now, but Davi suspected that the man and his wife were in an argument. Ever since they'd sat down, the air around their table felt too thick and silent for anyone to fall into casually.

"Sprite, right?"

He nodded again.

"I'll bring you guys a little sliver of cheesecake to share too. I think you'll love it," Davi said, walking off with his glass.

"But we didn't—"

"You didn't think you'd get a dessert to share? I know. Not such a bad day, right?"

At her last table, she scooped up the tent of folded dollars and crammed them down into the front pocket of her apron with the rest. She began to stack the plates and pile the wadded-up napkins onto the top, clearing enough space in the mess to where she noticed one of the paper placemats on the table was turned to its blank side and scrawled all over with a sharp-pointed, precise pen. She picked it up for a closer look, and there were three math problems written from top to bottom, the first one being an exercise in algebra and the last two requiring calculus. The engineers in town for the excavation project had been the ones sitting there, but they hadn't solved anything that they'd written on the placemat. They hadn't even tried.

Her eyes wandered over the problems, piecing together the needed steps to solve each, but she could already tell that she would have to check her old textbooks to refresh her memory on some of the exact operations. She folded the placemat twice and carefully slid it into her apron, reaching in before she did and balling up the wads of money to make as much space as she could. Tomorrow would be another lunch shift for her, and at least some of the engineers would be coming back in and finding their way into her section.

They've got a big surprise coming to them, she thought, smiling out the front window at the cars lining up at the red light.

*   *   *

Suppose you are in a situation where...

When I am in a room that has blank, I tend to feel...

She must have read and answered a thousand hypotheticals, but there were only a few pages left. As she suspected, the entire exercise felt like one big waste of four hours with a mess of questions that all gave away what the normal answer was supposed to be, but she'd been genuine and honest nevertheless, curious as to what sort of accuracy the test would produce. If Mills had the results ready in their next session, she had to admit she was actually going to be interested to hear something come out of his mouth. Surely, that wouldn't last.

Except for Calvin, all the dogs were asleep on their comforter, its corners nailed to the floor to keep it from bunching up under their ruckus. Davi looked up from the last page of her test to see Calvin sleepily licking his front paws, then the comforter, then his paws again.

"Hey, what're you doing?" she said, chuckling.

He licked the comforter three more times in a row, oblivious to her voice.

"You're strange. You know that?"

Propped up on her elbows on the floor next to him, she reached over and scratched behind his ear while he continued licking away, never breaking his rhythm or looking up with his contented, half-closed eyes.

When she shifted back to her original spot, her toe accidentally caught one of the legs of the easel behind her, and she spun halfway onto her back, anticipating having to catch the canvas before it fell on her. The easel only rocked twice before standing pat in the carpeting, and she relaxed, looking up to admire her work. Her plan for that particular canvas was a rendering of the exterior of The Copper Top with a '50's spin in changes to color, dress, and lettering, all smiling faces stopping for a chocolate malt on their way home from the roller rink. A few weeks ago, she'd gotten frustrated and given up on painting it to work on a new wax bumblebee candle, but the scene was still resting unfinished on the easel, waiting for lightning-strike moments when the right angles and strokes would come back to inspire her again.

At last, she flipped the test back to the front page and dropped her pen on the packet. She rubbed the fatigue out of her eyes with a lazy growl. In the living room, the moaning on the TV crept up in volume, and she quickly dove for the knob on her tiny stereo to drown it out. Stopping his hypnotic licking, Calvin crawled off the comforter and inched closer to her. He poked his nose into the back of her arm, and she hugged his head, kissing him between the eyes. With a grunt, he slung his rear end around, collapsed his body against her side, and laid his head back down on the carpet.

4.

On the end table, the top magazine's cover story read "The Y2K Bug: Is This the End?" on a background of neon green computer code. Davi shook her head, wondering whose job it was in the office to update the reading material.

She bounced out of her seat and started to pace around the waiting room's chairs. Her curiosity over the results of the test had become inconsolable in the days since turning in her answers, wrapping each passing hour in Christmas-Eve anticipation, and she was sick of sitting still in the dry, brittle office space. As she slowly weaved her way through the empty chairs, Janice huffed heavy, unapologetic sighs through her nose, and Davi could tell that her restlessness was driving her up the wall.

"So, what's up, Janice?" Davi asked aloud.

"Excuse me?" Janice asked.

"Nothing."

Mills opened his office door, and Davi instantly turned with the sound to retrieve her purse from where she'd left it on her seat. She threw the strap over her shoulder and briefly furrowed her brow at the way Mills looked standing in the doorway, his posture radiating a strange sturdiness that she didn't recognize.   Ordinarily, he'd be looking down or pretending to need something over at the counter with Janice while she approached, but that awkward energy was gone just then. To the contrary, she sensed only stocky composure.

Davi sat down in her usual seat, perching herself towards its front edge, and Mills wandered past his desk and over to the high-backed, upholstered chair in the corner of the room. As he sat down, he picked up a clipped stack of paper off the floor by his feet and moved his tie out of his way to the side before the heavy stack of documents slapped onto his lap.

"I hope you had a good week, Davi," he said. "As promised, I have the results of your examination here, and if you like, I'm ready to review them with you."

"Let's do it, Millsy. I didn't spend four hours taking the damn thing just to not know."

Searching his face, she couldn't detect a reaction to her having called him that.

"This assessment is a very sound and accurate tool, but before we begin, it's important for you to understand that it will still get some things wrong. Personalities and the human brain are too complex for a one-size-fits-all battery like this to be completely accurate. So, as we go over the results, I'd like you to tell me if anything that I say seems inaccurate in how you view yourself."

"I can do that," she said in a low voice.

Dread twinges began to spike through the back of her neck. Her eyes darted back and forth between him and the papers resting on his lap, and she shifted in her seat, moving back from the edge. Even more alarming than his posture, his tone and eye contact were commanding and authentic, a far cry from the clunky, steam-shovel manner she'd come to know.

"Alright then," he said.

He flipped the top page and wrapped it over, behind the large binder clip that clenched them together.

"The first item. Patient exhibits tendencies towards narcissistic behavior—"

*   *   *

The plate started to feel tacky in her hands. Rinsing the last suds off, she placed it in the dish rack and picked up another from the bottom of the sink. On the living room floor, Calvin was gnashing away at a squeaking chew toy of a stuffed pig he had pinned under his paws. Monty was curled up and asleep on the sofa, and Henry was lying by the bay window at the perfect angle for the vent in the wall to pour heat on him, well-accustomed to lavishing himself with creature comforts after only a few weeks home with them. Another dish went into the rack as Calvin's chomping filled the kitchen with squeak-squeak sounds.

Victor came out of the bathroom and walked up behind her at the sink while he finished buckling his belt. Feeling his breath on her neck, she arched her head away to make room for his and closed her eyes as he planted a soft kiss. He picked up a still-dripping dish from the rack and brought it close to his face. His jaws clenched as he looked it over, and suddenly, he punched her on the shoulder. Stunned from the contact, Davi stopped scrubbing and looked at him.

"What the hell was that?" she asked in disbelief.

"You fucked up the dishes. Look at that. What, are you going to eat off that?"

The dish gleamed in the bright overhead light.

"Yeah, I am. It's absolutely spotless. What'd you punch me in the arm for?"

Squeak.

"It's not clean. That's why," he said.

"Where? Where do you see anything on there?"

He gestured to two spots.

"Those are in the texture of the plate. Scratch it with your fingernail. It's not food," she said.

Squeak, squeak.

She turned off the faucet, dried her hands, and went into the living room. Lighting a cigarette, she watched him continue to examine the plate and then place it back in the rack. He turned and walked towards her.

"Look, I've seen it a few times now, okay? We can't eat off plates like that," he said, his voice rising in frustration.

"Every dish I clean is absolutely spotless, and you know it. I don't know what your goddamn problem is, but you know it. Just admit that you're wrong. You should never have done that."

Squeak, squeak.

"I just don't like it when—"

"You shouldn't have done that!" she yelled, emphatically jabbing her finger at him with each word.

Calvin looked over at her with his pig in his mouth, only to spit it out onto the floor and drop his face onto his paws. Victor walked over to the window sill and picked up her wedding ring where she'd placed it while her hands worked in the sink. He carried the ring into the living room and sat down next to her on the sofa, holding out his hand for hers. She blew her smoke into his face and opened her left hand, extending her fingers into his palm. He gently separated her ring finger from the others and slid the platinum band back into place.

"I'm sorry that I did that. Are you okay, baby?"

Davi rubbed her shoulder with her left hand and shrugged.

"I'll live," she said.

Victor headed back to the kitchen and opened the freezer. He pulled out the carton of mint chocolate chip ice cream and started to scoop some into a bowl, just like she usually did for herself after they'd finished dinner and she'd done the dishes. As he scooped, she put her feet up on the coffee table and relaxed, watching him with a punitive look. He came back and placed the bowl in her hands and kissed her on the cheek, his fingers sliding along her jawbone.

"I'm sorry," he said.

She put the bowl down to wait until she'd finished her cigarette while he went back into the kitchen, turned on the tap, and picked up the sponge from the bottom of the sink.

*   *   *

Her hand shot up to her mouth to stop her lips from quivering. Her heart felt like it was seizing on every other beat. She took a deep breath to compose herself. Oblivious, Mills flipped through another wad of paper.

"Item two. Patient exhibits a tendency towards histrionic behavior—"

*   *   *

"Victor."

Victor was glassy-eyed in his recliner, watching stock cars scream around the track down in Bristol.

"Victor, where are my paints and canvases? What did you do with my portfolio and everything else?" she asked with trembling panic.

"They're in the loft in the garage," he said.

"Why are they in the loft in the garage?"

...

"Victor?"

He sparked his lighter onto the end of a cigarette and looked back at the TV. Whatever he'd done, he'd emptied her entire studio with the exception of the painted glass pane in the window.

Davi hurried to the garage door and reached for the doorknob too quickly, making her grimace and taking her breath away. Her ribs on the right side were still tender, perhaps had even been cracked, but at least the cut the barrette had opened on her forehead was totally closed and healed with the two stitches she'd put in. She reached out to turn the knob with her left hand instead.

The garage was thick with a bizarre smoky musk that escaped into the house as soon as she opened the door, overwriting its usual smell of crisp, dry wood and clean fiberglass. The boat was in its place and spotless. Victor's tools were hanging in their cutout spaces along the pegboard wall. Still, the charred smell had to be coming from somewhere, and glancing up at the loft over the boat, she knew that he had done something and hidden it there, sequestering it from all the things he liked to keep tidy.

The ladder up to the loft popped and cracked under her weight as she reached up the rungs with her left arm and relegated the right to keeping balance. As she climbed, the stale charcoal got stronger, and with a step to go before she'd be able to see over the edge, she paused and closed her eyes. Her head pressed against the back of her hand, buying time to come up with a reason not to look. With her work snatched out of place while she'd been gone, the emotions that had gone into them felt stained. Worse yet, the ones attached to the older pieces that she didn't readily remember anymore felt completely erased, like they'd never happened at all. Slowly, she peeked up into the loft, spotting a bright blue tarp that looked new and out of place among the dusty boxes and containers.

Getting off the ladder with only one trustworthy arm was trickier than she'd expected, but once she had crawled her way in front of the blue tarp, the spigots in her eyes twisted. Tears streamed down her face of their own accord, springing leaks without her sobbing or feeling anything beyond impossibility. She sat down and crossed her legs, and her fingers gathered up a corner of the tarp and slid it back to see what it was that Victor hadn't been able to say.

Her portfolio case was ripped open, its zipper torn off track. The smaller, luckier pastel and watercolor pictures only had their edges singed, but most were shriveled into gray and black flakes that disintegrated and smeared onto her hands when she touched them. The bumblebee-shaped candle that she'd raised from molding to painted likeness to finished project was half its size, the thinner wax in its wings having deflated and collapsed onto its body. In shock, she cupped her hands over her face, obliviously smearing all over her cheeks the soot she'd picked up from sifting through the mess.

He had to have done it at home in the spur of the moment, probably borrowing Hank's fire pit for the night to protect the lawn. He could've made the decision right after she'd been whisked away by her father who'd come and taken her with him at gunpoint the morning after the party. Or maybe he'd done it when he was notified of the restraining order she'd had put in place. Worst of all, he might not have touched anything, right up until she'd called to say that she was coming back.

But why would there be anything left at all? Even the miserable pile of exploded pastels and warped chopsticks that used to be paintbrushes could have been much worse, completely burned into thin air. Had he felt guilty when he saw the colors bubbling and fading away? Is that why he'd eventually put them out and salvaged what was left of her work while still halfway recognizable?

She wondered what he'd looked like in front of the fire. She pictured him seated in a lawn chair, his face dancing in orange-red, his lips spread into a slight grin, his eyelids drooping with satiated anger. She pictured him on his knees, his fingernails digging into the patio as he howled bone-chilling remorse into the moonlight. Then he was the one with blank, assembly-line eyes, staring off into the treetops in detached repose. Then he was the one who climbed into the flames and snuggled his face against them, mad with desire and abandon.

A shiver ran down her spine when her foot touched solid ground again. She looked up the ladder's rungs from the bottom with smeared gray ash coloring her cheeks, carved through with dried black canals that started at her eyes and wrapped under her chin, tracing the last trails of a sun-baked soul.

*   *   *

Mills looked up. She nodded through wrenching sobs to encourage him to continue. He looked back down reluctantly.

"Item three. Patient exhibits tendencies towards manipulative behavior—"

*   *   *

Her instincts were right. The dogs were all missing from the bay window. She fumbled with the metal trash cans and lids, clanking them together with each step that she jogged up to the side of the house. What raised her blood pressure more than anything was that whatever had drawn the dogs away from their usual spot hadn't been anything Davi had heard, even while standing right in front of the house.

She opened the front door to fresh, watery smears of blood all over the carpet and linoleum. Smokey was slowly pacing around Slick who was sitting back on his rear and staring at her with wide, headlight eyes. In a few steps, she passed Calvin who walked past her with his head hanging low. Monty barked quickly when she turned the corner, and Zeke trotted the opposite direction into the other room. Then, the blood trail ended.

"Henry!"

His body was down on its side and motionless. The fur on his back was scruffed up in strange ways that he would never have tolerated without licking back into place.

She scooped him up and desperately grabbed at his face to turn it towards hers. He was pure deadweight, and the fingers she slid under his head felt wet against each other, sticky with blood and saliva. Cradling him tightly against her, she kissed him along the crooked scar on his mouth where she always had and stuffed the ribbons of his ripped throat back inside him. Calvin sniffed in their direction from a distance while she rocked him back and forth in her arms.

She didn't have any idea how she would ever get the red out of the carpet, his blood having soaked it in so many places. Her keys hung on the rack by the door, right where she'd put them for years after that first time she'd dropped them on the counter while looking through the mail and Victor's jaws had clenched all the way over on the recliner. Her daily list of chores in his handwriting was waiting for her on the kitchen island. Henry was dead in her arms. One by one, the strips of a shredded document fell back into place, and even the dam of mood stabilizers had to break and give way under the pressure.

The phone never rang for her anymore. Letters never came. Her boys were everything she knew and loved in the world now, and even they had turned on each other. Even the very stillness itself had betrayed her, breaking her most cherished hunch that nothing could happen to her without first making a sound.

Her face dropped into Henry's neck, and their bodies shook together. *This could be me*, she thought over and over on an endless loop. *This could be me.* She looked into Henry's empty eyes and apologized. She didn't know why.

*   *   *

Mills wrapped the wads of paper back over the clip and flopped them back onto the front of the stack. He swallowed deeply as Davi held herself across her stomach.

"Are you alright, Davi?"

She nodded and reached for a handful of tissues from the box on the table. The test had not often missed its mark, and only because the sobbing had upset her stomach terribly over the course of the hour that he'd been reading had she stopped now. Mills being the one to deliver the autopsy results was just insult on top of injury, but at least he didn't look like he was brimming with self-satisfaction over it. To the contrary, he seemed deeply uncomfortable.

"Like I said before we started, this test cannot be completely accurate, and I think it has some things wrong about you," he said.

She wiped her nose on the back of her hand. This was not the plan. Mills was only the rubber stamp for Goldstein, and

Goldstein was the one who called the shots when it came to turning off the flow of medication. Mills was only supposed to know what he needed to know to satisfy that objective, and now that he was on the inside and knew it, everything became much more complicated.

She didn't want to be the person who the test results described. Still, she knew that she was and stopped dabbing at the makeup running down her face.

"I really need you to help me," she said.

5.

The Silverado's engine faded away as it turned onto the main route and out of the neighborhood, and Zeke's paws flailed through the air and wrapped around her waist. She hugged him back and hurried to acknowledge each dog's excitement before their frantic jumps left her with long arteries of nail scratches down her arms and legs. The scene was always the same for them on weekday mornings at quarter to eight. The door would rattle shut, Victor's engine would rev in the driveway, and she and her boys would clamor all over each other, overjoyed to have tensionless reign over the entire house.

Davi retrieved her green notebook from her studio and tossed it onto the kitchen island. Mills had given her the notebook last month, requesting she keep a journal of her thoughts, feelings, dreams, memories, and whatever else as they proceeded through their work together. Since Victor almost never went into her studio, she'd agreed to take it, instantly considering hiding places, but even more foolproof was keeping the notebook entirely blank when she wasn't actively writing in it. Fortunately, convincing Mills to permit her to mail her entries to the office in advance had posed no problem. He hadn't even bothered to ask why.

She pulled the stool under her and picked up her pen. Her hands still didn't feel like they remembered how to write, her fingers pinching the pen in a way that strained the muscles in her palm with overkill, and while she knew the journal entries weren't being graded on their prose, she was self-conscious that Mills would read her sentences and think her to be moronic from their simplicity. She doodled some letters in cursive on the page while she waited for a writing topic to come to her. Picking up her pen to look them over, she curled her lips in disdain at how the letters were coming out wobbly instead of graceful, all quivering with newness.

She rested her cigarette on the rim of the ashtray while she reached behind her shoulders and tied back her hair. In the corner of her eye, the list of chores that Victor had just reviewed with her sat across the island. She'd dutifully stood next to him and nodded over each item as he covered it, as though the list was somehow news, as though any of it ever changed. Now that she'd noticed his loose-leaf chicken scratch resting in her line of sight, it became like an itch in her vision where even if she looked straight down at her notebook she would still feel her focus stuck on his writing instead of hers, inexplicably magnetized in its direction. With a sigh, she lunged across the island, wadded up his list, and threw it over her shoulder onto the floor.

*   *   *

"This is a knight. It moves like this," he said, sliding the piece over the board.

"In an L-shape?" Davi asked.

"Yep. And it's the only piece that can jump over other pieces. None of the others are allowed to do that."

Her father took a sip of his soda and placed the glass bottle back on the table. Davi picked up a knight and rubbed her fingers over its grooved head. She liked that it had special abilities and a carved mane.

"And this one is a bishop. It can only move diagonally," he said, moving the piece along a black diagonal to demonstrate.

"Daddy?" she said, putting her knight back on the board.

"Yes?"

"Do they have horses at the zoo?"

"I don't know, but I'm sure they have zebras. Those are just about horses," he said.

"Can we go to the zoo soon? We haven't gone in forever, it feels like."

"Absolutely not," he said with a grin creeping onto the side of his mouth.

She smiled and pushed the pawns around the board as he chuckled and bit into his sandwich.

"You know you want to go to the zoo. Don't lie," she said, kicking her feet in the air under her chair.

"If I'm going to the zoo, I'm not taking you with me. That's for sure," he said, overly serious.

She rested her elbows on the table and dropped her face into her hands, feigning hurt feelings. He chuckled again, his eyes playfully smiling.

"I guess I'll never get to go then," she said.

"Oh, come on. Of course, we'll go, Spock. Now, do you get how bishops are allowed to move?"

"Yes. So, how do you win?"

"Okay. This is the king," he said, holding up a piece with a cross on the top of its head. "When you have a piece that is attacking the other guy's king, that means his king is in check, and you say 'Check' to him."

"How come you say 'Check'?" Davi asked.

"You just do," he said. "That's how the game is."

She picked up her rook and placed it on the same rank where he'd dropped his king.

"Check," she said.

"Right. So, you win when his king is in check, and at the same time, he can't do anything to stop it. That's called checkmate. You win when you get checkmate."

"I think I get it," she said.

"You ready to give it a shot?"

She nodded and rested her chin on top of her folded hands, loaded with determination.

"Wait, what's this one again?" she asked.

"Mm," he said, swallowing another sip of soda. "That's your queen. That's the most powerful piece in the game."

*   *   *

Her pen waltzed along the page, and the more she wrote, the more she could see her penmanship improve, the muscles in her hand gradually coming to remember all the small, fine movements they used to make together. After all, they still understood tight, orderly nuance when the job called for a paintbrush instead of a pen, a bumpy canvas instead of a smooth page. What they lacked now was the understanding of how those same skills could be applied down the line.

Sticking her pen behind her ear, she looked over the journal entry with paranoid attention to detail. Mills still knew nothing about Victor or her marriage, and she read and reread every word to ensure that she hadn't inadvertently given something away now. Sufficiently trusting Mills in order to confide in him wasn't what concerned her, though holding him in any regard still felt brand new. The problem was her suspicion that he would be bound by law and professional ethics to contact the police if he became privy to circumstances that endangered her, and she wasn't about to let him take that risk on her behalf.

On her way to the mailbox, she held the envelope up to her forehead as a visor from the sun. She wanted to believe that her eyes were somehow transitioning away from being purely indoor and nocturnal, but they weren't convincing her so far. If anything, they were more strained by the bright sunlight than ever before. They didn't tear up as much, but they ached menacingly under the workload, promising to deliver a splitting headache if she pushed them far enough. Considering how tired she was, she tried to keep them closed as much as she could until the flag was up on the mailbox and she was back inside.

Glancing at the side of the house as she dragged her feet back up the driveway, she remembered the garden she used to keep there, and at the simple thought of its existence, the dampness came back through her knees, recalling being burrowed down into the grass while she reached into the tomato plants. The warm threads of spring woven into the brisk air brought the garden scents into her nose, even with nothing around but the fresh mulch that Victor had scattered by the bushes. She could still smell wafts of pumpkin and squash in the passing breeze to the point where she had to open her eyes again to make sure that the garden was actually gone.

The kitchen clock read quarter after nine, and she decided to let her body collapse on the couch. The first round of vacuuming wasn't for another hour and forty-five minutes, and she hadn't slept a wink since yesterday afternoon. As she dropped onto the cushions, the dogs all took their cues, circling about and flopping down in the spots they each liked best. They were used to staying up through the night with Davi who had learned not to sleep around Victor if she could avoid it, and even though her body was trained to rest while he was at work, she would still be over the moon if it would let her string together three consecutive hours without jerking itself back into consciousness.

Her eyelids started to give up and flutter closed, but sheer habit was making her fight the urge to fall asleep. Her mind began to wander back to the journal entry she'd just mailed, and she wondered what Mills thought of the letters as he read them, curious if any parts of them surprised him. She'd written about how marvelous it had felt to emerge from the drug-laced cocoon she'd known for years. She'd mused about the past and how she had lost control of it, only to see it begin to blend haphazardly into the present. She'd detailed her atrocious, erratic nightmares, from which she would awake like she'd been shot from a cannon. Pushing back against the pillow, her hair brushed in front of her nose, and the wonderful springtime scents came again, as though stuck in the strands. Maybe next time she'd write about all the things her memory knew by her nose and vice versa.

*   *   *

At the kitchen table, Davi's math book was open to a page covered in diagrams of circles and their radii. She yawned and flicked her pencil in her fingers so the eraser would make soft tapping sounds against her notebook.

"Would you quit it?" Mona said from across the table.

Mona was trying to memorize state capitals, but some names she didn't know how to pronounce, like Montpelier and Tallahassee. Her testing how to say them in whispers under her breath had been irritating Davi just as much.

"Stop sounding out the names, you idiot. I can't concentrate either. And state capitals don't matter, you know. They just make you memorize those."

"Whatever," Mona said.

Thumping steps started to descend the stairs, and both of them went quiet and looked back down into their books. Their mother stamped into the kitchen, on a beeline to the cupboard by the fridge.

"Are you guys doing your homework?" she asked casually at a shocking volume.

"Mm-hm," Davi said.

"Good. Because you're not going to watch cartoons until you're done. Ha!"

"It's nighttime. There aren't any cartoons on at night," Mona said quietly. "And Davi is too old to watch cartoons even if they were on."

Their mother splashed a glass with a third of tonic water and reached into the cupboard for the plastic jug of Beefeaters to make up the difference. Davi took a sip of her soda and solved the next problem in her assignment with a few taps on her calculator. She took a deep sigh as her mother downed a gulp of her freshened drink and grunted contentedly.

"What are you girls working on?" their mother asked, turning to the kitchen table.

"Homework," Davi said.

Coming over to look at their books, their mother slammed her glass on the table harder than she seemed to mean, sending some of her drink sloshing over the rim and onto the pages of Davi's notebook.

"Mom! I have to turn this in tomorrow," Davi said.

Her mother chuckled, wiping the page with her hand to dry it off, but suddenly seemed to remember something else. Her eyes caught fire. She leaned over right in front of Davi's face, and her acidic pine-cone breath still had enough proof to sting her eyes.

"Don't you ever raise your voice to me like that," she said through gritted teeth. "You understand me?"

Mona reached over and grabbed Davi's notebook, blotting the spill away with her sleeve and making sure not to smudge the pencil marks.

"There. It's fine, Davi. See?" Mona said.

Begrudgingly, Davi took her notebook back from Mona and closed it to its green cover just in case any other accidents were in the offing. Their mother's breathing shallowed out, dropping to normal, and she stood back up while Davi crossed her legs and looked down at the floor.

"Okay, I'm going back upstairs. Get all of your stuff done properly, girls."

Their mother leaned over and kissed Mona on the cheek, leaving her to wipe extra gin and tonic from her face. She came over to Davi and kissed her just the same, but unlike Mona, Davi left the slobber there, too irritated to wipe it off.

"It's not good to mess up in school," she said before chuckling and climbing the stairs.

Imposing silence flooded the kitchen. Mona looked over at Davi who was staring off into the wall across the room.

"How do you say this one?" Mona asked, turning her book towards Davi and gesturing at the map inside.

Davi opened her notebook and tore out the damp page to copy its answers onto a dry one in the back. She glanced over at Mona's little finger gesturing to the edge of the Rockies.

"Shy-ann."

*   *   *

The vacuum's motor whirred louder when it was locked upright and stationary on the carpet, and Davi switched it off while she fussed with her t-shirt, tucking in the part that had been catching on the handle while she steered. None of her clothes fit right anymore, and her appetite never seemed to appear over the course of the day. Everything was baggier on her, almost comically so, and if she was only going to be able to eat a few bites a day, she didn't see any way around having to convince Victor that she needed to buy smaller clothes.

"I'm not done yet, guys. Stay back where you were," she warned.

The dogs were beginning to wander out of their hiding places and into the living room when she turned the vacuum back on, sending them scattering away all over again. She rounded the corner into the dining room with the bay window, and Smokey's eyes popped open in panic that he'd been discovered and cornered by the fabled machine that she dared to tame, her hand wrapped around its throat. He stabbed his head downwards at the vacuum and then recoiled back, seemingly trapped in the choice of whether to stand and fight or make a break for it.

"Well, go on," she said, holding the vacuum still and gesturing for him to escape through the other side of the room.

Upon hearing her voice, he looked up at her and wagged his tail, and she rolled her eyes and laughed.

"You lummox," she said while he happily wagged away.

She pushed the handle down, forcing the vacuum head to lift off the carpet and roar at him, and he snapped out of the indecision and dashed away, clamoring into the studio where she would be going next. As she moved each chair around the table out of the way and back again, she began to smile at how Smokey's face had instantaneously flashed from gripping terror to tender delight, eventually coming to laugh herself to tears the more she thought of his ears propping themselves up on his head in confusion then falling backwards with dopey relief.

Next, she pushed her way into the studio, chasing all the dogs out while she changed outlets. The stenciled geometric patterns she'd sketched and then painted onto the window pane threw blues, greens, and auburns all over the carpet and the vacuum as it ran beneath them, but the studio still felt under repair, having even now failed to amass enough new pieces to replace the number that Victor had burned a year earlier. Fresh ideas were just hard to think up, and she vowed to hold each one sacred if they ever did decide to come to her again, to bask in their electricity like they deserved. Expertly, she steered her way around the skinny easel legs without jostling the canvas and then headed out the door.

Back in the bedroom, she zoomed around and under the bed. Then, she opened the closet doors and rammed the vacuum into the shoes and boots on the floor, trying to get to the last edge of carpet. Victor's shirts drooped low on their hangers, swaying lightly in the motor's air current, and back in the dark corner of the closet, Davi momentarily caught the grim steel of one of the rifles, just above where its wooden stock ended. She closed the closet doors and pulled the vacuum away.

Just as she pulled the plug out of the wall, a knock came at the front door. She steered the vacuum in front of her as she went to answer it, its long cord snaking through the carpet behind her.

"Oh, hey, Ker. Come on in. I've just got one more room, and then I'm done," Davi said, leaving the door open.

"Vacuuming again? God, it's crazy how clean you keep this place. Can I hire you for my house?" she joked, heading over to drop her purse on the island.

"Well, with all the animals, the hair just gets out of control if I leave it."

Davi moved to her last wall outlet and switched the vacuum on to do the hallway. Ordinarily, the last stop on her rounds would be moving the couch to do the carpet below, but with Kerry there, deciding whether she would find that unusual was a tough call. For now, she decided to leave it be and make up for the cut corner when it came time for the second session at two o'clock.

"Okay, sorry. I just had to finish that," Davi said, unplugging and winding up the cord.

"What are you apologizing to me for?" Kerry asked, opening the fridge, looking around, and closing it without taking anything. "I'm the one who just stopped by while you were busy getting things done."

"I don't know. Just sounded right," Davi said.

Kerry sat down on the couch and packed Victor's bong with her feet stuttering in excitement in their heels. For a stay-at-home mom, Kerry dressed richly in a strange manner, as though she was about to attend an art exhibition or a charity gala, only stopping by first to purge her aristocratic guilt over the common man and his seedy plight. She looked out of place all around town, not that Davi was in a position to throw stones of that nature.

"So, what's been going on over at your place?" Davi asked.

"Not a thing," Kerry said. "Sam is over her friend's house, so I ran to the store to get a few things for dinner. Just bored, and I thought I'd stop by to hang out and get a little high with you before I did anything else."

Kerry sparked the lighter and drew the flame into the bowl. When the glass cylinder turned chalky white, she released the pressure and sucked it all down.

"You must really be bored, Ker. That was a big hit."

"Well, I'm frustrated too, dammit. I called Danny's office earlier to ask him a tax question, and he's away on vacation for a week. So says his bitch assistant anyway. I wonder if she actually tells him that I'm trying to reach him sometimes."

*　　*　　*

The phone rang on the kitchen wall, and Davi's feet jolted off the coffee table. She must've dozed off after coming back from stoking the anachronistic wood-burning stove in the basement. A phone call at this hour was almost certainly a telemarketer who could be dispensed with quickly, but regardless, sleep would now be impossible with the shocking alarm of the phone still shivering down her spine.

"Hello?"

Someone was on the other end of the line, caught in an uncomfortable pause.

"Davi, it's Mona."

Davi froze. Mona's voice sounded so different in her head under the thick tarp of medication smothering her senses, and she panicked that Mona was hearing someone else entirely through her receiver too. Henry looked up from the bone he was chewing to growl softly at Monty who walked away, confused.

"Oh, er— Hey, Mona. How've you been?"

"I'm doing well. Everything's going really well," Mona said.

"Um, good, good," Davi said, twisting the long phone cord around her finger. "I'm glad to hear that."

Mona cleared her throat on the other end of the line.

"Okay, look. I'm just gonna say all this at once. I know that we've lost touch for a while now, but I wanted you to know that

I met this guy about a year ago – his name is Declan – and we're getting married in September. I'm telling you because I wanted to know if you would be in the wedding party. Like I said, I know it's all just right out of the blue, but I really wanted you to be a part of it."

"You want me to be a bridesmaid?" Davi asked, her fingertips levering their nails into the skin on the right side of her neck.

"If you want to. I mean, it would mean the world if you would. I've called a couple of times before, but Vic always answered and said you were out. You just never called me back," Mona said.

Davi had never even known that Mona had been trying to reach her.

"I see," Davi said. "So, it's in September?"

"The end of September."

With a dreary winter overcast outside, Davi could see her vague, translucent reflection in the kitchen window and wondered what Mona would say if she were to see her scabbed face, missing tooth, bizarrely whitened hair, and extra weight. She expected and could handle wild-eyed disbelief from the rest of her family but not from Mona. If she saw it in her eyes too, then maybe there wasn't anything left of her that anyone would recognize. Still, she had nine months to get herself together and had missed Mona's voice more than she'd realized.

"Okay. I'll do it," Davi said.

Mona sighed lightly into the phone. Davi could feel her relief through the wires.

"Thank you. I'm so happy you wanted to, and I promise you'll love Declan. I promise he's wonderful. You'll just love him."

"I'm sure I will," Davi said.

"I'll call you in a few weeks and give you more details. If you don't hear from me by the end of February, will you call me yourself please?"

"Okay, I promise," Davi said, suddenly nervous about hanging up the phone. "It's really nice to hear your voice."

"It's nice to hear yours too," Mona said.

"Okay. Erm— I guess we'll talk soon."

"We will. Bye, Davi."

"Bye."

6.

As soon as she sat down on the toilet, she could see the towels were the wrong length on the rail. She wondered if Victor had moved them deliberately but doubted it, considering that the days where she missed such obvious errors were long gone. Besides, at whatever length the towels were actually hanging was hardly relevant anymore. They were hanging at the length that he said they were, no matter what a ruler might have read. Their sloppiness before her eyes still bothered her, and she reached over from the seat and pulled them down about a quarter of an inch to the center of the caulking, just above the fifth tile from the floor.

Davi gathered up her breath and held it, trying to force her first bowel movement in days, but the hopeful feeling she'd had in the grocery store had vanished as soon as she'd stepped in the house. The laxative bottle in the medicine cabinet was tempting, but she put it out of her mind completely as a viable option with the time already approaching one in the afternoon. Taking a dose probably would help before Victor got home at three-thirty, but after that, the residual pressure that would mount in her gut through the night, until quarter to eight the next morning, would make for time-stopping agony.

Resigned to constipation, she pulled up her pants and went over to the sink. She noticed the bathroom door behind her was all the way open to where the knob touched the wall, just like the old rules would have required, and she scrunched her face into the mirror, unable to place just how long she'd been doing that with neither purpose nor need. Now that she thought about it, the open bathroom door did have a perverse quaintness to it, a strange appeal in the relative sense, and she decided to let the whole matter go, drying her hands and adjusting the hand towel back to its proper length.

In the kitchen, Monty was sniffing up at the groceries she'd dropped on the island before having run to the bathroom. Davi grabbed his inquisitive nose and talked into it like a microphone.

"How now, black cow?" she said.

Monty wagged his tail back at her like a sail flapping in the wind and poked his nose at the corner of one of the brown paper bags where the chicken was.

"Keep dreaming, mister."

Beside himself with excitement, he began to spin around and hop from side to side. In the process, his nails clicked up and down on the kitchen floor, attracting everyone else who wanted to see if he was getting a special treat. As well-trained as her boys were, Davi started to hustle to put the groceries away before a feeding frenzy erupted.

"Do you see what you've done?" Davi asked Monty while she dug the chicken out of the bag and threw it into the fridge before he got even more worked up.

With all but one of the grocery bags folded, she wiped her hands clean against each other and held them up in front of their eyes, as though to show the dogs that everything was put away and that they were out of luck. But none of them batted an eye, all focused on the one paper bag that was still standing atop the island. Smokey barked up at her once.

"Hey. No," she said firmly, pointing at him.

One by one, they all sat down in front of her, except Monty who licked his lips inconsolably at the fact that she was in fact hiding treats to share with them. Davi looked at him sternly, and he tried to sit like he'd been taught but couldn't resist shooting back up once she started to rip open the plastic bag of jerky. Right away, she put the bag back down on the island out of his sight.

"Sit," she said, singling out Monty.

Monty sat back down with his rear still wiggling on the floor, and Davi decided that that was going to have to be close enough for now. Calvin, Zeke, and Slick were relaxed and dutiful as usual, but she could see that Monty and Smokey needed more training around food. The two of them weren't all to blame this time however, not when she had intentionally wound them up by making their treats a surprise.

Calvin got his jerky first with a kiss on the snout and trotted off to eat in the other room. Slick was next, then Zeke, then Smokey. Monty looked around in a panic that the others had gotten their snacks and left. She shook her head at how he tortured himself over food, even managing to turn what should have been a delightful surprise into torment. Finally, she gave in to his desperate face and snuck an extra treat into his mouth that he didn't expect. He snatched them both up and ran off to the living room with his prize.

*   *   *

Davi peeled her denim jacket off her shoulders and fanned her face. With desperate gulps, she drained the entire cup of water the nurse had given her for the ride, and her mouth still felt cottony. At an intersection, a Rottweiler stared out the back of the sedan in front of them with his tongue hanging out of his mouth. When she fixed her eyes on him, the dog's gentle face began to warp into something unrecognizable, and she had to look away. She sighed, and a little, involuntary sound of despair escaped with it.

Her mother hadn't been as furious with her as she'd expected picking her up at school, but she might just have been waiting until they were alone to raise her voice. No matter what was in store, fear of her mother's wrath came a distant second to the fact that she had lost control over her body and didn't know how long it would last.

"So, they told me that you told them that you smoked something before school," her mother said from behind her sunglasses, the wipers streaking back and forth across the windshield.

"Yeah," Davi said.

"What was it?"

"It was just pot," Davi said, closing her eyes. "I mean, I thought it was."

"I guess you had that one wrong."

She concentrated on working her tongue around her mouth to gin up as much saliva as she could. At the tail end of another long exhale, the little sound escaped from her mouth again in quivers. Her mother reached over and rubbed her thigh.

"Just breathe, kiddo. It has to end eventually."

"Okay," Davi said, stretching her arms away from her body to let her diaphragm expand for larger breaths. "I'm sorry."

"I'll bet."

Davi would have preferred her eyes shut to stem the tide of subtle hallucinations, usually on the frayed edges of her vision, but closing them made her feel dizzy in a hollow, disembodied way. She squirmed in her seat to find a way to get comfortable and settle down while her mother wiped a finger under her sunglasses.

"What does it feel like?" her mother asked curiously.

"I don't know how to describe it," Davi said. "My eyes are all scrambled, and I'm burning up."

Her mother switched on the air conditioning and pointed all of the vents she could reach towards Davi.

"Do you have any idea what it could be?"

"No, but it's definitely something. It's just scary," Davi said.

The rain started to pick up, and the sound of the drops pummeling the roof and windshield were war drums to her ears. She kept telling herself that it was all in her head and that the world hadn't suddenly, maliciously changed around her. Rather, she was the one that was different, and the funhouse mirrors that had sprung up around her in first period would disappear back into the shimmer soon enough.

*   *   *

Davi pulled the slide on the bong and inhaled. She passed the pipe back to Kerry on the couch on her way up to fill the dog bowls in the kitchen.

"Do you ever feel like something is missing from your life? Like something important?" Kerry asked.

"I guess so. I'm not sure what you mean," Davi said, assembling the dog bowls on the island.

"I mean, isn't it so easy to start something important like a career or what-have-you, wake up one day down the road, and realize none of it makes sense? What you're doing doesn't make sense. It's hard to remember how it ever did."

Kerry smelled faintly of some sort of cherry liqueur and was smoking more than usual. The booze odor lingering around her was disconcerting, especially with the afternoon hour and Kerry only having ever come over smelling of exquisite perfume or nothing at all, but while Davi got the bag of kibble from the floor of the pantry, she couldn't avoid getting lost in the luster of Kerry's appearance. Her short blond hair was freshly cut into a trendy flip style over the left, and she was wearing a new white top and navy blue skirt combination that looked fantastic against her tanned skin.

Davi moved Kerry's Coach purse off the island and onto the counter, just in case any food scattered off the bowls as she poured. The bag's style was beyond dispute, but feeling how light it was when she picked it up, Davi suspected that there couldn't be too much inside, aside from makeup, a wallet, and chewing gum wrappers. As gorgeous as it was, she would have sooner spent the money on sketchbooks with finer quality paper and just kept her ratty old t-shirts and sweatpants.

"Is everything alright, Ker?"

The probing question popped out of her mouth while she'd been entranced with the purse, and she hoped she hadn't just inadvertently set a precedent of such things being asked in their friendship. Kerry nodded and crossed her arms and legs.

"How's Tom?" Davi asked, filling the bowls.

"Tom's fine. He's his usual steady, reliable self. Solid," Kerry said, trailing off. "The thing is that he's always working. Oh, or he's exhausted from working. That's getting pretty old, I don't mind saying."

"Does he travel?"

"No, he's around plenty. It's just that he's running his own business, always on the phone or the computer, and when he's not doing that, he has to give Sam time too. So, I just miss him."

"Do you—"

"And Tom provides everything me and Sam need," Kerry said quickly. "So, don't think I'm one of those thankless bitches that just runs their men into the ground. I know how hard he works for us, and I won't knock him even a little for that."

Davi met Calvin's gentle eyes as she put the bowls on the floor. She rubbed her face against his, and he licked her cheek.

"Do you ever tell him that you need more of his time?" Davi asked, coming back into the living room and lighting a cigarette.

"I don't know. I feel guilty saying that to him with as much as he has on his mind, but I probably should. I need more of his attention, I think," Kerry admitted.

"At least give him a fighting chance against Danny."

"Oh, I just lust after Danny playfully," Kerry said with a dismissive hand wave. "Who wouldn't? He's only a fantasy. I just tell you because I think it's funny."

Davi glanced over at her boys lined up eating next to each other to make sure no skirmishes were brewing between them. Monty may have been the glutton of the bunch, but Zeke ate the fastest and had started snapping fights before by poking his snout into other bowls where it didn't belong. This time, he again finished his bowl first but walked off into the living room dutifully in her direction. She scratched under his chin with approval, and he sat down in front of her, basking.

"And Victor? How have things been between you two lately? You know, I've still never met him, but that picture of you guys on the wall? My God, what a stud," Kerry said.

"He's good. He's very busy himself."

The smoke from Davi's cigarette was beginning to waft in front of Kerry's face, and Kerry got up to move to Victor's recliner. On her way, her heel nicked Zeke's tail as she stepped over him, and he yelped in surprise.

"Oh, no! Is he okay? I'm sorry, Zeke. Come here."

*   *   *

The entire transaction would have been at least two minutes faster if she had just hustled to the counter ahead of that obese woman. Davi could tell through the window as she walked up to the store that she was going to be a problem, oozing her way to the register with her arms full of cookies and six-packs. Now, she was going to have to figure out how to explain the unusual amount of time it took to check out.

"Davi Ross?" a vaguely familiar voice called out behind her on her way to the Legacy.

Davi turned, and a fit blond woman in a track suit was squinting at her, closing in from across the parking lot.

"It is you! Oh, my God! Come here!"

Caught by surprise, Davi allowed a hug but drew away quickly when the woman's hands on her back made the skin underneath them feel like they wanted to be scratched with a cheese grater.

"Wallace. It's Davi Wallace now," Davi said, holding up her left hand and flicking her ring finger against her thumb.

"No shit!" Kerry exclaimed while holding up her sparkling left hand. "And I'm Kerry Cavanaugh now! No way, this is so exciting!"

Davi smiled lightly at Kerry, mainly out of a mimicking reflex that recognized her smiling at her first.

"When did you get married?" Kerry asked.

"Oh, just after I left school," Davi said, nodding slightly.

"You left me alone in that terrible English class, and there was nobody else who was cool to talk to in there for the rest of the semester," Kerry said.

Davi's hand began to slide up her sweatshirt towards its favorite spot on her neck, but she restrained it. Kerry looked beautiful, almost to the point of intimidation, and Davi unconsciously turned the right side of her body slightly away from her.

"I'm just teasing. I'm so happy for you," Kerry said. "So, where do you live now?   Tom and I just moved to the neighborhood a few months ago, so we don't really know anyone yet. We like it, though. It's nice to have a police station so close too. I don't know. Just makes me feel safe."

"I live by the police station," Davi said.

"The one on Foals? Get the hell out of here! Which house? This is crazy."

"The blue one with the bay window in front."

"Are you kidding me? I drive past your place every day. I know exactly which one it is. We just moved to the other end of the street, like nine, ten houses down. The red one on the left side if you're coming from your house, just before you get to Partridge."

"Beats me," Davi said, itching to reach for the door.

Kerry's eyes shined into hers without a trace of hesitation or awkwardness, which felt far more bizarre than if she had recoiled in horror and dashed into the convenience store. Davi flung her keys up with a wave.

"Well, I hope I see you again, I guess," Davi said.

"Wait, let me give you my number," Kerry said as she reached into her purse. "I've been a little bored lately. There's only so much work a girl can do around the house before she loses her mind, right?"

"Yeah."

"I don't care if we just find a bar and go get a beer one afternoon or something."

"I mainly smoke pot," Davi said, opening her car door and throwing her bag on the passenger seat.

"Oh, my God. I love you. Yes, let's do that one of these days. That sounds wonderful."

Kerry stuck the note with her phone number on it into Davi's hand and looked poised to hug her again, but Davi dove into the Legacy, now frantic to get home.

"I have to run. Good to see you, Ker."

"Call me soon. We have so much to discuss," Kerry said.

"Okay," Davi said, closing the door behind her.

She peeled out of the parking lot. The odometer was going to be on her side, but the time stamp on the receipt promised to be a major complication.

*   *   *

With only a few minutes left in the session, their conversation had reached a natural stopping point. Mills opened a drawer and pulled out a Snickers bar. He pushed his chair back from his desk so he could swivel to the side and cross his legs.

"What time do you get to work, Mills?" Davi asked.

"I get in around seven most days."

"And it's almost seven at night right now."

He shrugged as the candy wrapper crinkled in his hands.

"That's the job. Ordinarily, I'm not here this late, but—"

"But I'm the problem child that needs the extra time and attention?" she asked, gesturing towards his candy bar with a little space between her thumb and forefinger.

"That, you are," he said, breaking off a piece about the size of the space she was holding up and lobbing it over to her.

"Thanks," she said.

She chewed and sighed through her nose. She hadn't realized how hungry she'd gotten until the chocolate lit up her taste buds.

"I've been thinking," Davi said, swallowing the candy. "People tell you a lot of horrible things in here, huh?"

"Sometimes," Mills said.

"Does it ever affect you?" she wondered.

"It can. I imagine it's similar to what police go through in that the job gets you accustomed to seeing people malfunction. You get used to seeing dramatic pain, and when you see it enough, it can make you miserable because you can start to think that that's the whole world. And it's not."

"So, what do you do if you start to feel like that?"

"I take my wife out to dinner. I watch a ballgame. I play with the kids. I get perspective," he said.

She pulled her purse off the coffee table and sat it on her lap. As he took another bite of his candy bar, she reached in to find a stick of gum.

"It sounds like a lot of stress," she said.

"When a patient discusses their issues with me, it's a question of taking them in intellectually instead of emotionally. They're just puzzles to solve, dots to connect, and you can't connect them if you let yourself get distracted emotionally."

"I see," she said.

"And that doesn't mean I don't care because I do. It's just about striking a balance for the sake of achieving the optimal therapeutic result."

"The optimal therapeutic result," Davi repeated slowly, savoring the sound. "And how far am I from that?"

"I honestly don't know," Mills said.

"If you did know, would you tell me?"

"No."

Davi smiled but not so wide that her lips would separate and reveal her gap-toothed grin.

"Honesty. That's nice," she said.

He checked his watch, and she scooted off the edge of her seat, knowing that was what he always did when he was wrapping things up,

"Well, very good session today, but it is time for me to get out of here. You too, for that matter. I'm sure your husband is anxious to see you."

Her body jerked short at the doorway and launched all of its sensors at once back towards Mills to see if he had noticed the reaction. When she turned around to see him organizing papers into folders with his head down, her shoulders relaxed, and she let herself breathe again.

7.

"Wow, this is great, Ker. There's a little tang in there too. I didn't expect that," Davi said.

"I added some lemon zest to the recipe. It always seemed like it could have used some extra pop when my mother made it for us growing up."

Davi cut the side of the fork through her sliver of apple pie, standing and eating another bite by the island to avoid Monty's guilt-inducing stare. He'd been broken of the habit of begging for human food, but she could never figure out how to stop him from watching her eat from the living room floor with droopy, hard-luck glances that broke her heart. As for the pie, she was surprised how much she liked the peculiar shock of citrus in with the sugary apple. The contrast made the whole pie seem sweeter.

"Did you know that tax avoidance is a different thing from tax evasion?" Kerry asked.

"I didn't."

"Tax avoidance is legal, and tax evasion is what the IRS will come after you for. Who knew, right?"

Davi shrugged, chewing her last bite down even though her stomach wasn't interested in processing it.

"So, what did Danny say about the trust you guys want to set up for Sam?" Davi asked, putting her dish in the sink.

"It's all pretty standard. It's just insurance for Sam in case anything happens to us, and Tom and I think it's a good way to keep savings for her college too when the time comes."

Davi brought her brush over to Smokey on the sofa to comb out the loose hair his shaggy coat was shedding in the warmer May weather. Kerry edged over to the far side of Victor's recliner, warily eyeing the brush and seeming to anticipate the messy whirlwind it might kick up.

"And how has he been?" Davi asked.

"Oh, really good," Kerry said excitedly. "You can tell he's been working out too. His jaw looked squarer, and his shoulders are filling out his suit differently."

"I was talking about Tom," Davi said, glancing up from Smokey's coat.

Kerry's face flushed red as she put the bong back on the coffee table.

"Tom's good. Working hard, like always. How's Victor?"

"He's about the same," Davi said, feigning renewed interest in the grooming.

"Victor, the man of mystery," Kerry mused as she reached over the sofa and scratched Smokey's head.

"Tom's just as much a mystery to me, you know. Danny too, for that matter."

"What about me? Am I a mystery?" Kerry asked.

"Do you want to be?"

"Fuck yeah!" Kerry said with righteous disbelief. "Who wouldn't want to be mysterious?"

"I wouldn't," Davi said to herself, suddenly hearing the ticks from the clock on the kitchen wall.

"So, what do you think? Am I a mystery?"

"In your own way. Yeah," Davi said.

"What do you mean?" Kerry asked, moving to the edge of her seat and reaching for the bong on the coffee table.

"Well, you come by in the afternoon, we hang out, get high, and I don't see you in other situations. Oh, and I know you're a very good baker now as well."

"So, what else would you like to know?" Kerry asked.

From the pitch in her voice, Davi sensed there was a correct question that Kerry was waiting to be asked but couldn't imagine what it might be.

"I don't know, Ker. You're putting me on the spot."

"Ugh, that means I'm obvious and boring," Kerry said, rolling her eyes to the ceiling.

"It doesn't mean that at all," Davi said, taking her comb off Smokey's coat. "Maybe it just means I'm a lousy detective."

*   *   *

Davi swirled little doodles in midnight blue towards the bottom of the canvas, testing how her new brushes held the paint. Their hairs were stiffer than the old ones and didn't call for her hand to be stabilized as much in order to spin off smooth, tight lines. All of her tools felt nice and sharp, but she still struggled to summon to mind an image that inspired her. Perhaps she was pushing too hard. Keeping things simple was the best way to get her feet wet again. She swished her used brush in a small glass of water next to the easel and shook her head a little to reset.

Going back to basics, she decided a full moon over a seascape would make a comfortable starting premise, amenable to improvisation should smaller ideas occur to her along the way. For the base color of the sea, she folded some royal purple in with the midnight blue on her makeshift palette and swabbed a big brush with generous amounts of the mixture over the bottom of the canvas. Then, she picked up her putty knife and carved its edge through the wet paint to pull out some lines for the tops of small cresting waves. Mixing some white and silver with a little gray, she traced patches of reflected light onto the tops of them, just below the spot she had planned for the moon. A small dab of purple went into the white-silver-gray mixture to deaden the effect as she went further away from the image's light source.

For the top half of the canvas, a dark black in textured swirls seemed an obvious choice for the night sky, and while other possibilities fluttered through her mind and begged for consideration, she dismissed them in favor of simplicity. There wasn't any rush to get fancy, and if she wanted to feel the creative sparks flying off the flint again, building confidence had to be the top priority. Besides, the image's perspective already looked tilted and inconsistent, and she began to worry that perhaps her fundamentals had lapsed just as much as her creativity.

Through the walls, Victor's groans from the living room started to become audible in the studio. Normally, she would have had her little black stereo next to her to combat the sound with a track from The Cranberries or Alanis Morrisette, but it had fizzled out the previous day. Now temporarily without recourse to block him out in the other room, she could only hope that he would hurry up and get to a scene that struck his taste so he would finish and go to bed. Davi picked up her little palette again and added a few more lines of moonlight on the calmer ocean around the cresting waves.

His moaning got louder and turned throaty, and Davi raised her brow and rolled her eyes in unison. *Now comes the swearing,* she mused, and Victor started to breathe heavier and swear, no sooner than she'd had the thought. She nodded her head in bemused distaste and tried to refocus on the canvas, but what her ears picked up kept drawing her attention away, obstructing her creative intuition from immersing itself into the image. She sighed and swished the brush covered in purple-blue in the glass of water, his moans peaking in snarls and growls. Sitting back, she decided that the moon had to go in place before the night sky, and if the edges blended together when it came time to add the black around it, then so be it.

"God, yes! Maeve! Fuck!"

Victor shouted the name again, his voice diffusing into ecstasy. Dropping her brush on the palette, Davi spun around towards Calvin with her jaw dropped wide open.

*   *   *

"You know, I don't think it's fair that Tom was all Mister Sex Machine before we got married, and after the ring, I get no action. That's like entrapment."

"Have you said anything to him about it? How else is he supposed to know?" Davi asked.

"How is he supposed to know? Just check the credit card statements and see how much money your wife spends on batteries, Tom. Then, he'll know I'm not satisfied," Kerry said.

Davi chuckled and pushed against Smokey's side to make him shift his weight. His left side had been pressed against the couch and still needed to be brushed out.

"Maybe he's not satisfied either," Davi said.

"You're taking his side?!"

"I'm not taking anyone's side. I'm just saying that if you're not having sex, then he's not either. And if he's not having—"

"What if he's having an affair? Do you think that could be?" Kerry asked with a pinch of anxiety in her voice.

"Why would you say that?" Davi asked.

"I don't know. Why else would a man not want to sleep with his wife?"

"Well, has he done anything unusual lately? Does he disappear for long stretches of time?"

"Not really. It's just work, work, work with him."

"There you go then," Davi said.

"Maybe it was the pregnancy," Kerry said, folding her arms over her stomach and staring off into space. "God, that wreaked fucking havoc on my body."

Smokey's coat felt sleeker, and the little ball of harvested fur didn't seem like it was going to get any bigger. Davi ran her palm down his side one last time, collecting all that she could off him, and walked to the kitchen to smack her hands clean over the trash can.

"It's not fair that men get better as they age," Kerry said. "You see a guy with a head of thinning, silver hair, and he looks distinguished. If it's me, it looks like I've been knitting socks in my rocking chair all day and can't afford a proper dye job."

"Right," Davi said, clearing her throat.

"But their sex drives apparently completely end somewhere in their mid-thirties. So, that's the catch," Kerry said.

"There's always a catch."

Kerry reached for the remote and turned the TV off, even though the sound had been on mute since she'd arrived. She closed her bloodshot eyes and lightly rubbed her eyelids. She had eye drops in her bag but never used them until she was just about out the door.

"So, tell me a crazy story of yours. I talk too much sometimes," Kerry said with her eyes still closed.

"I don't really have any," Davi said, sitting back on the sofa. "I accidentally smoked PCP once before class in high school, and that was fucking horrific, let me tell you."

"Hm. Not what I expected you to say."

"What do you mean?"

"I guess I was thinking more like sex. I should have been more specific. Jeez, never mind me. I have sex on the brain," Kerry said.

"You sure do."

"So, it didn't feel good?"

"The PCP?"

"Yeah."

"I have no idea if it would be fun, like if I had bargained for it, but when you don't know you took something like that and feel your body going haywire, it's just panic."

"The feeling of being out of control didn't feel good at all?" Kerry wondered.

"Like I said, maybe it would have been the greatest thing if I had been prepared—"

"But then you wouldn't have been out of control. Being prepared for it means you still want to be in control of it."

"I suppose that's true," Davi admitted.

Drawing her hand to her mouth to smother a yawn, Kerry arched her back in a stretch. Her dress' snare-drum fabric drew tighter across her ribcage, bringing out its lines and contours with elegant elongation.

*   *   *

Her father hiked up his pant leg to kneel down and retie her shoelaces that had come free and were dragging all over the pavement.

"They're all pink!" Davi squealed.

"They're flamingos. You know they're pink."

"I know, but look how cool they look!"

When she felt the knot's tension get tight on her instep, she broke away to run over to the fence of the flamingo enclosure and push her face against it. About a dozen flamingos were standing in the pond water on the other side.

"How can they move around without falling over when their legs are so skinny?" she wondered to herself amazedly.

"Maybe they're not as heavy as they look. Maybe they're just a bunch of pretty feathers glued onto a crow."

Davi kicked him softly in the shin for making fun of them and then hugged his hip right after. In the pond, some of the flamingos had twisted backwards to hang their heads on their bodies to rest. The others whose heads were upright made a wavy S-shape with their long necks.

"They're just so odd," her father said upon further reflection.

"Don't they do anything?" Davi wondered.

"Well, it's not a circus where they're trained to do things. These guys live here and relax. They look like they're just hanging out to me," he said.

"I guess."

Her father looked over at the informational plate in front of the enclosure.

"Says they're Caribbean Flamingos, and they're pink because of the food they eat."

"What they eat turns them pink?!"

"That's what it says. Algae and tiny crustaceans."

Davi swung one of her legs around behind her while she went quiet and wondered how much she would have to eat to turn pink like they were.

"Yeah, I know what you're thinking, Spock, and you can forget it. You're no flamingo," her father said.

She smiled up at him and bugged her eyes out in bashful surprise. He must have known she was plotting something from the silence.

"How much longer do you think everyone else is gonna be in the bathroom for?" Davi asked impatiently.

"They'll be back soon. Mom's with them."

One flamingo reached back to dig its beak into its feathers while the rest stayed still, all perched on one leg.

"Do you think they like being here?" Davi asked.

"One thing's for sure: as long as they're in here, they never have to worry about being hunted by guys like that back there," he said, throwing his thumb over his shoulder towards the bear exhibit they'd passed earlier.

"I just wish they had more room is all. They look like they don't have enough places to go."

"I think they like being here. It's their home."

"Hope so," she said.

Reaching for the chest pocket of his shirt, her father took out the map he'd picked up at the entrance and unfolded it to plan the best route to see the zebras before they had to head home. Meanwhile, she let her fingers go from the chain link and waved at the flamingo that had twisted around to poke into its feathers. The bird stopped for a second to look back and then plopped its head down on its feathers to rest.

*   *   *

"Don't you ever feel like you just wanna break out and lose control and be in danger and feel alive?" Kerry asked.

"Everyone feels like that once in a while," Davi said.

"But tell me something, are you happy here? I feel like I should be much happier than I am."

Davi shrugged.

"You know, living in suburbia with the SUV and the kid and the husband and the big house. Why does it feel so empty?"

"Well, what else do you want?"

Kerry exhaled a big cloud of smoke and raised her eyebrows at Davi while she coughed into her hand.

"Oo, good question. I want Tom to— I don't know," Kerry said, shaking her head. "I want him to be something I know he can't be."

"What's that?"

Kerry cocked her head, seemingly fifty-fifty on what she wanted to say. Then, she slapped her palm against her knee.

"On the rare occasions that we do have sex, he's just so predictable, lazy too since he put on a little weight. I'm still attracted to him, but there's just no effort. No passion. Nothing worth a damn."

Davi nodded and took the bong from her. Kerry had first come over when Davi had been finishing the morning vacuuming, but it was already nearly two. She wasn't sure how she would be able to do the same chore in front of her twice in the same day without drawing attention to the behavior. Instead, she sat and hoped that Kerry would get a sense of the time, heading out of her own accord before it became an issue.

"I want to know what it's like to be with a guy who will like commit felonies over me, you know? Like he just gets so jealous and possessive over me that he completely loses his mind, maybe kills someone who gets in his way just to take me. Arrgh!" Kerry said, balling her hands into fists and smacking them onto the top of her legs.

"Felonies?"

"Back when I was just out of college and living in New York, I saw this guy, Harris, a few times. He was English or British or whatever, so he had one of those lovely accents they have that sounds like diamonds pouring out of their mouths, right?"

Davi chuckled and pretended to understand. Kerry's comment just before that was still tumbling around her head, struggling to find context.

"You would have thought he was super uptight and proper, or at least, I did when I first met him. Very sophisticated. But when I got him into bed, he was like some kind of demon. Yanking my hair out, smashing my face against the wall, choking me until I blacked out—"

"Ultra aggressive."

"Yeah, but more than that. Like fucking sadistic. It was like I drove him so crazy that he hated me for it," Kerry said wistfully. "You don't think that's sexy?"

"I get it," Davi said.

"And I didn't even appreciate it at that age. He was older, and it just felt too rough and a little scary. So, I stopped taking his calls. What a shame," Kerry said.

"I see."

"Are there actually women out there who prefer soft, gentle sex? Who are these people?" Kerry asked, picking up her bottled water.

"I don't know. Unless you mean—"

"But I shouldn't make fun. I'm lucky to get that much out of my husband."

Calvin crawled over from beside the sofa and licked the top of Davi's foot. She looked down at him and smiled.

"I think of that night more and more often, you know. It's like it haunts me. I left his apartment, and I was bruised and ravaged and just fucking taken. And I— Just don't let yourself have regrets in life. There's no worse thing in the world."

"I think everyone winds up with regrets, no matter what they do," Davi said.

"Then err on the side of having gone for something when you wanted it. Just go for it. Today," Kerry said.

Davi nodded like she understood, but her nerves were acting up, allowing only a fraction of the conversation to register. It was now three minutes after two, and something inside the center of her right hand felt like it was vibrating, as though the vacuum handle was already pressed against it with the motor running.

"I'm sorry, Ker. I've got a few errands to do before Victor gets back. I completely forgot," Davi said.

"Oh. Okay," Kerry said tentatively.

Kerry collected her bag from the island and fished around for her sunglasses and eye drops as she headed to the door.

"Hey, I didn't just freak you out with what I said, did I?"

"Oh, no. Not at all. I meant it that I just had some things to do that slipped my mind," Davi said.

"Okay," Kerry said, turning around and then right back in a flash. "And you'd tell me if something was wrong, right?"

"Ker, I would say something. I swear."

"Okay," Kerry said, finally appearing to believe her. "Sorry. I'm just a little self-conscious, and you're like my one friend in town who's a really good listener. I didn't want to make anything weird."

"Don't even worry about it," Davi said.

Kerry reached for the door and left her hand on the knob, sighing deeply without turning it.

"Does it make me a bad person that I would fuck Danny if he wanted to?" Kerry asked. "Because I would."

"I know you would, Ker."

Kerry dropped her face towards the floor and flung her car keys around her index finger.

"I just don't remember what it feels like to be wanted anymore, and it's driving me crazy," she said.

"How could you even say that? Of course Tom wants you. Look at you," Davi said, rubbing her hand on Kerry's shoulder blade.

"Yeah, I guess he does," she said without turning around. "But not the way I want him to."

Kerry opened the door and walked to her Cherokee. Before she started the car and backed out, she dropped the visor and took off her sunglasses to put in some eye drops.

8.

Davi stumbled out of the bathroom and burped up a thick, bilious taste. Her stomach was launching a full-on mutiny, which put it in lockstep with the rest of her body that morning. She hadn't slept a wink in forty-eight hours, and the world around her was beginning to take on a wispy, ethereal quality like a waking dream, batting its eyelashes through her consciousness.

She collapsed on the couch to let her stomach settle, deciding to shirk the litter boxes for a few more minutes. The sickness was brewing up from the memory blast that was still burning ultra-vivid, and only mere luck had placed her next to the bathroom at the moment when the sudden explosion of nausea had become non-negotiable. Even that was thin consolation though, only accommodating a trifling symptom. The source of the disease went down deeper to that feeling that came to her sometimes and peeled her mind back a few frames behind her body, far enough away for each to become sick with worry about the other.

She knew what caused these episodes, the memories that flashed into her mind tracing the lines, but it wasn't always this way. In fact, she'd hoped that she was somehow past this, as though her mind ought to have already vetted this method of coping and abandoned the concept in its prototype stage. Now, she became gravely concerned that this was not coping at all but rather horrendous disorder, an overloaded circuit that had blown long ago in the one place where damage could not be tolerated.

You're not your body. You're your mind.

As soon as an incident ended in the house, her mantra would get stuck on playback, spinning like a favorite record, but at times like these, hearing it cycle through her thoughts was a cruel backfire of what she'd trained her brain to do. Yes, she believed in the truth of the statement, but when she found herself in these moments where the problem itself was her mind, there was nothing consoling about constant bulletins that the capitol itself was under assault. To avoid panicking, she focused on the mundane and tried to delight in the simple things to bait her mind into downshifting from the epic to the routine.

On a tree branch outside the kitchen window, a cardinal was resting and occasionally singing a song into the breeze. His red feathers ran into a black mask around his eyes and beak that might have looked ominous on another face, but against his red, it looked correct, like nature had matched its colors well this time. His head made instantaneous flicks in attitude, snapping to its next position faster than her eye could track along the way. Maybe he had little traumas and worries rolling around like dice in his head too. Maybe everyone did and just pretended that things were fine when they weren't fine at all and never had been. Maybe he on his branch knew it more than most and decided to sing, not because he was particularly happy or had a song he found special but because one choice was just as good as another.

His chirps were doing the trick, and while the keyhole images of hands on her face were still coming back to her, the cardinal's unwitting soothing was gratefully accepted. When he hopped into the air and vanished from the window pane, Davi reached down to pet Slick who was lying at the base of the couch. She suspected he gravitated closer to her at times like these, as though he could smell the rot in her thoughts and wanted to be nearby on the off-chance that his proximity distracted her from them. He picked his head up just in time to lick her fingertips as she pulled them away.

She began to feel like she wanted something substantial to eat but dismissed the idea amidst the continuing turbulence. She felt chilly but was sweating all over, tears running out of her eyes without her having cried them, and just then, the fluttering flipbook sensation came again and bulged nosedive pressure into her ears. Out of reflex, she closed her eyes and jerked her head abruptly, and the pressure dissipated just as mysteriously as it had appeared.

She began to think that her discontinued drug cocktail hadn't been as useless as she'd thought, some part of it having smothered these attacks. Now, she found herself without recourse to hold them at bay, but Mills couldn't be told. If he knew, all that could follow would be questions, driving towards the same secrets she'd taken such pains to ensure always rested just outside his view. Somehow, there had to be a solution outside of the pills and doctors, not necessarily even a permanent one. A stopgap measure would do if it bought enough time for her to escape the house for good. Maybe this was a blessing in disguise, serving notice that, no matter how refreshed she'd been feeling by her work with Mills, her happiness could only ever be short-lived and relative as long as she stayed near Victor.

A knock came at the door, and Davi considered letting it go unanswered. She knew it had to be Kerry but couldn't assess the risk of letting her in, her mind too lost in nightmare twitches to calculate it. Since Kerry had to know she was home though, she got up to answer the door before things got more complicated.

"Hey! What's up, sister?"

"Hey, Ker. Come on in," Davi said, turning away quickly.

Kerry dropped her purse on the island, and Zeke and Calvin both intercepted her to say hello on her way to sit down. She flapped her hands near her face, trying to stave off sweating.

"You believe this damn heat today?" Kerry said. "Unbelievable. And I'm the one that's always too cold."

Davi nodded and watched Kerry load up the bong with dismay. She'd made the mistake of smoking in this state once before, only to find that it spun her out and augmented the torment, the extra dose of paranoia scrubbing out any relaxation. Exactly how she was going to explain to Kerry why she wasn't smoking with her without triggering a flurry of questions seemed impossible.

"Guess what? Tom's parents are going to take Sam for a week, starting on Monday. Just a little quality time with her grandparents. That means Tom and I are going to get to be alone together for really the first time since she was born. Do you have any idea how exciting that is?"

Only pieces of what Kerry was saying were coming through, but the words and phrases she did catch were being repeated and amplified in her head against her will. Three- and four-word chunks kept popping out of Kerry's mouth and into her head, only to be relentlessly revved like an engine whose gas pedal was stuck against the floorboard. The looping repetition got louder and faster until eventually disintegrating into meaningless, garbled sounds as her brain tired of that bunch, discarded it, and snatched a new set to begin again.

"Anything to drink?" Davi asked.

"I already got myself a Diet Coke," Kerry said, holding up the can she'd gotten out of the fridge. "You didn't notice?"

"Sorry, I missed that."

"You been smoking all morning without me? I need to catch up."

With a jolt, the words 'all morning without me' began spiraling through her head, but Davi managed to nod quickly anyway, eager to adopt the cover story of being far too high to communicate before she missed her chance. She got up and went to the fridge to get her own can of soda while Kerry leaned over to grab the bong from the coffee table.

"You know what I watched for the first time in forever the other night?" Kerry asked, exhaling smoke. "The Phillies. That's how little I had to do. What do you do at night anyway? You ever go out to have a drink or anything?"

"Not really. I don't re— No," Davi stammered.

"I see."

I see. I see. I see. Icy. i c. Eye z. I Z.

"I picked up some new clothes for Sam over at the mall the other day. These tiny little shoes I found for her? They have the cutest buckles on them. You wouldn't believe it."

The cutest buckles. The cutest buckles. The cutest buckels. Thuh qtest buckals. thuhkewtisstbuhqelllsss.

It was as though her brain was using the words for gauze, absorbing weeping fluid from its blisters and then disposing of them once the bandages were saturated. Whatever was happening, her teeth were gritted from the merciless speed of it all, and she was terrified by her total inability to resist spinning the next thing she heard into oblivion. She wanted Kerry to shut up just to clear her head, but if Kerry stopped talking, then Davi would have to speak. Perhaps answering the door hadn't been the smartest option after all.

"Tom got kind of mad when he saw the receipt, though. He says that it makes no sense to spend money on clothes she'll just grow out of. Maybe he's right, but who cares? They were so damn adorable."

Makes no sense. Maeks no cents. maycsnosentzzz.

Leaning against the island, Davi slapped down her unopened can of soda behind her and stared at Kerry in breathless horror. Slowly, Kerry's face and body began to lose all coherence, breaking down into a constellation of disjoint, vaguely related satellites that somehow failed to add up to a complete person. Her energy was too sapped to regroup, and she began to sob into her hands in despairing heaves. Kerry put the bong down and leapt to her feet.

"Whoa, Jesus. Hey, hey, hey. What's going on?"

Davi shook her head side to side to knock the question out of her ears, lest something inside would be tempted to answer. Kerry came over to her and rubbed her arms.

"Oh, my God. What could be so wrong? It's okay, okay? It's okay."

"It's not," Davi said. "It's not."

Kerry's eyes were already glassy red, but Davi's hysterical tears seemed to have sobered her up right away. Behind her fingers, her eyes couldn't decide if they were better off open or closed.

"What is the matter?" Kerry asked, incredulous.

Davi shook her head again through the sobs. Kerry wrapped her arms around her and rubbed her back lightly.

"Just breathe. Whatever it is can't be this bad, right? Nothing's worth this," Kerry whispered into her ear.

Slowly, Davi felt her mouth prying open to speak. She closed her eyes and moved her hands to the sides of her face to squeeze it together in case it tried to come to pieces too.

At first, her whispers came in jerking, whiny hiccups, starts and stops that rendered them unintelligible. She exhaled deeply and began again. Calvin picked his head up off the carpet and stared at the huddle. His mouth tightened as though he was preparing to bark, but he relaxed and watched intently instead.

She whispered little puffs of air into Kerry's ear, and Kerry turned her head towards her with piqued interest. Having already broken its containment protocol, Davi's mouth now raced to dump the toxic sludge inside her that was corroding everything it touched. Slick sat up and looked over at Calvin who shot him a look back. Suddenly, Kerry backed away from Davi and stood in front of her at a loss.

"Are you kidding?" Kerry asked.

Davi shook her head and covered her mouth to physically push the wails back down her throat. Kerry looked around the room with her lips parted in disbelief.

"I don't know what to say."

"Me neither," Davi said.

Phantom hands were groping her all over, and she couldn't shake the sensation that they were pressing on her nerves from the inside.

"You're telling me that you have these men who take you and fuck you as hard as they can, and you're fucking complaining about it?!"

Davi gasped. A dulled ice-pick pain started to throb behind her left eye.

"Jesus Christ, look at you. You should be dropping to your knees and thanking your fucking lucky stars that any of them would touch you, let alone fuck you like that," Kerry said, outraged. "I'm coming in here day after day and bearing my soul to you – like an idiot – that I can't get what I want from Danny, and you've had it the entire time. You don't just have it. You have it with four fucking men who fuck your brains out with your hideous sweatshirts and your fat ass and fucking scabs all over your face. God fucking dammit!"

*   *   *

Whenever Victor turned on the boat's engine, the feeling passed instantaneously. It was only when they stopped to drop their lines and drift in the current that the queasiness began to build and churn inside her. Choosing to fish the inlet where the ocean met the bay hadn't helped either. The choppiness there was constant.

"I just don't think we're going to get anything," Davi yelled from the bow.

"Yeah, we will. We'll pull something out of here. I need more squid on my lines, though," Victor shouted back over the sputtering motor.

Davi burped, the last of the residual nauseous pressure in her stomach escaping. She cut two thin pieces of squid on the cooler lid and headed for his poles, relieved to feel the boat cutting through the waves instead of bobbing around in them. She uncurled the old strips from the hooks and threw them overboard. Pierced through the mouth, one of the minnows began to flop about on the deck as she squeezed a fresh strip on the hook along with him.

The engine snapped back off. Victor had brought them back to the spot near the bridge where they had started only a few minutes earlier, compensating for where the current kept taking them.

"Drop mine in too. I'm gonna grab a sandwich out of the cooler. You want one?" he asked.

"No, thanks. I had one already," Davi replied through renewed flashes of hot saliva and cold sweat.

Looking only at the horizon was the advice Hank had once given her to combat seasickness. Supposedly, the fact that the horizon was fixed and immobile was supposed to trick a sloshing equilibrium into thinking itself stable, which wasn't working. Hank had probably just made the whole thing up to sound smart. The whole notion didn't even make sense, now that she really thought about it. How could anything at all appear stable to rocking eyes, unless what they saw was rocking along with them?

"The waves are making me a little sick to my stomach, babe," Davi finally admitted. "It's freezing out here too. Can't we just come back on the next nice day?"

"Just a little longer. I'm dying to pull one of those big flounders up. They were saying they'd been biting all up in here back at the bait shop."

Putting the rod over the side, she dipped the minnow on her hook into the water's surface. Then, she released the line, and the minnow disappeared, the sinker sending it and the squid racing towards the bottom.

She spit into the water and felt more and more like vomiting could only be delayed for so long. Back on the stern with the motor, Victor peeled the saran wrap from his sandwich while Davi perched up in her seat to prepare to jettison her head over the side when she needed to.

"Plenty of fish in the sea, my ass," she said, spitting again in frustration.

"Look, just a few more drifts, and if we don't get a bite, we'll head in," he said.

Feeling the sickness rising into her esophagus, she dropped the butt end of her rod on the deck and collected her hair into her left hand. The wind was blowing into her face when she looked over the side where her line was, so she hurried to the other one, launched herself toward the railing, and threw up overboard. Euphoric relief wiped away the nausea as she angrily blew her nose into the water.

"I hadn't counted on seeing that again so soon," she said to a chunk of her sandwich as it floated away.

"Hey, did you just puke?" he asked, putting down his pole.

"Yup. Just like I told you I would, dummy."

"Shit," he said. "Okay, start chucking the bait off your pole. I'm going to leave mine down for five more minutes, and then we'll get out of here."

After the tackle was back resting on the deck, Davi threw the squid away and carefully levered the hook out of the minnow's mouth without tearing it more than she had to. If looks counted for anything, the little piece of bait wouldn't make it far on its own, but just as soon as she opened her hand in the water, the minnow darted away and vanished back into the cloudy green deep.

*   *   *

Davi grimaced as Kerry slammed the door. All of a sudden, the house felt massive around her, as though whole wings had been built onto it that she had no way of monitoring or keeping under control. With a burst, she dragged and shoved the sofa in front of the door. Calvin lifted his head off the carpet and stared at what was happening.

The back of the couch refused to come flush against the wall, and she pulled it away and slammed it back against the doorframe. The puffed fabric and upholstery looked as though it would give if someone wanted to force the door open, so she started to pound on it with her fist to try to bring out sharper, uncompromising angles. The fluffy couch pillows were even more useless and intolerable. She plucked them off and threw them back onto the living room floor.

Then, there was the back door. She experimented with stuffing Victor's recliner down the tight hallway and into the laundry room, but its leg rest kept opening when she pushed against it in the wrong places, getting the whole thing wedged between the walls. Instead, she went to the bedroom and took the night tables by the bed. Victor's night table had some loose change and a matchbook on it, which she mapped onto the carpet in their same relative locations. When she came back for hers, the lamp went on the floor gently, and everything else got swept off.

Once they were in place against the washing machine, the night tables and a dining room chair seemed an adequate brace for the back door. Passing back down through the hallway, her mind flickered surreal confusion seeing Victor's lamp sitting on the carpet in the bedroom, but there was still work to do. An invisible propeller drove her to check every lock, close every blind, and barricade every door. Monty sniffed around the carpet where the couch usually sat. Something about what he smelled made him lightly scratch at the ground.

Standing by the island and looking into the living room, she noticed the dark scruff marks running through the carpet where the legs of the couch had dragged against the grain. The couch stuffed by the door had caught on some drapes that were now going to be creased. With the house as secure as she could think to make it, she gradually became aware of how heavy she was breathing. Her shirt was sticking to her sides, so she took it off and wiped her body with it. Slick sat down in front of her and looked up dutifully.

Her heart was beating way too fast, and now that she'd stopped long enough to notice, its furious pounding scared her. She slid down onto the kitchen floor with her can of soda and concentrated on controlling her breathing. Slick turned away from her, partially sat on her feet, and looked around with his ears perked on his head.

Slowly, her thoughts wandered back to Kerry and what she'd said, and her brain shorted out and reset back to blankness. Then, the steaming premonition returned that doom was on its merry way to test the doors and windows she'd just sealed shut. Reaching up onto the island, she grabbed her shirt and smoothed away the beads of cold sweat on her forehead. The soda began to even her out, and after a big burp, she couldn't resist chuckling weakly at the sound.

Her chuckling rose into laughter. Tears came out of her eyes, and she curled up on the floor in a fit, holding her arms across her stomach, squeezing her sides together. Slick looked back over his shoulder and then quietly walked to the other room. The kitchen linoleum against her left eye socket somehow soothed the stabbing pain she felt behind it, but as she pressed against it harder to enjoy the sensation, she worried that her makeup might be staining it. Suddenly, the joke was over, and she sat back up clearheaded.

"What time is it anyway?" she wondered.

The clock read a few minutes before noon, and Victor's list of chores began to roll through her head like movie credits. She got to her feet and went to the bedroom to swap for a new shirt. On her way back, the spot where the couch belonged caught her eye.

"Jesus. What the hell am I doing?" she asked herself.

Rubbing the strain out of her forehead, she pulled the vacuum out of the closet and plugged it in. There were two small clumps of light cat hair that she'd missed under there earlier.

9.

"Got any bright ideas, Spock?"

She canvassed the chessboard. Few of her black pieces were still on it, and those that were had been isolated in different corners of the board, ready to be captured whenever he felt like taking them. Her father sat back down with her peanut butter and jelly sandwich and slid the paper plate across the table to her.

"I don't think I can do anything," she said.

"Tell me why."

She exhaled through her nose in frustration and kicked her dangling feet around in protest.

"Just tell me why you don't think you have any moves," he said.

"It was only my first time playing!"

"Relax. I'm not rubbing it in. You just won't get good at it until you understand what you did wrong. Got it?"

The last few drops of soda slid out of his glass bottle. Davi sat up and rubbed her eyes. The sun was much lower in the sky outside than when they'd started.

"You took all my pieces. That's why I can't do anything. I'm out of pieces," Davi said.

"I took your pieces because you had no plan on how to win. Your only plan was to react to what I was doing, and you wound up one step behind the whole way," he said.

"I think you cheated," she said, picking up half her sandwich and taking a begrudging bite.

"I won't want to play with you anymore if you act like this when you lose. You did alright for your first game."

"I guess."

The sandwich was a nice consolation prize. She couldn't stay mad at him, even with the losing board staring her in the face. He'd even cut the edges off the bread.

"Wanna watch TV?" she asked, perking up.

"The Phillies playing?"

"How should I know?"

"Yes, I'll watch TV. We'll find something," he said, as he tucked her captured pieces into a drawer on his side of the board. "By the way, when you think you've lost and you don't want to play anymore, you knock your king over."

She coiled her finger up, ready to send the disgraced king skidding across the board and onto her father's lap with a spiteful flick, but he grabbed her wrist before she could.

"Maybe don't take me so literally. Just place your king on its side instead, okay?"

Her little fingers grabbed the king and tipped him onto the board like she was pouring salt from a shaker. When she let go, the curvature of the piece made it gently rock back and forth across the black and white squares.

"And then say that you resign."

"Like, I give up?"

"Right," he said.

She picked the black king back up to his feet and tipped him over again.

"I give up."

"Close enough," he said with a chuckle.

They shook hands over the table, and he put the rest of the game away while she took her sandwich to the other room. She turned on the TV and flipped to channel four to see if there was a baseball game on for him.

*   *   *

In over a month, Kerry had never called or come back, and by now, Davi knew not to expect her. Deep down, she blamed herself for the trauma of what Kerry had said. Back when they'd reunited while she was out buying Victor's cigarettes, she'd sensed the foolishness in relying on her, even through the pharmaceutical straitjacket. It had been something about how Kerry's eyes saw, too eagerly groping away at the objects of their interest like a teenage boy's fingers unclasping a bra. Confiding in Kerry had been a mistake for so many reasons, and she would never have exposed herself to the risk but for those paint-shaker emotions that had forced her mouth open to stabilize from the outside what she could not from within. Even still, she had to admit that she missed her, if only because the silence now was so numbingly total.

Lying in bed, Davi stared at the lower corner of the left closet door by the hinges. There were things back there that had never crossed her mind before today. Things made of heavy metal, that exploded, that ended other things. They sat on their rears in the corner behind Victor's boots. Never before had she given them even a passing thought, but now her eyes reached out for them with the weariness of a homesick traveler who'd been only yards away from the taxi line before being snatched back inside to be put under indefinite quarantine.

Perhaps the only sensation that would register would be something small and unexpected like an eardrum blowing out. Gunpowder would probably spray out of the muzzle and land ignited on her skin. Other than that, surely there would be nothing more than a huge concussive blow, followed by smoking release. The experience might be no different than a cannonball off the high dive into a warm pool, an instant of tension as the skin of the water warped under the force before it accepted and incorporated her into itself.

If she felt it at all, a broken eardrum would hurt the most, surely many orders more excruciating than the way her ears rang under Victor's fists. Scattered embers on her cheek would be a breeze after all of the lit cigarettes poked into her arms for a laugh on idle Sundays. The mega concussion was no threat, considering the headache afterwards would never come. In imagined pieces, the whole affair seemed so easy. It would only take placing her face on the typewriter reel and striking the period key right into her forehead, and there would be no more of this distasteful grime that felt like it was infecting her down to her DNA.

So, then why was it so difficult to move? Her heart brimmed with gallons of desire, but her body had scarcely moved an inch since she'd gotten settled in bed. She thought about the rifles and shotguns in the closet with such obsession that she became convinced she'd already gotten up and was holding one, that is, until she would move on to think of the next step only to look down to find her hands innocently empty. It all seemed so easy, but she hadn't moved. She had put herself through this with several paintings. An exciting idea or perspective would come through her mind just right, but when she tried to put it on the canvas, the concept seemed ineffective or lost in translation. How natural it was for her hands to fail yet again, especially with such an important piece in mind.

Such artistic things, guns were. They were brushes whose hairs held only reds in dark crimson and only painted them with anarchic splatters on unsuspecting canvases. They were only used by the boldest artists who felt the world's whimsical agony and longed to flow into it. One more moment of pain perhaps, and then it would be done. One last painting of a world gone mad, in the abstract.

*   *   *

The lawn chair creaked under her weight, and Davi didn't trust it not to collapse. The criss-crossing nylon straps were frayed and felt like they weren't interested in putting up with too much more. She crossed her legs and leaned her weight to the left to see if she could avoid falling through and having the hollow pipe frame fold on top of her like a mousetrap. One of the fibers stretched and popped as she shifted in the seat, and she decided to abandon her comfort and sit forward, concentrating her weight into the backs of her thighs and onto the uncomfortable but relatively sturdy metal pipe in the front of the chair. A heavy thud reverberated through her chest.

"Are you sure you're allowed to do this?" she asked.

"I called those idiots weeks ago. They told me the sidewalk was my responsibility," Victor replied.

He swung the sledgehammer down onto the concrete again, and the tile sunk into white powder where the head had fallen. Victor had become maddened by a particular block in the sidewalk in front of the house that had always been slightly forked up into the air for as long as Davi could remember, but something about the previous winter had caused the raised end to crack and crumble. With the weather finally warming up, he'd had enough of looking out on the yard he worked so diligently to groom, only to see its symmetry spoiled by one lousy, broken tile on the perimeter.

He bent over to pick up the pieces that had come loose, reached into the trash can with them, and placed them down at the bottom quietly. She could tell the work was harder than he'd expected, but even she had thought the tile would lift straight out of the ground. Davi smiled at his frustration, at a loss to think of anything else to do with herself. He had made her come outside to watch him pull the block out while simultaneously insisting that she not help.

"You smile too much," he said, sniffing his runny nose and dragging the sledgehammer back off the concrete.

"You always say that," she laughed.

"You laugh too much too."

He swung again, and even though the hammer head pulverized the raised end of the tile, one corner kept driving deeper into the ground on an angle. Still, most of it had come loose, and he bent down to pick up the pieces to place in the can. The last half of the block resisted his wrenching hands for as long as it could, until finally giving in to his crowbar and lifting out of the ground too.

"Son of a bitch," he said, looking down into the open plot.

"What is it?"

"There's a damn tree root under there. That's what was prying it up."

"From this tree?" she asked, gesturing to the one a few yards away.

"No, from the one on Mars," he said, testing the root with the heel of his boot.

"There aren't any trees on Mars, genius."

"Yeah, whatever," he said.

Resting the head of the sledgehammer on the sidewalk and letting the handle point straight up, he put his hands on his hips and stared at the exposed root. If he poured a new section of concrete, the root would just get bigger and crack it again, and if he was thinking of cutting the root out to bring the ground level, he'd have to first plan how to make his saws effective with him having to angle his arm four inches below the ground just to reach the cutting point and with concrete obstructions on both sides that would limit the sawing motion.

Davi sipped her drink and looked at the hole in the sidewalk with a shake of her head. The entire affair was an utter waste of time from her seat. Even with how easy the job had looked from the bay window, removing the block would never have crossed her mind. To him, the situation must have seemed so different. Indeed, his tools, wheelbarrow, bag of quick-drying concrete, and the sweat on his brow stood testament to how much it bothered him, but she couldn't help but be astonished at the beating he'd delivered on the tile for what seemed such a forgettable violation.

With the chair's metal pipe having numbed her legs, she took her chances on sitting back for the sake of blood flow, knowing that they wouldn't be going back inside until the block's entire plot had been excavated and recast in an image that fit his definition of quality.

*   *   *

She wondered what her death would be like for Victor, especially if he had to be the one to find her. Even though he and Henry had always hated each other, she still remembered how Victor had been affected when she'd told him months back that the other dogs had attacked and killed him. That day, Victor dug the hole in the backyard with Henry's body on the ground beside him, covered in an old blanket, and when the grave was nearly deep enough, he spiked his shovel into the emerald lawn and leaned his head against it. Through the window pane, she could hear his wails echoing against the fence walls around him.

Davi had never understood why he'd done that, and maybe Victor didn't even know himself. Lying in bed now however, she suspected that it was because he had loved Henry. It was just so hard to see at first. Those glossy childhood storybooks in gold leaf she had read as a little girl never contained a word about what love really was. Their authors just wrote what sold to children who knew nothing of passion or how it could blur all the lines.

There were no princesses in tiaras who feigned swoons in the mirror against canopy bedposts, who stood under full moons, pressing calligraphy to their chests. There were no princes who sang up to balconies in Romance languages, who forfeited their deeds to bloodline inheritances with sublime, refreshed priorities. How sad all these stories were and how false. The truth was far more violent, and if there were ever to be a true love story, a knife's edge was the only pen that could write it. Only then would the page itself show the weight of what love really meant, falling to shreds and ribbons.

Picturing the scene to which Victor would return in a few hours, she knew he would cry like he had with Henry because he loved her just the same. He loved her. She could feel it, and the broken teeth and bruised skin had only ever proven the depths to which it had driven him. Nowhere in the universe's laws was it written that love and violence had no business with each other. Indeed, they were cause and effect, forever in orbit.

His love was no different from her dogs playing in the snow on any given icy morning in January. They would all burst through the door and fall over each other to be the first to run into the fresh blankets, their paws punching holes in what had been a flat, uniform top, their nails reaching deep enough to scratch up the topsoil and scatter it into the air, and by the time they'd had their fill, flecks of brown mud would be mixed all through the pristine white. All of their bounding about made the snow a choppy mess, but they loved it. They loved it, yet it was destroyed because they loved it. Their passion for it created their violence towards it, and the snow's destruction showed that it had had the priceless honor of being beloved in this saddest of worlds, this lonesome pigsty.

The ghastly depression into which Davi had sunk began to subside as she came to realize for the first time in years that Victor did love her. She was the one who'd had everything scrambled and upside down. Love was never about appreciation, respect, or anything like that. Love was about fusion. Love was about being ground into dust and inhaled by the other. Love was about being owned, the highest realization of the human experience.

Wasn't that what love was?

*   *   *

Blades of plastic grass spilled over the sides of the wicker baskets, the candy inside still untouched. Daphne and Mona had briefly pouted about not being allowed to eat some of the foil-wrapped chocolates earlier, but they weren't complaining now. At dinner, the two girls had discovered that sweet potatoes were sweet enough to temporarily substitute for candy and had nearly eaten themselves sick on them. Now, they were reduced to holding their bellies on the couch, drooped over like wilted daisies.

On her way back from the bathroom, Mara dropped a few jellybeans in Davi's hand, smuggled from the baskets without their mother or younger sisters having seen. Getting to dig into the Easter baskets was an event to their mother, and they didn't need Daphne and Mona tattling because they were left out. Davi fished a black licorice one from her palm and munched slowly to avoid detection, but her father had caught the handoff from Mara and shook his head at Davi with a smirk. She smiled back at him broadly to flaunt the smashed jellybean on her teeth.

"Oh, that's a good look," he said.

"What is?" Mona asked from the couch, looking like she was beginning to feel livelier.

"Nothing," their father said as Davi snapped her lips back over her teeth. "You know what's a shame is that I didn't have time to make an Easter egg hunt this year."

"What?!" Daphne said in shock, shooting up in her seat next to Mona.

"Yeah. Mommy's probably throwing away all the candy about now too. It's for your own good," he said.

Daphne turned and consulted with Mona in suspicious whispers. Their father always hid Easter eggs all over the house and pretended he hadn't, but this time, the younger girls seemed to have bought the charade. With Davi starting high school next year, she and Mara were too old for Easter egg hunts anymore. Instead, they had helped him hide some for their sisters before they'd gotten up.

"He's teasing," Mara explained.

"Daddy!" Daphne yelled and catapulted herself onto his lap with slapping windmill arms.

As small as he was, her tiny hands still found gaps in his defenses, all the way to ticklish spots that made him laugh aloud and tickle her back. The racket brought their mother in from the kitchen where she'd been doing the dishes from dinner. Davi slid a jellybean between her lips without realizing she was standing there.

"Abe," she said.

"What do you need, dear?" he asked, still tickling the hysterical Daphne on his lap.

"I need you in the kitchen for a moment. And you," she said more ominously, pointing at Davi. "You get in there too."

Mara raised her eyes at Davi, as though to blame her for not being supremely aware of her surroundings while enjoying the contraband. Davi poked her in the side of her belly as she got up. Irritated, Mara slapped her hand away.

"What do you need?" he asked in the kitchen.

"I need you to dry some of these pots for me. I'm running out of counter space," she said.

"Okay," he said with a look of confusion. "Couldn't this have waited?"

"So, what were you eating?" her mother asked, turning towards Davi before Abe had finished his question. "Hm? Looked like something out of an Easter basket to me."

"What's the big deal? I'm not a kid like Daphne or Mona anymore," Davi said.

The heavy breathing through her mother's nose started, and Davi instantly regretted her tone, blasé and dismissive.

"You know what your problem is, kiddo? You've got no goddamn respect," she said with her face moving closer to Davi's. "No respect for my rules, no respect for where you come from, and I'm sick of it, I tell you. I'm sick of it, and there's going to be an end to this. I am sick of it!"

Her voice climbed towards a shout, and the sounds of the girls laughing in the other room went quiet.

"Birdie," her father said softly.

Her mother turned her head to look at him, and when she saw the confused, troubled look in his eyes, her jaw released the cracking tension on her teeth. The rips of air through her nose calmed down next, and Abe looked back towards the counter and picked up a pot to dry.

"Tell Daphne and Mona they can open their baskets when we're done with the dishes," she said to Davi, turning the faucet back on and plunging another pot into the water.

*   *   *

Calvin walked into the room and around to Davi's side of the bed. Lost in her thoughts, she didn't realize he'd come in. He poked his snout up towards her, but she was closer to the center of the bed than usual. Too short to reach her arm with his nose, he backed up a few feet and growled in a deep, low throat. When she still didn't turn her head, his growl rolled into a quick yelping bark, and Zeke wandered over to the bedroom doorway in curiosity.

"Not now, Cal," she said blankly, staring at the closet doors.

He barked twice more at her, and Slick, Monty, and Smokey joined Zeke in the doorway with their ears raised on their heads. When she didn't react, he started to bark constantly, just like he would have had he been at the front window and seen a dog passing by that he didn't know. The four others watched with confusion from the threshold, looking back and forth between Calvin and Davi. Finally, his yaps pierced the haze, and annoyed, she picked up Victor's pillow and threw it at him.

"Cal, stop it!"

One by one, the four others came through the doorway, filing into the bedroom to study Calvin as he darted around the front of the bed. The hair on his spine was rising slightly, and he stabbed his front feet into the ground every time he shot forward to bark. His barking was so constant it seemed like he would have to eventually pass out from not breathing. Smokey looked over at Slick, his eyes glassed with panic.

She threw the covers off her legs and stormed by them to the kitchen. Grabbing the bag of dog food off the floor of the pantry, she lined their bowls up on the island and poured the food in a constant stream up and down the line, scattering bits all over the island and onto the floor. Calvin kept barking at her throughout, even while a splash hit his paws. Indifferent to the mess, she flung the metal bowls onto the kitchen floor and headed down the hallway. Only Monty wandered over to smell what was in his before turning back to put his eyes on Calvin and Davi.

Almost back to the bedroom, a wet nose and mouth nipped her heel, and she wheeled around in disbelief. Calvin had lightly bitten her and then started his barking all over again. She wanted to holler at him, but the surprise of his teeth grazing her skin overwhelmed the outrage. Standing in the hallway, she watched him barking up at her face, yelling himself hoarse. Behind him, the other four weren't eating anything she'd just put down. All around their paws, dog food had bounced onto the floor and carpet, and suddenly, her brain clicked.

"Hey, come here," she said gently.

She squatted down and patted her hands together to lure him towards her. Slowly, he came forward, hanging his head low and wagging his tail nervously. Sitting in the hallway as she did, she slid her arms around his neck and smoothed down the upraised fur on his spine and the back of his neck. He pressed his head against the side of her face.

"I'm sorry, baby. Forgive me? I'm sorry," she whispered.

She let him go slowly to catch his face and kiss him on the top of the nose, and he licked her back on hers. At once, Monty turned to bury his snout into his bowl, and Zeke galloped after one of the cats. Davi got back to her feet, and Calvin spun around himself in front of her legs, anxious to see where she was going. On her way to the couch in the living room, she could see the dog food all over the floor needed to be cleaned up and hoped, just for today, that Monty would be hungry enough to shoulder the workload.

10.

"Called strike three, and Trammell is retired. He got him looking. That's Wolf's fourth recorded out of the game, all of them by strikeout. But the Phils still find themselves down two to one in the top of the second on this perfect night for baseball here at the Vet."

In the background of the radio broadcast, light cheers and commotion emanated from the stadium crowd. As the summer had gone on, Davi had found herself craving baseball more and more and wondered what she was seeing in it. Maybe it was the game's general pace, occupying a peculiar space between entertainment and tranquility. As nice as it was to hear the sounds of the game on the radio, she hadn't paid attention to the Phillies in years and no longer knew any of the names on the team. They still weren't any good and had been written off from going to the playoffs from the start of the season, but it all felt wonderfully fresh to her ears, which had become accustomed to a steady diet of canned sitcom laughter and racetrack sonic booms.

Getting the Legacy up to sixty-five made the engine work harder than it remembered how to do, and rattling noises in the dashboard popped up when she pushed it all the way to seventy, the steering wheel shimmying back and forth in her hands. The other cars were flying right by her, but she didn't feel comfortable accelerating to match. Driving on the highway felt strange enough without the car feeling like it could fly apart at any second.

Her tongue continued sliding over the right side of her mouth, inspecting the new tooth that had finally been implanted the previous week. When she smiled, it certainly looked the part, but she had a nagging sensation of having something stuck in her teeth since its arrival. Before she'd started the car back at the house, she'd tested her grin in the rear view mirror from all the angles her eyes could hit to see if the tooth looked as strangely as it felt, and everything had appeared seamless then as it did now. Nevertheless, her tongue refused to relent in poking around what it had come to know as a canyon in a land of mesas.

"Bordick swings and sends a grounder down to third. Rolen plays it, fires to Travis Lee, and Bordick is out by a few steps."

She'd decided not to tell Mills about the suicidal fantasies that had crept up on her. Bringing up such extreme emotions while continuing to obstruct any view he had of the inside of her marital life would be playing with fire. Surely, he would sniff that pattern out eventually, and once he did, an unstoppable mudslide of outside interference would begin. She knew that he sensed she was omitting something, having gained expertise in reading her body language and syntax, but making Mills explicitly aware of the thoughts had no positive outcome for her, especially if his primary solution was going to incorporate a renewed array of anti-depressants.

The last rays of sunlight leaked over the treetops flanking the road, and Davi tamped down bouts of worry over seeing Mara, Daphne, and Mona for the first time in years. Ever since

she'd gotten the phone call from Mona back in January, Davi
had rehearsed little conversations in her head to ease the
paranoia that her sisters wouldn't recognize her in her present
condition and come to discard her as a lost cause, if they hadn't
already. The three of them had stayed bonded with each other,
leaving her as the only one to have wandered off and gone dark,
and after so much radio silence, she expected them to have just
flipped the channel rather than wait to hear her voice come
crackling back through the white noise.

"The two-two pitch. And Jones strikes out swinging. That's
five K's for Randy Wolf through two innings, and the side is
retired. Marlon Anderson, Gary Bennett, and Wolf due up in
the bottom half of the second."

The crowd's cheers on the radio rose in appreciation of the
pitcher's performance just before the feed cut to commercial.

*   *   *

"You have the chips?"

"Maybe," Davi said, sneaking another into her mouth and
crunching into it.

"Well, cough 'em up. Here, take the pretzels," Diane said,
flipping the bag into the backseat with Davi.

Davi wiped the greasy salt onto her jeans and handed the
chips up to Diane.

"Turn the radio down a little. It's getting late," Davi said.

"I'm just going to turn it off. It'll kill the battery if I leave it
on all night," Diane said.

She turned the key, and the Vega went quiet between the
sounds of their snacks being torn apart. The emptiness of the
parking lot felt vast without the music.

"So, what are you going to do now?" Diane asked.

"What I've been planning to do all along. I'll finish senior year, and then we'll get the band moving across the country."

"How're you going to pay for that?"

"I'll have to work some jobs, waitressing maybe. Whatever's quick. Whatever I can walk into and start working the same day. Jay and Bobby have a car, so we could all fit in there," Davi said.

"Your mom would never speak to you again."

"Big deal. We're almost all the way there right now."

Diane looked down at her bag of chips with soft disappointment. She'd always had a strange bond with Davi's mother but knew better than to take her side just then while they were preparing to sleep in the parking lot.

"What did you tell your mom?" Davi asked.

"I said I was sleeping over Beth's house. It'll be fine."

"Cool," Davi said, slinging her bookbag full of clothes against the interior and laying her head down on it. "I just wish I could get on with doing it already, you know? With the band, I mean."

"I'm enjoying hanging out with you too," Diane said with a sarcastic smile.

"You know what I mean."

"It does feel like time stands still in this town, doesn't it? I've been ready to start my life for years now."

"Yeah," Davi said. "It's like I'm dying here."

"That's a little dramatic, don't you think?"

"I don't think so. Feels very real to me," Davi said.

"It's your mom, isn't it?"

"She's why I'm in your backseat tonight like a cheap date."

"You scare her, I think," Diane said. "I don't think she knows what to do with you."

"I don't think anything scares her," Davi said.

"You don't know what she thinks," Diane said, waving her hand dismissively.

Diane crushed the empty bag of chips in her hands and stuffed it back in the plastic bag they'd gotten at 7-11. Their candy bars were still waiting at the bottom.

"Hey," Davi said.

"Yeah?"

"Thanks for staying with me tonight."

"It's cool," Diane said, slapping the salt off her hands. "It's crazy, you know."

"What is?"

"The idea of running off with your band."

"Sometimes, crazy is all you got," Davi said.

"I like it," Diane said. "I mean, I know your mom wouldn't, but just forgetting about everyone else for a second, I like it. My kind of crazy."

"What do you like about it?" Davi asked, spinning off her back and propping her head up on her elbow. "I was starting to think you thought it was stupid."

"It's exciting. I like the way it makes me feel when I think about it."

"You and me both," Davi said, turning again onto her back.

Diane squirmed around in her bucket seat. She'd given Davi the backseat so she could lie down and relax, which was working. The glow from the few streetlights was making her sleepy, despite the lot's quiet eeriness.

"What if you guys break up before senior year is over?"

*   *   *

"Gaahhh!" Mona screamed, throwing her arms around Davi's neck.

"My mascara's starting to run," Davi complained as she sniffled and hugged back.

"Just shut up and take it, you bitch," Mona said.

Mara and Daphne came out of the living room and whispered to each other in the foyer behind Mona. Mara went to get some tissues from the other room before the tears got out of control, making them look like circus clowns left out in the rain. When Mona finally let go, Mara tugged at one of the whitened streaks in Davi's hair as though to tease her, and Davi read the initial trepidation in Daphne's eyes before they hugged.

At last, Davi made it into the house with Mara and Mona whisking her back to the living room while Daphne detoured to the bathroom to straighten out her makeup.

"What do you want to drink?" Mara asked.

"A Diet Coke, I guess," Davi said, taking a seat.

Before they'd lost touch, Mara had had a full head of steam in corporate banking, and from the looks of the sumptuous living room, her trajectory had continued as planned.

"Okay, let me get my presents for you guys before I forget," Mona said, hurrying upstairs.

"Presents?" Davi asked.

"You know, for being in the wedding party," Mara said, handing her a can of Diet Coke.

"Oh, right," Davi said, nodding intently to suggest she'd only misheard.

Mona hustled back down the steps with three thin boxes, stacked on top of each other.

"You didn't even wrap them, you big slug," Daphne said, coming back from the bathroom.

"What are we, nine?" Mona said. "You can't see what it is because it's inside a box. For all intents and purposes, it's wrapped."

Mona plopped a box on each of their laps and sat down in the chair next to Davi and took her soda can to hold while she opened hers.

"Oh, my God! I love this," Mara said, opening her gift.

"And it matches our shoes for tomorrow too," Daphne said.

Davi fished through the tissue paper inside the box to find a pewter clutch with rhinestone designs on each side. Hers were little flowers.

"Oh, wow. It's very pretty," Davi said.

"I'm glad you like it," Mona said to her.

"Speaking of our shoes," Daphne said. "Could you have possibly found a strappy sandal that hurts any more than the ones you picked?"

"Toughen up, bitches. Beauty hurts," Mona said, handing Davi her soda.

"Seriously, I wore them for an hour as I was making dinner the other night—"

"Did you make sure to splash some spaghetti sauce on them while you were at it?" Mona asked.

"My place is all carpet except for the kitchen and bathroom. I couldn't test them out anywhere else. Anyway, I felt like I wanted to have my feet amputated after it was over. The straps are so thin and flimsy. You have to grip down so much just to get stability," Daphne said.

"They're brutal," Mara agreed.

"Were they that bad for you, Davi?" Mona asked.

At no point had it even occurred to Davi to walk around in the heels before the wedding to test out how they would feel. After she'd picked up the outfit, everything went straight onto the top shelf of the closet, safely away from any renegade pet hair. She'd just assumed her feet were going to hurt by the end of the night no matter what.

"I mean, I thought they were okay," Davi said, bringing her hand up to lightly caress the skin on her neck.

She felt stupid as soon as she'd said it, realizing that that wasn't how the sisters all spoke to each other when they were alone like this. Somewhere in the back of her mind, her brain knew it was on the wrong script, but exactly how she was going wrong was unclear. Still, she knew enough to know that the three of them knew she'd just lied about having tried on her heels and hurried to begin a new thought before the awkwardness set in.

"So, what's Declan like?" Davi asked.

"He's definitely got a big dick," Daphne said.

"I agree, but only because it's Mona marrying him. That's how you know," Mara said.

"My God, listen to how you guys talk. You jaded whores," Mona said as she scooped a slice of sharp cheddar onto a cracker.

Maybe it was the pace of the interaction, flying by at a speed that seemed impossible to hit. As long as the conversation was just between the sisters, any of them was liable to mow through rolodexes of family and friends, blowing them all to smithereens with strings of exaggerated insults and vulgarity, and they were all so quick on the trigger. Davi was trying to keep up, but the steering wheel kept shimmying in her hands.

"But he's a nice guy? I don't even know what he looks like," Davi said.

"Oh, yeah. He's wonderful. Daphne loves him as much as I do, and they're fabulous together. They really are," Mara said more seriously.

Mona rummaged around in her purse and pulled out her wallet. Flipping it open to the photos, she handed it to Davi and lingered over her shoulder as she started to leaf through them. Davi turned sideways in her seat so that Mona wouldn't be right behind her as she looked. The sensation of anyone standing behind her was like an open flame on her neck anymore.

"I forget where we were in this one," Mona said, explaining the first photo. "Some amusement park thing he took me to when it was early going. I thought it was a cute idea on his part. Really, he could've taken me on a tour of the sewage treatment plant and been way ahead of the guys I'd been seeing. Just lazy, thoughtless jerks. You haven't had to put up with the singles scene for a while, so you've been lucky."

Mona trailed off slightly at the end of her sentence, betraying a brain that had wanted to throw the emergency brake but hadn't gotten to the lever before its mouth had jumped the tracks. Mara's and Daphne's side conversation got briefly quieter at the same time. Davi tensed up and nodded slowly as she flipped to the next picture.

"And that's us at a Phillies game. I think we were playing the Expos, and—"

"They were losing three to two the last time I heard the score in the car. They're playing the Mets tonight," Davi interjected.

"Oh, I didn't know. I haven't been watching them lately. I'm pretty sure they're already eliminated from the playoffs. Big surprise, right?"

Mona's smile beamed in the photo at Veterans Stadium. Their faces were all red like they'd been sunburned from the day at the game or tailgating in the parking lot. Davi laughed and pointed at the big whitened areas their sunglasses had left around their eyes.

"Mm," Mona said, overly serious. "Believe it or not, that was deliberate. I was dabbling in trendsetting at the time, and Declan was like, 'Hey, no one's really gone for the human raccoon look.' So, I figured, fuck it. I'll roll those dice."

"Believe it or not, I don't believe you," Davi said, laughing again.

"What we do best is play Dungeons and Dragons and watch Star Wars. The sun offends our inner dork DNA," Mona said.

The last photo looked like a professional shot, but the spontaneous quality of the scene made Davi think that maybe they'd just gotten lucky in the moment and handed the camera off to an anonymous virtuoso. Next to a street sign that went too high and out of frame, Mona and Declan were leaning on a raised brick ledge in front of an aging property in the city, looking into each other's eyes with an intensity that seemed impossible in its casualness.

"Wow," Davi said.

"Right? How great is that one? You know who took that for us? Debbie Gibbons," Mona said.

"Jeez. It feels like forever since I've heard that name. She's a photographer now?"

"She's been a photographer for the last four years. You'll see her tomorrow. She's going to be shooting the wedding."

How crazy Mona and Declan were for each other was apparent from the pictures, not even because they looked like they were doing anything particularly fun. Rather, their images together belied some invisible magnetism that mesmerized to the point where nothing else in the shot seemed to exist. Declan did seem like he had a nice face, but even if his accurately reflected his nature, Davi still didn't know big things like how he spoke or his general manner. Regardless of Mona's infatuation, she decided to reserve judgment until they'd properly met tomorrow.

Mona put her wallet away, and the room went quiet as the side-by-side conversations happened to end at the same time. Desperate to change the topic before one of them started inquiring into what she'd been doing with her time, Davi raced through a confetti of ideas, at a loss to find anything that even remotely approached interesting common ground. All of her thoughts were Victor and Mills and disappointment and lacerations, and she was stunned how difficult it was to remember small talk.

"You still work at whatever bank that was when you first moved out here years back, Mara?" Davi asked.

"It was bought by Chase two years ago, but yes, same general management structure and location," Mara replied.

"Did the Y2K virus ruin anything with your computers? I remember seeing it on magazines all the way through the winter, and they said it was going to be this whole big thing. But it didn't seem like anything happened," Davi said.

"It's not really my thing, you know, computer software stuff, but my understanding was it was much ado about nothing. If it was ever a legitimate problem, the papers hyped it to the point where everyone went crazy to get it fixed before the computers all exploded at midnight on New Year's or whatever was supposed to happen."

"Y2K bug," Mona said to Davi.

"What did I say?" Davi asked.

"You said Y2K virus."

"But that's the papers for you. Whatever sells, right?"

"Whatever sells," Davi nodded and repeated to herself what Mara had said.

"It wasn't a virus?" Mara asked.

"It was a programming bug, which means it was somebody's mistake. A virus is intentionally malicious computer code. You don't know anything," Mona said.

Mara laughed and threw a wedge of cheese that hit Mona in the forehead, even as she dove backwards away from it.

"I'm not getting married tomorrow or anything. By all means, throw a bunch of stuff at my face."

"Oh, it was just cheese," Daphne said.

"This coming from the one who just got done begging for a bone saw because her shoes hurt," Mona said, picking up the cheese that Mara had thrown and eating it defiantly. "Wonder Woman you are not, my dear."

*   *   *

"So, you're just swinging by?" Davi said over her shoulder while she finished washing the knife and fork from her late lunch.

"Vic must have gotten hung up, but I called him this morning and said I'd pick him up at three-thirty to get over to set up a deer stand. Sorry about that," Hank replied.

"Oh, please. I wasn't doing anything. Well, other than this, but you know what I mean," she said, drying her hands and sliding her wedding ring back onto her finger from the window sill.

While Hank relaxed with a beer in Victor's recliner, she came back into the living room and sat on the couch next to Monty who promptly rolled onto his back in his usual manner of requesting that she rub his stomach.

"How has school been?" Hank asked.

Davi looked down at Monty's belly and started to scratch, beginning to feel the extra blood heat up her face.

"I'm kind of taking a little break with school at the moment. Victor and I have been talking about it a lot, and you know— I'll go back, but it doesn't make sense to do right now, like from a money perspective as well as— I'll go back, of course. It's just for now."

"What were you good at?"

"Just anything really. I could do it all, Hank," she said, driving the end of her sentence directly into a wistful smile.

"Like math too?"

"Well, I'm not really into math, but sure. I think the last thing I studied in math was linear algebra. Matrices, eigenvalues, abstract stuff. You don't really know what any of it means in the grand scheme when you learn it. I never knew how to apply it to real world problems, but I knew how to use it theoretically."

"What the hell is an eigenvalue?"

"Don't be too impressed. I just know the word. I already forget what they are," she said.

"Who said I was impressed?" he asked with a wry smile.

No matter what he said, she could tell he was deeply impressed, oscillating between leaning forward to hear more and then back in quiet surprise. Knowing she was always awake late, Hank came by sometimes in the middle of the night when Victor was asleep to talk with her in the kitchen about his problems and tell her what a great listener she was. His asking her about the things she enjoyed or did best was a nice change of pace.

"There's clubs for really smart people, I think. People with high IQ's."

"What, like MENSA?"

"That was the one I'd heard of before," he said, snapping his fingers. "Maybe you could join that to take the place of school for the time being."

"Maybe," she said politely.

Hank nodded in her direction with raised eyebrows to reiterate that he liked his idea. Davi knew it would never happen, but Hank was right insofar as he meant to imply that whatever exam battery that may be required wouldn't be the thing that stopped her.

"Well, what are you guys going to do out there today? Just get set up, or are you staying to hunt a little too?" Davi asked.

"Not sure. I've got one or two spots in mind, but we'll probably just get set up, spread some yams around, and head back on Friday to take some shots."

"Gotcha," she said.

Hank crossed his camouflaged legs and reached back for his beer on the coffee table.

"Eigenvalues. Huh. That's some crazy shit," he said as he tipped the can back.

*   *   *

"So, how are your dogs?" Daphne asked.

"They're very good. I've got five of them now. They're all good boys," Davi said.

"What are their names again?"

"Calvin, Slick, Monty, Zeke, and Smokey."

"Must be a lot of work to take care of five dogs, yeah?"

"Yeah, but they're my boys. So, it doesn't feel like work as much, I guess," Davi said.

Mara returned from the bathroom and plopped back down on the couch.

"Where's Mona?" she asked.

"She went upstairs to show us the tiara that she's going to wear tomorrow," Daphne said.

"It looks amazing with my dress!" Mona yelled down from somewhere upstairs.

"How did she hear that?" Daphne asked.

"Have you seen it yet?" Mara asked Daphne.

"I have. It's interesting, I think."

"So, it's hideous," Mara said.

"See, I know you're going to think so because it's kind of loud and a little ostentatious, but I think she makes it work."

Davi got up to get a chair from the kitchen. Mona wanted her to do her hair that night and makeup the next morning, and Davi needed to sit her down and look her over to make a plan of what would work best. As she carried the chair back into the living room, Mona resumed her cross-house conversation with Daphne and Mara with yells from upstairs.

"Daphne always had better taste than you, Mara," Mona shouted.

"What's taking so long? It's just a little crown for Christ's sake. Slap it on your head already," Mara yelled back.

Mona started down the stairs with one arm over her head, holding the tiara in place. Excitedly, Daphne patted Davi on the hip while she stood by the chair she'd set down. Mona turned and came into the room.

"My God, you weren't kidding," Mara said.

"Oh, I think it looks cute," Daphne said.

"See? Daphne likes it," Mona said.

Tauntingly, Mona did a little celebratory dance of hip shakes in Mara's direction before sitting down in front of Davi.

"Now, I've got the full picture. The crown, the dance moves. Fright Night oh-one," Mara said.

"You wish you'd thought of this for your wedding. Admit it," Mona said as the hair was swept away from her shoulders. "What do you think, Davi?"

Mona looked up at her, hopeful that she thought it looked as good as she did.

"Um," Davi said, taking a moment to clear her throat nervously. "So, Declan has a big dick, right?"

Davi plucked the tiara off her head just before it would have fallen off while Mona flung herself forward, doubled over laughing.

11.

A steady draft was finding its way into the back rooms of the church, and Davi could only shiver in her backless dress until the wedding was ready to begin. Daphne pulled a few tissues out of the box to bring up the aisle with her for the ceremony, and Mara was clearing her young daughter's hair off the back of her neck to see what part of the necklace clasp kept snagging on her skin.

"You didn't bring a sweater or anything, Davi?" Mara asked, pulling a beige cardigan over her arms.

"I'm okay. I didn't know it was going to be chilly at all in here to be honest," Davi said.

"You sure?"

"Yeah, I was out in the church a few minutes ago, and it's not like this. Maybe they're running the air conditioning back here."

"Some women probably get nervous and sweat their makeup off as they wait," Daphne said.

"And some would have a glass of champagne about now too. That'll get you flushed," Mara said before pausing and looking confused. "They do that before weddings, right?"

"I don't know. Probably," Daphne said.

"How do you feel, Claudia? Are you warm enough, sweetheart?" Davi asked Mara's daughter who nodded back.

"How did Mona's makeup turn out?" Daphne asked.

"She looks great," Davi said. "I think she's just super nervous. Once I was done, she told me to fuck of— I mean, get lost. Excuse me," Davi said, finishing her last few words looking at the floor.

Mara looked Claudia over to see if the swear word had registered, but the little girl was less interested in their discussion than she was with how her shiny black dress shoes made pleasant clacks on the stone parts of the floor like she was a tap dancer. Daphne stacked her pile of tissues and folded them over and over into a ball she could palm against the stems of her bouquet.

"You want some tissues too, Davi?"

"Waterproof eyeliner," she replied, pointing to her eyes.

"Well, what if the tears run out of your eyes and down onto your face. You know, as tears are wont to do," Mara said in a silly voice.

"I'll put some together for you. I don't even know why I asked when they're right here in front of me," Daphne said.

The wedding planner poked his head through the door and spoke to Mara who was closest.

"Just another couple of minutes before we'll go. Everyone about ready?" he asked.

"I think we're all set," Mara said. "Not sure about—"

"I'll check on Mona," Davi said.

Mara called Claudia back over for one last look at her outfit before she gave her the white satin pillow with the wedding rings tied to it. Davi opened the door to Mona's room to find her sitting in the exact position she had left her a half hour earlier, blankly staring into the mirror with her tiara sitting atop her pinned-up hair and a straw dangling out of a soda can on the vanity.

"Almost time to go, Miss America. I don't know how you've been feeling in here, but I'm getting a little nervous myself," Davi said.

"You're nervous? I'm about one slammed door away from taking a hostage right now," Mona said.

Davi closed the door extra softly behind her. Resting her hands on Mona's shoulders, she looked with her into the mirror.

"Well, you look fabulous."

"Thank you. You did a great job."

"So, what're you nervous about?" Davi asked, lightly rubbing her shoulders. "You look great, you love this guy, everyone's here for you. What more could you want in a day?"

"I don't know. Nothing, when you put it like that. It's just the end of the line in a way, you know? Of course, I love him. It's just the drama of it all—"

"The tiara was your idea," Davi muttered, smiling into the mirror.

"Very funny," Mona said.

"Look, I know how it feels to sit in your chair. The good news is the ceremony is over before you know it. The walk down the aisle is a little intense, but once the ceremony starts, it flies right by. You don't even remember it."

"And everything else?"

"The reception is just like that too," Davi said.

"No, no. I don't know," Mona said with a tone that seemed like she did know but couldn't say. "I mean, what if he's not the right guy and I don't know it?

Davi gulped and shifted her weight on her feet. The way Mona's eyes had flashed towards hers in the mirror when she'd asked the question betrayed something deeper on her mind.

"Then, you'll take steps. Just like you always have," she said, taking a breath. "Just like I am in my life right now."

Mona quickly snatched some tissues out of the box to dam up her eyes.

"Are you really doing that?"

"I am. And one way or the other, I'll get this thing figured out, and it's going to be okay," Davi said, turning loose a guilt-ridden sigh. "I'm sorry I've made you worry so much about me and that I lost touch with all of you. That was my fault."

Mona got up and threw her arms around her while they both maneuvered their arms behind the other to press tissues against their eyes.

"I'm so glad you're here," Mona said.

"Me too. Thanks for calling me."

They let each other go, and Davi examined Mona's face, seeing that she had some touchup work to do. There was only so much the tissues could defend against.

"Okay, now quit that," Davi said, fanning her hand towards Mona's eyes. "You're ruining my masterpiece."

The organ piped up through the stone and wood archways. Davi only needed a minute or two with her pencil, and they would be ready to go. Through the door, she heard someone enter the other room in a rush.

"Okay, ladies. It's showtime," the wedding planner said, bringing his hands together in a clap.

"Davi and Mona will be out in just a minute," Daphne said, amidst a flurry of clicking heels.

"We need them now. Everyone is ready to go," the planner insisted.

"Unfortunately for everyone, there's no wedding without the bride, and she's not quite ready yet. They'll just have to wait a minute. If the organ player is paid by the song, I'll cover the extra hymn or whatever the hell he's playing right now," Mara said.

Davi and Mona suppressed their laughter while Davi steadied her hand to finish her right eye.

"God, Mara."

"We'd better hurry, or they'll throw us out before you get to exchange the damn vows," Davi said, zipping her makeup bag and straightening her dress in the mirror.

Davi bent over and scooped up as much of Mona's train as she could, and they headed into the other room. Before she knew it, Daphne was next to her, gathering into her arms the hanging folds that Davi had missed.

"I think I got the rest," she said.

"There's two of us back here, Mona. Don't walk too fast," Davi said.

Rounding the corner into the back halls, Daphne, Davi, and Mona got a better rhythm to their steps, but the wedding planner and Mara were getting away from them, even with Mara holding Claudia's hand and swinging her forward every few steps to the little girl's delight. Near the antechamber where they would double back for the procession into the main hall, Mara took a misstep in a small patch of the floor that turned to cobblestone.

"Watch your heels here," the wedding planner said over his shoulder. "It's a little funky for a few steps."

"Those two are going to have problems later. Calling it now," Daphne said.

"That's if she makes it up the aisle without breaking her neck," Mona said.

"Hey, I hear you making fun of me back there. I wear flats to work," Mara called back to them. "You hear them, Claude? Your aunts are picking on me."

"They don't mean it, Mommy," Claudia said with a chastising whisper loud enough for all of them to hear.

Once they reached the front of the church and could see into the main hall, the wedding planner threw the bouquets he'd been carrying back into Daphne's and Davi's arms and disappeared around the corner. All three sisters swarmed Mona like worker bees, fluffing the train of her dress and making sure no strands of hair had come loose from their pins. Claudia waved to Mona from behind the bustle and smiled while the rings clinked together on the pillow hanging by her side.

"Okay," the wedding planner said, trotting back into the room. "We'll get going just after the next song change in a few seconds. Remember to breathe as you're walking. Okay? Remember to breathe. Everyone looks beautiful. Little Claudia, all set?"

The sisters gradually stopped fussing over Mona's dress and took their spots in front of her. Davi looked over Daphne's shoulder to peek into the church and saw that the front pews were loaded with guests, many more than she'd counted when she'd last poked her head out to look. Suddenly, her nerves exploded in protest, having lost the distraction of fretting over Mona all morning. These weren't interchangeable cardboard cutouts in convenience stores and gas stations but family and friends. To be the center of their attention for even just a hundred paces was no easy reunion.

The organ music changed, and on the wedding planner's signal, Claudia began to walk down the aisle in bouncy steps, flinging her pillow around with her.

"Claudia! Hold it with both hands," Mara whispered while she was still close.

Davi wrung her hands on the bouquet and concentrated on breathing. The thought of looking into the crowd during her walk down the aisle made her dizzy. If she smiled into the pews, couples might be giving her side-eye glances as they leaned their heads together to hear the other whisper about how much she'd changed or how surprised they were that she'd showed up at all. Staring straight ahead the whole way with animatronic fixation seemed incorrect in its own right, but nothing else was coming to mind. Watching Mara and Daphne go first couldn't hurt. Perhaps there was some obvious tradition about where bridesmaids looked during their entrance that she was forgetting. The wedding planner gave Mara her cue, and she set off down the aisle behind Claudia who was already nearly at the altar with the rings.

Daphne looked down and took a deep breath before stepping up to go next. Kneeling down to the side of the aisle, Debbie snapped photos of Mara just before she got to the seats filled with guests and trotted around the outside of the pews up to the front to take a couple more that included the crowd as part of the shot. Daphne took her first step down the aisle, and Davi was next. If she could have slowly melted away into the stained glass and carved, hooded saints just then, she would have jumped at the chance.

"Almost. Remember to breathe the whole way. And go."

Davi took a wobbly step forward as Daphne fell in line next to Mara on the side of the altar. The organ music was so much louder in the hall, echoing off the towering ceilings. The two strands of black beads hanging from the back of her collared dress kept tapping together against her skin with each step. All of the eyes in the church trained on her, and she pretended Mona was just one step behind her, their gazes instead reaching out to see the bride over her shoulder.

As she neared guests, Debbie returned from the front of the church and knelt down to get her first round of entrance shots.

Staring down the lens as she approached, Davi realized that she couldn't remember the last time she'd had her picture taken.

"Come on, Davi. Give me something," Debbie said with a smile from behind her rig.

She stopped walking in the middle of the aisle and turned to Debbie's camera while hurried glances chased hissing whispers through the pews. Putting one hand behind her head and the other holding the bouquet on her jutted-out waist, she cut her eyes at the camera and struck a pose.

*   *   *

Having scrubbed the boat clean inside and out while Victor put away the tackle box, rods, and the rest of the gear, her muscles were still burning against the sheets. Even though it was only midday, she desperately needed a nap to take refuge from her throbbing shoulders and seasick stomach. The world was pitching and rolling behind her eyes, and lying down made the hangover from the waves all the worse.

Victor sat on the bed beside her to take off his shoes, neatly placing them on the other side of his nightstand. Stretching back onto the bed, he put his arm around her, and Davi curled against his side, resting her hand on his chest. Being cuddled up next to him always made her drowsy, but the vertigo sensation kept forcing her eyes to pop open and remind her stomach that it was no longer on the water. The part of his shirt that was by her nose still smelled of salt water, exacerbating the queasiness with every inhale.

"Take this off please," she requested, lightly tugging at the shirt material.

After he'd lain back down, she drew into the same spot against his chest. With his bare skin under her cheek, her thoughts drifted to sex, and just as quickly, she recoiled in tentative repellence. The last time they'd made love he had asked in the middle of it what she thought of Hank joining them with a strange smirk, the question itself somehow becoming less disturbing than the look on his face. His smile at that moment, all mischief and appetite, lingered in her mind even now.

A certain bent pattern had been emerging in the past year, but she couldn't quite put her finger on what her intuition was sensing. All she had to go on was a fuzzy hunch that the doors he held open for her were beginning to feel less like thoughtful gestures to unburden her day and more like guarantees to himself that he would know exactly where she was at all times because he would be escorting her the whole way. Just then, the nauseous malaise cleared a bit, and she snuggled her face into his chest to try to seize the opportunity.

"Hey," he said.

"Yeah?"

"I'm sorry that I made us stay out there when you weren't feeling well. I don't know why I did that."

"It's okay. I'm just glad I made it overboard. And to the side where the wind wasn't blowing right back at me. That would have been terrible," she said.

His body moved slightly underneath her as though he was nodding in agreement, and she squeezed him across his ribs to thank him for apologizing. He hadn't done so after that shove in the backyard the prior week when she'd missed picking up one of the dog squats that he'd stepped right into, but then again, she hadn't demanded it of him either. Gaps in decorum were easy to overlook in the heat of the moment.

His torso began to spasm under her head, and she lifted her face off him in confusion. When she looked up, he was hurrying to wipe tears off his cheeks.

"What's the matter?" she asked.

His mouth opened to speak but clapped back closed as he sobbed into his hands. Davi sat all the way up on the bed next to him, alarmed by his sudden despair.

"Hey, what's the matter with you?"

He left his face covered while she rubbed his arm softly to calm him down.

"I can't—"

"Hm?"

"I can't believe how strong you are," he said through the tears.

Davi sat next to him and furrowed her brow, wondering why such a thing would make him cry. Meanwhile, her fingertips traced the outline of their favorite muscles of his, unconsciously signing her name across the slopes.

*   *   *

"So, what do you think of Declan?" Mona asked.

Davi's feet were feeling the toll of a night on the dance floor, and she took a seat with Mona at an empty table to take her heels off and fan herself with a seating card. A wreckage of icing-frosted forks and tossed napkins was scattered around the tablecloth, left behind in the party's wake.

"He's very nice. You were right. More importantly, you two look great together. Very happy, very natural."

"I'm so glad," Mona said, reaching up to remove the hairpins around her tiara. "This thing, on the other hand, is pissing me off."

"It must have gotten loose while you were dancing," Davi said.

"Could you give me a hand?"

Davi pushed herself up with a grunt. Her thighs were hollowed out, and the muscles in her feet were all seized up with sharp, tiny strains that totaled up in a steady throb through her arches. Apparently, her legs used different muscles to dance because she could clean the entire house every day for weeks and not once wind up with them reduced to quivering jelly.

"Did you have a good day?" Davi asked, working away on Mona's hair.

"Well, I spent most of the reception getting congratulated by people, talking to everyone. Uncle Ray had me cornered for a good twenty minutes telling stories until Declan came and pulled me away."

"You want your hair down now too?"

"Please," Mona said.

Davi started to remove all the pins she could see. With Mona's hair so thick, she was bound to miss a few, unless Mona could feel them pulling on her scalp and point them out. Watching her fingers search through her hair, Davi thought of Victor, the dogs, and home for the first time all day. They seemed so far away just then.

"Did you see Mom and Dad yet?" Mona asked.

"Not yet."

"Do you think you'll go over to see them before everyone goes to bed?"

"Yeah. I just wasn't ready for it earlier."

"I know what you mean," Mona said.

"Here's this," Davi said, handing her the tiara. "Now, you don't look like a Romanian princess anymore."

"Thank you."

"Sorry, my feet are absolutely killing me right now," Davi said, collapsing back into her chair. "I got all the ones I could see."

"It's fine. Fuck me, it already feels so much better. Total relief," Mona said, scratching her scalp.

One by one, the band members slowly filtered back into the room for a few more songs before they wrapped for the night. While she'd been dancing, Davi hadn't realized how many guests had already left for their rooms. The party was almost over.

"I should go over to see them. It's later than I thought," Davi said.

They got up and hugged. Mona's hands pressed against her back and slid around, jostling the hanging beads on her dress, and lost in the moment, Davi didn't want to let go. The trumpeter with the band blared a loud practice note that startled them both into a laugh, and Davi kissed Mona on the cheek.

"I want to be involved in your life and you in mine. So, please don't stop calling and talking to me when you get home," Mona said.

"Okay," Davi said. "I promise."

"You staying for brunch tomorrow, or are you going to head back?"

"I'm going to drive back tonight. I'm just wiped out. Everything's been great, but it's just exhausting for me to—"

Mona raised her hand to cut off her explanation and hugged her again.

"I'll call you when you're back from the honeymoon in a week or two," Davi said.

"Okay. I love you," Mona said.

"I love you too."

Davi picked up her heels and started to make her way across the dance floor towards her parents' table. Thankfully, the band was starting to play a slower number to wind down the night, giving her a good shot of making it to their table without another old friend ambushing her and pulling her out to dance on her spent feet. Halfway there, she crossed paths with Debbie who was taking the camera strap off her shoulder and cracking her neck.

"Hey, Deb. Walk with me for a minute? I'm just heading over to see my parents before they leave," Davi said.

"Man, I haven't seen them in years. Maybe fifteen years? You think they remember me?"

"Maybe, maybe not. Hard to know what to expect with them."

"Sorry we didn't have time to really catch up, but Mona wanted a lot of shots of the reception. People partying and laughing and falling over, that kind of thing. You want to maybe grab lunch sometime?" Debbie asked, handing her a business card.

"Absolutely. I'll call you, and we'll figure out what to do."

"So, what have you been up to all this—"

"Hey, Mom. Dad," Davi said, just within earshot of the table.

Her mother looked worn out, the lines on her face now proper creases, and Davi could practically smell the liquor oozing through her pores. Her father got up and gave her a big hug, but her mother was only willing to muster a fleeting smile and soft hello. Just like the last time they'd seen each other, Abe was bloated, the color of his face uneven with a subtle blotchiness. Davi could tell that his usual laughing, kissing self had been absent from the party because he was uncomfortable being seen this way and knew how the alcohol was affecting his appearance, forcing a deniable interior onto the surface and into the open. She could sympathize.

"You guys remember Debbie?" Davi asked.

"Hi. I'm Abe," her father said, shaking her hand with a smile but clearly not remembering who she was.

"Maeve," her mother said.

Debbie smiled back and politely excused herself to finish packing away the rest of her gear.

"So, what did you think of the wedding? Mona had a great time, and Declan seems wonderful," Davi said.

"It was very nice," Maeve said blankly.

"How's everything back at home?" Abe asked with a look of muted concern in his drooped, mismatched eyelids.

"We're working things out as best we can. Marriage is tough, you know? People make mistakes," Davi said, her eyes bouncing about the room.

Abe put his hand on Maeve's leg under the table and looked over at her, but she didn't noticeably react. Her cup of coffee was nearly empty, and he got to his feet to get her a fresh one.

"So, things are going well, are they?" Maeve asked.

"Yeah," Davi answered, fidgeting with the edge of the tablecloth now that Abe had gone to the bar.

"You look like you've lost a lot of weight."

"I have. Just haven't had much of an appetite."

"You could stand to eat more. Your face looks drawn this way."

"Maybe you're right," Davi said with an irritable sigh.

"You're going back home tonight?"

"I think so."

"Gotta keep Victor happy, I suppose," Maeve said, dipping her words in backhanded iciness.

Her drinking was as bad as it had ever been, and Davi had seen it through times when she couldn't imagine how it could possibly get worse. Now, Maeve barely seemed to be in there at all, and Abe looked well on his way after her into the abyss.

He'd stood by her through everything, and Davi knew he always would. He'd never asked her to change, never needed her to, and there was something beautiful about that. Still, it had been dawning on Davi more and more through her time with Mills that love of that brand became poison when the ratios were off.

"I want to know something."

"What is it, Mom?" Davi asked, turning to look back at the dance floor.

"Did I play any part in making you the way you are now?"

Lurking behind every encounter Davi had had since last night was that unspoken topic, and she was caught off guard that Maeve would be the one to finally broach it, especially in such a low, grave tone. Davi placed her palm flat on the tablecloth and dragged her fingers back while the threads ran beneath them, through the linen.

"I don't know," Davi said solemnly.

Maeve took a sip of her coffee and nodded. Two tables away, Mara was getting Claudia's things together, and Davi got out of her chair, anxious to catch them before she headed home herself.

"I'll finish my coffee, and then I'm going to bed," Maeve said.

"I'm going to say goodbye to Mara, and then I'll be back to see you and Daddy before you head up to your room," Davi said, waving over to Mara for her to wait a moment.

"Mm-hm," Maeve muttered as she put her empty cup back down in the saucer and rested her cheek on her hand.

12.

The vacuum zoomed over the living room carpet for its eleven AM treatment. The cold had arrived earlier than usual that fall, and regularly stoking the wood-burning stove in the basement was now cycled into Victor's list of tasks every morning. Even though she'd gone down there at ten, a chill was already beginning to creep through the insulation again, and she reminded herself to throw a few more logs on the fire once the carpets were done.

After nine months with Mills, Davi sensed for the first time that their work was paying real dividends, the world now crisp with potential instead of drooping under soggy gauze. She hadn't yet cracked how to escape the house once and for all, but her confidence in manufacturing a solution was climbing, which Victor must have been noticing himself. He was hardly placated by time-stamped receipts and odometer readings anymore, and almost every trip she made out of the house resulted in a fight when she came back, leaving Davi to marvel at how little she was cowed by his disconsolate outbursts. The more furious he became, the more desperate he looked, and while the tables were plainly turning, she worried about what new levels he might be driven to because of it.

147

Davi closed the vacuum inside the closet. Just as she reached for the knob to the basement, the phone rang on the kitchen wall.

"Hello?"

"Davi? It's Diane! What the hell?"

"Oh, my God. Diane," Davi said, her head beginning to spin like chloroform was coming through the receiver.

"How could you come to Mona's wedding and not make plans to see me while you were out here? I can't believe you," Diane said.

Davi was sure she'd heard that Diane had moved to Richmond or Roanoke or somewhere deep in Virginia years ago but couldn't remember where she'd gotten that idea. Probably just some passing rumor that had lodged in her mind because she'd needed it there.

"Shit, I'm sorry. I was kind of overwhelmed with seeing a lot of people, and I— What can I say? I'm sorry," Davi said.

"Hey, I was only teasing. So serious," Diane said, chuckling. "So, I heard the wedding really came off. Debbie told me."

"Oh, you talked to Debbie? Yeah, it was a great party, and Mona and Declan definitely had a great time. That's the main thing, right?"

Diane's end of the line stayed silent for a second longer than felt natural, and Davi gulped, anticipating the onslaught.

"You know, there's a weird hesitation that people do when I ask about you," Diane said.

"Yeah?"

"I'm not prying, but everyone just kind of goes blank slate on me," Diane said, pausing again. "How come they're doing that?"

Davi tried to erase Kerry from her thoughts. She and Diane had been through too much together to bear such a comparison.

"Okay," Davi said. "I'll explain. You got a little time?"

Davi started to detail her daily routine, and Diane filled the empty spots with gasps and curtailed questions. She described how she'd had to ask for the money to have her tooth fixed from the same man who'd knocked it out. She explained how quickly and often she'd had to redefine the concept of normal and how frighteningly easy it was to do. She talked about how entire months could pass like days when sleep was always just out of reach. She even told her what a relief it had been to discover that bags of frozen vegetables were easier on swelling skin than ice packs. She told her everything.

"I'll fucking kill that bastard," Diane said.

"I'm sorry to spring it all on you like that, but I'm figuring things out here. I've been seeing a shrink since March, I'm off all my meds now, and I'm getting it together. I don't want you to worry."

"Jesus Christ, Davi. I haven't heard from you in years, and now I call you to hear that you're being beaten, abused, dehumanized, and you tell me not to worry. Do you understand how that sounds on my end?"

Davi closed her eyes and rubbed her forehead.

"I guess not. I'm sorry. I'm out of practice on some things, Diane. But I am getting things in order. I just haven't figured how to get out yet."

"Where are your parents?"

"My parents have enough problems. My dad is drinking all the time now with her. They're in no condition."

"So, what do you need me to do? Tell me what you need to have happen in order to get out of there," Diane said.

"I'm going to head around town and find a job. I wanted to start that by now, but I don't know when I can spare being away like that. That's a little risky."

"Find an apartment. I'll send you the money for the first month's rent and security and whatever else they need from you."

Tightrope tension stiffened Davi's spine. The last thing she needed was well-intentioned recklessness from those in whom she chose to confide, and the risk of others not understanding how dangerous their help really was had been almost the entire reason that Diane was the first of her former circle of close-knit friends to hear about how she'd lived the last few years. As much as she didn't care to admit it, the rest of the reason amounted to nothing more than simple, garden-variety embarrassment.

"No, don't send me anything here," Davi said quickly. "I won't get it, and he'll figure out that something's up. This only works if I can keep him complacent and thinking he's in control of everything like he has been."

"What if he tries to—"

"I'll handle it, Diane. I promise I'll handle it."

Diane's end of the line went silent.

"What the fuck am I supposed to do here?" she finally said in frustration. "I'm sending you money. Don't even try to talk me out of that."

Davi racked her brain. There was only one option to accommodate her safety if Diane was going to be this insistent.

"I'll see if you can send it to my psychologist's office. Victor lets me go there without any problems. I told him I needed to go to learn how to become a more compliant wife for him, and he bought that."

"My God," Diane said breathlessly. "He's out of his mind."

Davi was sure Mills would accept the package that Diane wanted to send, but implicit in that arrangement was the inevitability that he would want an explanation as to why her home address was somehow unfit. Perhaps it was time that she took that chance with him. In order to make a run for it, she needed a job, some money, and a place to stay, and a gloomy reality had been sinking in over the months since the wedding that she couldn't pull all that off alone. An apartment could not be landed without money, money could not be had without a job, and a job could not be worked unless she had her own place. If Diane could safely send her a month's rent to start, that might create enough momentum to break the impasse.

Davi hung up the phone and saw it was nearly noon. Maybe she had time to run to some of her old jobs around town and see if her former managers still ran them. Bella Florist was a good place to start, sure to avoid Victor's radar as a place to search once she'd left since they hadn't yet met at the time she worked there. Even better for the sake of returning home quickly and sparing enough time to cross off the remaining items on Victor's list, the florist was only a couple of miles down the road. Davi snatched her keys off the hook by the door and hopped in the car.

As she drove, she refused to look down at the odometer, unwilling to watch its wheels slowly turning over as quiet reminders that she was leaving a trace. Victor would notice even the slightest difference in the numbers he'd seen before leaving for work that morning, so there was no reason to watch them spin once they'd crossed the point of no return, this time the seven in the tenths place circling downward to where the horizontal top of the number became visible.

Maybe she could tell him that Mills needed to see her for some sort of emergency. Maybe she could stop at an auto body shop and see if there was a way to crack open the steering column and manually roll back the digits. Briefly, she fantasized about driving in reverse the entire way home, deftly navigating the intersections with her mastery of going both forwards and backwards simultaneously. Whizzing into a spot in the strip mall parking lot without having arrived at a solution, she popped out of the car and burst into the florist's, hopeful that the mounting pressure on the ride home would lead to a breakthrough of ingenuity.

The young woman behind the counter leapt off her stool when she heard the sudden bang of bells against the top of the door glass. She dropped her magazine onto the counter and half-glared at Davi who marched right up to her.

"I used to work here, and I'm looking for Frank to see if I could get my job back," Davi blurted.

The young woman's gaze lightened, and her head drifted backwards.

"Unfortunately, he had a stroke last year and had to retire. I run the shop now. I'm his daughter, Cait."

The possibility that Frank might not still work at the flower shop hadn't crossed Davi's mind. Everything about the sign and façade out front looked identical to what she remembered, and she fell flat-footed staring at Cait, unable to muster any sensible continuation.

"I might want an extra hand soon, though. I'm getting married in February, and I'll be around less," Cait said.

"What do you need me to do?" Davi asked, dropping her purse on the counter.

"Well, I'd need to talk with you first, have an interview, see your résumé."

"The last job I worked was as a waitress at the Copper Top Café over the bridge seven years ago. But I worked here the job before that."

"I see," Cait said tentatively.

"So?" Davi asked. "What do you think?"

"Um, I really don't know what you mean."

On the wall behind Cait, the clock read twenty after twelve, and Davi decided to cut her losses. Cait's shoulders were becoming closed and rigid, telling Davi that she was coming off too intense, and Davi reached into her empty purse for a pen. The only paper on the counter was the lingerie catalog that Cait had carelessly dropped there, thanks in part to the commotion Davi had caused with her entrance. Davi grabbed the catalog and flipped it over to write in the white space on the back.

"I understand that you might be seeing me as a little weird right now. I was expecting to see Frank, er— your father. I'm just writing my name here to leave with you. I would give you my number, but it— I'll take your number and call you in a few days, okay?"

"That's fine," Cait said, an irked look crawling across her features as she looked down at her catalog.

Davi snatched up her keys and made for the door. She needed to rethink what she was doing. There was a distinction between urgently looking for a job and running around like a chicken with its head cut off, and from the way Cait had reacted to her, she suspected she was presently on the wrong side of the line. Davi caught the door before it closed behind her and poked her head back inside the shop.

"I'm sorry to hear about your father. I hope you'll send him my best," Davi said.

The bells on the door jangled through the glass behind her as she lit a smoke in front of the store. Her inability to converse without everything coming out in fits and starts boggled her mind. She was just guessing with people, going through the motions, which was a strategy that had never failed her while she was sedated and aimless. Only now that she was attempting to actively reenter society were the cars all piling up in her thoughts with every interaction, serving notice that the eloquence and charm she had once found so effortless had atrophied with everything else. She threw her cigarette against the blacktop by the Legacy's front tire and squished it, having smoked only a few puffs.

"Fuck it. I'm not going home yet."

*   *   *

"Because I don't fucking feel like it right now. That's why. Got it?"

Confusion spread over Victor's face. Her going out to get his Winstons at the store had become so assumed and automatic that he appeared to forget how to address any resistance. At first, he seemed to think she was kidding, but now that she'd dismissed him again, his eyes turned against themselves, each blaming the other for having missed the warning signs of her growing stronger. She had told herself that she wouldn't argue, that it was too risky to put him on his guard with her still riding high from Mona's wedding, but his unease was more of a rush than she'd expected.

"Then, get the trash cans from the curb," he muttered with his last cigarette popping up and down between his lips.

"Fine."

She let the screen door slip off her fingertips behind her, turning slightly as she did to make sure he wasn't rushing after her to pull her back inside and away from neighborhood view. Instead, the door flapped gently shut, and Davi exhaled a deep breath she hadn't realized she'd been holding.

"Well, hello, Miss. Haven't seen you around here in a while," she whispered, barely suppressing a smile.

Victor's lawn was putting up a good fight against the autumnal chill, especially in comparison to the neighboring properties whose lawns already had splotches of lighter green running through them. Walking along the driveway, she could see the beauty in it now like she never before could, beauty that wasn't about fragrance or vibrancy or eclectic colors but rather sheer determination. Brute force. Relentless will. That was the story written on every root if she were to bend over and peel up a corner like Astroturf. With her garden only a memory, she wondered if she could make a lawn do that too.

The trash collectors had flipped the metal lids off the cans by the curb and left everything scattered on the asphalt, which was unsurprising since they couldn't even be bothered to stop them from crashing into the ground with loud tin bangs at seven in the morning. She righted the cans and lifted one with each arm once the lids were back in place. When she turned around to head back towards the garage, Victor was coming out of the house.

"I'm going out to get smokes. I'll be back in a few minutes. Here, I'll take one of those up," he said, gesturing for the trash can in her left hand.

"Okay," Davi said with surprise. "Thanks."

Victor walked down the driveway, stuffing his keys back into his jeans pocket. He reached out and plucked the lid off the can she was holding out for him.

"No problem," he said.

BANG!

The two cans clamored on the driveway like heavy cymbals as her hands went straight to her nose. Mind-erasing pain reverberated through its bridge and pulsed into her eyes, flooding them with water. The snowfall feeling of a runny nose came almost immediately, the blood streaming so fast she could already feel drops running over her upper lip. Victor's chest heaved in front of her, and he unclenched his fist, dropping his lid onto the concrete.

Her brain was still rattling around as she bent over to pick up the trash cans and lids again with her tongue searching around for any loose teeth and thankfully finding none. The ringing in her ears made her eyes wince shut as she walked past him. Once she'd clapped the trash cans down in front of the garage where they belonged, she wiped the back of her hand under her nose, smearing it with a thick, red streak from her wrist to her knuckle.

"I'll be back in a few minutes," Victor said, opening the door to his truck and stepping up into it.

Davi went inside to the bathroom and turned on the faucet. In the mirror, her face was a bloody mess and excruciatingly tender along the bridge of her nose. She pressed her nose between her two hands and gently wiggled them back and forth to see if it was broken.

"Son of a bitch," she muttered, wetting a washcloth under the water. "Not smart, sister. Not smart. Now, you'll have to explain this to Mills. No way this clears up by Tuesday."

She stuffed some wadded-up toilet paper into her nostrils and pinched them closed. Her nose wasn't broken, but putting pressure on it still buckled her knees. Her eyes watered up again and rained tears down her cheeks as she pinched, but the bleeding had to stop.

*　　　*　　　*

Davi's car screeched into a parking spot. Kellerman's was farther from home than Bella Florist, and the traffic on the main route had been atrocious. Now, it was five after one, and Davi was only willing to spare time to speak with those who had previously known her, those who would be able to reference that earlier model to sand down the edges of her present jigsaw sketch. Dealing with anyone else would only amount to waste and the spoiling of an opportunity with avoidable mistakes.

The automatic doors zipped open, and before anyone could ask any questions, Davi made her way into the back and upstairs to the manager's office, relieved to find that 'Michelle Grove' was still written on the removable nameplate.

"Hello?" Davi said, pushing aside the half open door.

Michelle tilted her head slightly over her shoulder, her attention still focused on her computer against the wall. Her hair was much grayer than Davi remembered, but Michelle also had to be fifty by now. At thirty-five, Davi had lost even more color in the streaks in her hair than all of Michelle's put together.

"Hey, Michelle," Davi said.

Michelle swiveled her chair around towards Davi with a look on her face that suggested she recognized the voice but somehow found it impossible to have heard it. Upon seeing Davi, she began to sob, cupping her hands over her nose and staring at her through the tears. Davi closed the door to the office behind her.

"Please don't cry. I need a job, and I need it right now."

"Just come here first," Michelle said, getting to her feet.

Michelle came around the desk and hugged Davi tightly in her arms. Michelle's hands on her back made the hair on Davi's neck stand up, and her body pressing against hers electrocuted her brain, as though one of her metal fillings had bitten into foil. Davi pushed her away suddenly.

"Sorry. Don't take that personally. I— Please don't take that personally."

"No, it's fine," Michelle said, wiping her face. "You're hired, you're hired. When do you want to start? I was just working on the schedules for next week."

"I'm not sure yet. I still need to find a place to live."

"I'll get everyone to look around for apartments for rent in the next day or so. Would that help?"

Davi cartwheeled inside. If Michelle's digging turned up even a couple of leads, she would be saving her untold hours of scheming and sneaking around, and Davi would be less likely to face a demoralizing carousel of landlords balking at her strangeness and refusing to rent to her because of it, all of which seemed a likely destiny if Michelle's falling to tears at first sight was any indication.

"That would be fantastic for me," Davi said. "I have to run right now, but I'll explain everything, okay? I'm sorry to just barge in here like that. I'll call you."

"Okay, I'll get some addresses for you," Michelle said.

It was one-thirty. If she made it home by two, she would have about an hour and a half to do the carpets for the second time, put wood in the stove, and take care of all of the cats and dogs. As long as the traffic was thinner and she rehearsed her story on the way, she was confident she had enough time for everything. Remembering something halfway down the stairs, Davi snapped her fingers and jogged back to Michelle's door.

"Thank you, Michelle," Davi said, leaning through the doorway. "It's great to see you again."

13.

The early December day was oddly balmy, even with the wind insistently swirling through her hair outside the car. Davi had been able to see the apartment tucked back into the woods all the way from the main route before the turn onto Riverside, but the countless leaves that would return to the trees would obscure it completely come springtime. Combined with Kellerman's being only a few streets away, Davi now understood why Michelle had come across so assured on the phone when reading off the address, hurrying through the other three with an uninterested tone. She must have scouted the location herself and realized its advantages.

Unfortunately, the street and driveway by the big powder-blue house in front of the apartment wouldn't likewise improve their covers with a change in season. The Legacy would be easily seen from the main route by a searching eye, and while not an altogether singular car around town, she imagined that Victor would be of a mind to investigate each one he happened upon when the time came. Still, nothing posed as significant a probability of discovery as working at Kellerman's, and if parking was the only permanent drawback to the apartment, she doubted anywhere else could do better.

Walking up the front house's steps towards the wide, spacious porch, she realized that she'd been so anxious to chase Michelle's leads that she'd forgotten to call the house in advance to make sure the owners were going to be home and taking visitors. Halfway up the steps, she flung up her hands in disbelief, letting them slap down against her thighs. There was just too much to plan and take into account, especially considering she was still burning through huge amounts of energy on all of her usual tasks at home. With a shrug, she continued up to the porch and rang the doorbell. At some point or another, luck was just going to have to throw her enough breaks to smooth over the oversights.

The heavy door opened with a squeak at the end of its arc, and a little, old woman pushed on the handle to the screen door. Davi reached out to hold it open for her.

"Hiya there," the woman said.

"Hi, Miss Elliot?"

"Yes."

"I've been looking for a place to rent, and a friend of mine found out that you were renting your apartment out back. I was wondering if I could take a look at it," Davi said, reciting the brief script she'd rehearsed in the car.

Miss Elliot scrunched her nose to push her glasses to a different angle in front of her eyes.

"I apologize. I should have called. My friend just called me an hour ago, and I was so excited that I forgot to call and let you know I'd be coming," Davi said.

Miss Elliot nodded but still looked confused by either Davi or her explanation. The feeling of her soft eyes being suspicious of her was disheartening.

"You're the one Michelle said would be coming by today, aren't you?"

"I— Well, I don't know. My friend's name is Michelle. That's true. I just don't— She didn't tell me that she'd been here to see you," Davi stammered.

"Yes, she was here earlier. We spoke for a little while before she had to leave for work. Nice woman. Seemed concerned about you," Miss Elliot said, leaving a probing, upwards hook on the end of her sentence.

"She's like that," Davi said.

Miss Elliot nodded again, and her nose allowed her glasses to come back down to their original place. Breaking a gentle smile, she took Davi's hand and patted it on the back.

"Don't worry, dear. I think you'll really like the place when you see it."

Miss Elliot reached to the side of the doorway and got her cane. Then, she reached up and lifted a set of keys off a rack by the door. Davi wished she hadn't kept them there.

"Is it cold out?"

"It's windy. Not on the porch, but it was very windy walking up. You might want to put something else on."

From the threshold, Miss Elliot stuck her cane out parallel to the ground and looked up searchingly to the roof overhanging the porch, as though stretching out her palm under suspicious clouds to feel for raindrops. Davi chuckled, and Miss Elliot winked at her.

"No, I think I'll be fine to walk to the backyard. As long as there isn't anything on the ground, I'll be okay from here to there," she said.

Davi pushed the screen door closed behind her to make sure it stayed fastened shut in the wind, and by the time she turned around, Miss Elliot was already almost all the way down the steps. Davi caught up to her at the bottom where the wind was whipping, unabated.

"Woo, you weren't kidding. If you wouldn't mind," she said, reaching her hand into the crook of Davi's elbow for balance. "Just so one of the gusts doesn't pick me up and toss me into the trees."

"Of course," Davi said.

"And call me Gladys," she said in a why-not pitch.

"Okay, Gladys. Thank you."

"And what will I call you, I wonder?"

"Call me Davi."

"Davie Crockett?" she said with a wink.

"Davi Ross," Davi said, winking back.

Around the back of the house, the apartment sat towards the side of the yard, elevated a couple feet off the ground with a wooden latticework skirt to cover the gap. The woods didn't start until about ten yards behind the apartment with one lone tree permitted to grow to the side of the front door. Its stripped-down, winterized branches partially rested on the roof with one branch occasionally tapping against the siding in the bigger gusts.

Gladys handed Davi the key ring and waited at the base of the four-step staircase, twirling her cane around in her hand.

"The top one sticks a little. Just pull the door towards you as you turn it," she said.

The door opened, and Davi turned to give Gladys a hand up the steps. At the top, Gladys wiped her feet and dotted her cane up and down on the doormat.

"So, this is the main room. The TV went kaput around this time last year, but you can always bring another one for yourself if you want."

"I won't watch much TV," Davi said.

"You don't hear that too often these days," Gladys said, pleasantly surprised. "Look around a bit. Tell me if it's missing anything you were counting on, and maybe we can let you borrow it from the house until you get settled."

The rooms were furnished, though meagerly, and the whole place had a dankness that said the woods outside were slowly creeping into the carpets and upholstery. The couch looked like it hadn't moved since the seventies, its light checked pattern in yellow and brown gradually fading on its way down to the carpet. In a more deliberate interior design, its look might have come off stylishly retro, but pushed against the lined, cloudy wallpaper with water stains in the corners, the colors looked tired and dated. At least the round, wooden table with two chairs tucked underneath still had a healthy sheen of laminate on its surface, which must have made the whole set newer than the couch by twenty years.

In the kitchen to the side of the main room, Davi twisted a knob for one of the burners on the apartment-sized oven, and the tapping spark lit the gas right on time. The cabinets had a couple of loose bowls and glasses that looked worth salvaging, especially one coffee mug with a smiling cartoon bumblebee printed on its side. The window over the sink had dingy, yellowing lace curtains, but with them pushed aside, the little view was nicely quaint in the daylight, the tops of the bigger trucks traveling on the main route visible through the skeleton trees. Even still, she could tell that her mind would be keen to conjure shapes and shifty silhouettes in the blackness if she dared to look up while cleaning a fork after dark.

"So, you'll be working over at Kellerman's is the idea?" Gladys asked while pulling out one of the chairs at the table.

"Yes, that's my new job. Michelle's my boss."

"I enjoy their produce. I don't know where they get their strawberries, but there's always nice cartons of them with never a bad one in the bunch. Well, maybe in the offseason."

By the standards to which Davi had grown accustomed, the bathroom was absolutely wretched, and she had to restrain the gnashing urge to clean it all on the spot. Picking up a new shower liner and curtain on her way over tomorrow was simple enough, but the shower itself looked like it hadn't been cleaned in months. The grout between most of its tiles had gone black with mold, and she had to look away before she was overwhelmed by the craving to spit on the wall and rub the grooves clean with her thumb, even if it took off the skin down to the bone.

"Your boss is quite something to help find you a place," Gladys said from the other room. "I had a wonderful time speaking with her."

"I used to work with her years ago, and we were friends. When I said she was my boss before, that was misleading. She's my friend too."

"Well, she's a good friend. Not everyone goes out of their way like that, even for friends."

"I know just what you mean, Gladys," Davi said, her eyebrows raised knowingly as she came out of the bathroom and passed through to the end of the hall.

New linens and sheets had always been on her list of initial purchases, but the bed was going to need more than that, having been left with only a miserable, stained mattress pad as a covering. Grabbing a couple pillows from the house would be a priority as the squished ones on the bed looked like they'd been due for retirement years ago only to be pressed back into action by a previous tenant who'd slept far sounder than she. Despite its temporary shortcomings however, the bedroom was the nicest room in the apartment, boasting a queen-sized bed, two night tables with lamps, and a cherry bookshelf along the far wall that she pictured filling with smaller canvases.

"Well, what do you think, Davi? The rent is three hundred a month, and as soon as you give the first and last month's rent, you can move right in. Same day."

"I think it's perfect," Davi said, coming back into the main room with a relieved sigh.

"Wonderful. Your search is over then," Gladys said, pushing herself out of her chair.

"Six hundred dollars and I'll be ready to go?" Davi asked.

"That's right."

"Would it be alright if I came back in an hour or two to pay you?"

"Well, of course. But there's no rush."

"I know. I just have to get some other things organized, and I don't want to miss you because I would like to move in tomorrow," Davi said.

Gladys poked her cane into the softer ground beneath the last step and reached her free hand for Davi's arm. With the extra balance, she stepped all the way down and straightened up her back.

"Whatever you have to do, dear. It's fine with me," she said, patting the back of Davi's hand.

Driving to Mills' office, she wasn't sure what to expect from him. He had agreed to meet her and hand over the envelope on his lunch break, between twelve-thirty and one, but when she'd called to ask him to accept Diane's delivery, he was outraged to hear the story of what had really been happening, how he'd been capably kept in the dark for months. By the end of the call, he'd calmed down, but she found herself still resenting his feeling betrayed by her, as though he had a special right to know such things. Telling no one about her home life was the baseline rule with everyone she knew. She had simply declined to make him a special exception.

On the edge of the shade, Mills was standing beside the tree in front of his office building when Davi turned into the parking lot. Outside of the office, he looked more frazzled and out of control, the wind making his hands chase his hair and tie as they flapped into his face. Davi checked the time on the dash while she drove towards him and had to slam her brakes to avoid T-boning a white Honda that had just begun to reverse out of its spot. She cringed behind the wheel, knowing Mills had seen that.

"Thanks again for agreeing to be the middleman for us. I just didn't have anyone else to ask," Davi said, leaving the car door hanging open.

"You're doing okay? How do you feel?" Mills asked.

"Well, I'm getting things done, and that's what I define as 'okay' at the moment. It just takes a lot of damn work to straddle two lives, but I'm a realist, Mills. You know that," she said.

He glanced off towards the cars motoring along the street, a look of muted aggravation resting in his eyebrows.

"I just can't believe that you would keep all of this from me," he said, handing her the envelope from Diane.

"I did what I had to do to get things done my way. There wasn't anything personal about it."

"We might have been able to find a discreet solution. You shouldn't have assumed a risk that size on your own," he said.

"It would have been better for you to assume it? Or Goldstein? And do what? Call the cops? I live within sight of a police station, Mills. It never even crossed my mind to go down there."

"Why not?"

Davi chuckled and shook her head, finally putting her finger on why he'd looked so odd outside the office.

"What are they going to do, let me live at the police station?" Davi said.

He nodded soberly, letting his hair and tie blow all over. Davi opened the envelope and flipped through the cash. Eight hundred dollars, just like Diane had promised. Now, it was only a matter of time.

"You have a safe place lined up?" he asked.

"Yes, I was just there. Very safe."

"And you'll be leaving tomorrow?"

"Leaving tomorrow around midday. I need to go back to meet the landlady to pay rent, my sister has a divorce lawyer lined up for me, my job is ready to go. I've got lots to do."

He slid his hands into his pockets and sighed deeply. Davi tucked the envelope into her purse.

"Look, I know this is all new to you, but I've been thinking it over for months now. I think of nothing else. This is as good of a shot as there's going to be for me. I didn't get into this mess overnight, and I'm not getting out of it that fast either. That's just all there is to it," Davi said.

"I would like to know that if things start to get out of control that you'll call me."

"That, I can promise you," she said, patting him on the arm. "Cheer up, huh? We've done a lot of work to get my head right."

"I'm very proud of the work we've done, Davi. Just please be smart about the risks you take."

She was sorry that she couldn't put his mind at ease and that he seemed to feel he had never truly earned her trust. At the car door, she turned and smiled back at him.

"Proud of you too, Millsy. You stuck with a real asshole and helped turn her back into a nearly functional person again. Now, we'll get to see just how good you really are."

"You were never that bad," Mills said.

"I was what I was," she said, shaking her head to dismiss his comment. "And I appreciate it. I'll call the office in the next few days to see what we can do about our next appointment."

She hurried to spin the car back towards the street. Gladys needed to be paid, and her usual chores had to be done. She reached into the envelope in her purse and pulled out the money. Six bills came off the top for the apartment and got stuffed into the cup holder, and the seventh hundred-dollar bill was going to be eaten up by the one-time moving purchases and incidentals. But the last one was all hers.

*   *   *

Heavy rain cascaded down the front window of the Copper Top. The storm had swept in so quickly that a dozen or so people had hurried off the street and into the café to escape it. Since the downpour had already dented the lunchtime business, Davi hoped the rain outside would at least last long enough for the refugees trapped at the front to stay and eat something out of a sense of obligation. After all, the pleasant summer days when people would wander the downtown and casually stop at restaurants for an impulsive bite didn't stick around forever.

With only two tables working and both having been served their main courses, Davi leaned on the counter in the back and flipped through the sports section of a newspaper that had been left on one of her tables by a snippy businesswoman who'd turned out to be a bad tipper to boot. The Phillies had lost to the Astros the night before but were still in first in the standings. Having woken up that morning with her cheek pressed against a page in The Great Gatsby, Davi was stretched too thin to watch every game. In fact, she rarely had time to catch any of them between waiting tables and studying, especially now that her English assignments called for reading books that bored her to sleep.

"Your guys look like they want their check," Mona said, coming back from the dining room with empty plates.

"The engineers or the younger couple?"

"The engineers."

Davi had a special bill waiting for them, covered with all of the work and solutions she'd prepared from their little pop quiz yesterday. Only two of them had come in for lunch though, each wearing unusual full-body slickers, one in orange and one yellow.

"Okay, guys. Thanks for braving the storm today," Davi said, dropping the check on the table.

"What's all this?" the one in orange asked, flipping the check around in his fingers.

Davi's face went red. Maybe they hadn't left the problems there for her to solve.

"Ah," the one in yellow said, snatching the check from his associate. "I was hoping you'd do something like this."

"So, you did leave them for me, right?"

"Of course. We were just curious."

"And?"

"Looks good to me," he said, pulling aside the yellow rubber to get to his wallet in his slacks.

"Yeah, you're impressed," Davi said with a defiant smile as she stuck a new straw in his soda and sipped it in front of his face.

"I was done with that anyway," he said with a shrug.

The two men got up and put their rain jackets on, the one in yellow waving off his colleague from adding any money to what he'd dropped on the table.

"What's with the full rain suits anyway?" Davi asked.

"We had to ride out to the dredge this morning, which is about two miles. The waves and mist spill over the side the whole way," the man in yellow said.

"Though I'm glad we left them on," the man in orange said, wandering over towards the front of the store to watch the rain pour down the glass.

Davi picked up the money on the table, and her pulse jumped at the sight of the corner of a hundred-dollar bill amidst the fives and ones. She signaled to the man in yellow to linger behind as his friend walked out of earshot.

"I think you've made a mistake. There's way too much money in here," she said, holding out the hundred.

The man in yellow smiled and held his palms up to her with a shake of his head.

"One of my colleagues bet me a hundred the other day that you wouldn't be able to solve what we gave you, and you did. I'll get my hundred back from him, and the rest of it was for the meal," he said.

"And if I hadn't come through? Would you have paid your friend?"

"Well, I was pretty sure, but if I'd been wrong?" he wondered to himself, trailing off into thought. "I can think of worse ways to lose a buck."

Davi popped up onto her toes and kissed him on the cheek. What a pity that she'd just recently met a gorgeous man, and now there was this one, somewhat nasal but surprisingly confident and charming. There just wasn't and couldn't ever be the same rocket-fuel blast of attraction to the man in yellow as there was to the quiet one, Victor.

*   *   *

Standing at the threshold of her studio, Davi contemplated how she would pack everything into the car. As much as there was to move, nothing could be touched now, but she knew things would happen quickly tomorrow and didn't want to have to make triage decisions on the fly when it came to the studio. Fortunately, all of the bigger items looked like they would collapse down to movable sizes, and the non-negotiable things that wouldn't were flat and easily packed in their own right.

Davi cracked open a soda and threw her dishrag onto the top of the kitchen island. She'd been moving at a lightning pace since getting home from the apartment an hour earlier and had caught up on just about everything on Victor's list. The only thing left was the counters, and after those were done, she'd have time to go around the whole house and make sure that her haste hadn't led to any cut corners.

Her stomach rumbled. Forcing measly bits of bread and lunchmeat down her throat was what she'd come to accept, resigned to the conclusion that whatever chip stomachs had that created hunger pains had fizzled out in hers, but all of the driving and scheduling and sneaking and plotting must have been more taxing than she'd felt while in the midst of it. She fantasized about preparing and eating one of the sirloins in the fridge with a side of green beans, but considering the hour, executing all of her chores to a tee on the last day that she planned to do them was more important. The soda would go a long way towards satisfying her hunger anyway.

She crunched up the empty can and shook the last few drops down the drain. On her way to the trash, a knock came at the door, and Davi's heart leapt into her throat. Hearing anyone knock at this hour would have been irregular on a normal day, but considering what she had planned for tomorrow, the unannounced company was downright alarming. Opening the door, Davi saw a woman with black, wavy hair clutching both of her hands on the strap of her purse.

"Hi, I'm here to see Victor," she said.

"Who the hell are you?" Davi replied.

"My name is Karen," she said, extending her hand.

"I didn't mean your name."

"I'm his girlfriend," she said, returning her hand to her purse strap.

Davi's eyes cleared. Karen looked to be a few years older than she was, but she was Victor's type.

"I'm his wife," Davi said calmly. "Would you like to come in?"

Karen stepped inside, not seeming particularly shocked to hear that Victor was married. A few weeks back, Victor had stormed into her studio, and Davi had fought him off amidst crashed easels and splattering paint. On his way out, he'd turned and told her that he would find someone else, and Karen must have been the one he'd picked.

"Can I get you something to drink?"

"Are you going to poison it?" Karen asked, only half joking.

"You can help yourself to a drink if you like. The glasses are in that cupboard to your right."

After running a glass under the tap, Karen sat on a stool at the island, and Davi leaned back against the counter across from her.

"What time did he tell you to come here?" Davi asked.

"Three o'clock."

The only thing to be gained from having Karen show up at the door before he came home was the sending of a message, and Davi understood Victor's messages very clearly by now. Like him, they had all the subtlety of a wrecking ball.

"So, you're the new woman in his life," Davi mused.

"Hey, he's been telling me that you two have been lined up for divorce for months now. So, don't get the wrong idea about me. I'm divorced myself. I know what it's like at the end. People do spiteful things to each other, and I don't want to be a part of that. I don't have anything against you."

"Are you sensing that I'm angry with you?" Davi asked.

"I don't know," Karen said, adjusting her seat on the stool. "Not really, I guess."

"You're right."

Karen nodded pensively and folded her hands on the island. Davi marveled at how obedient she already was, placing herself in a setting that screamed confrontation simply because he'd told her to. Regardless of why she was there, Davi felt obligated to tell her what was in store for her. Karen would never mention to Victor the things she told her, and even if she did, he would only enjoy it. Making Davi feel threatened and jealous was the entire point of Karen being there in the first place.

"Listen, I know that he seems like a great guy right now, very attentive, very charming. I completely understand. I just have to tell you, you're not safe with him. I don't care if you believe me because I know how it looks with me being the one saying it, but I have to say it. You think you have a great catch. But he's not right."

"Thanks for the tip," Karen said, opening into a grin.

"There's nothing he isn't capable of, and there's nothing I haven't put up with. Telling me when I can use the bathroom, monitoring everywhere I go, hitting me for no reason, rape every which way," Davi said, raising her eyebrows. "If you're the next one in his life, so be it. But I'm giving you the warning now that no one gave me. That's all I wanted to say."

"I don't believe you."

"I don't care if you believe me. I just had to say it."

Karen studied Davi's face with suspicious curiosity.

"If I'd been the one to tell you all of these horrible things about the man you were seeing, would you believe me?"

Davi knew firsthand that Victor's handsomeness had the power to blind, and if Karen was presently in the part of the sequence where she was content to be smitten, there was nothing Davi could say that would penetrate. Besides, she was too close to slipping the noose to stick her neck out for anyone. She'd ensured Karen wouldn't be some clueless lamb headed backwards into the shears. The rest was Karen's responsibility.

14.

With their ring hanging from her middle finger, the apartment keys dangled in front of her eyes. She caught them into her hand and ran her thumb over the grooves. In any sensible universe, the bumps would have spelled out 'Freedom' or 'Rebirth' in Braille, but in this one, the locksmith had probably just cut a random pattern into the metal with no mind paid to how special the keys might have turned out to be for the next person to hold them. Job 1748 – one lock, one key, one duplicate, end of order form.

Knotted cords in her belly ratcheted up their tension, sliding over each other with hiccupping jumps where two coils would meet, grind together, and finally pop apart again. She rubbed her palms against the couch and remembered fantasizing about today in countless daydreams, born into rising cigarette smoke. This was the day when everything was supposed to come into focus and make sense, as though all the puzzle pieces would suddenly gravitate together before her very eyes because they ached to be solved, but with today finally here, Davi didn't feel anything pure or complete. Today, and the last few days for that matter, had all been a blur, pulled into each other by rip currents of adrenaline and anxiety.

Her nerves gnashed all over, fully cognizant of the fact that the vacuum's motor hadn't vibrated through their synapses over an hour earlier. A point of no return was rapidly approaching, and if her nerves had anticipated the drama all along, she herself had been too preoccupied to sense it. When she'd opened the apartment door for Gladys and took the envelope from Mills' hand, the ultimate destination of where everything was headed had felt charmingly distant, always partially drowned in the thrill, but when she'd dangled the apartment keys in front of her face and realized they were there to replace her old ones, the breathtaking finality of it all had hit home. As soon as she walked out the door, she was never coming back here, this place she had known almost entirely to the exclusion of all other places for seven years.

She glanced around the living room, and scrapbooks of happier days she'd known in the house came back to her. She remembered cocky looks she used to give herself in the vanity when a new outfit looked just the way it had in the fitting room mirror, smiling at her curves and bopping her hips around to the rhythm of an imagined song. Those winking faces and their smirking inside jokes felt so foreign and unfamiliar, just like her more recent selves, lost in slaughterhouse resignation. Whoever all these people were, they were dead, now little more than graffiti murals on the backs of her eyes.

Davi sighed and rubbed her forehead. She had to force herself to embrace change, just like Mills would advise. For months if not years, she'd craved to make the moves she had in the last few days, and the only reason she was bucking away from them now was because she'd become married to their impeccable hope instead of their concrete existence, never having dared to imagine that she could be without the company of her conundrums. Yet, they were indeed solved, and realizing their impermanence left her awestruck. Even if Victor found her that night and everything started again from the beginning, she could never forget how the dominoes looked down on their faces, would always remember the poise to be found on the far side of duress.

Compulsively, she reviewed every single item she needed to take and cross-referenced each with the memory of her hands packing it into its specific bag, then with the snapshot of that same bag being shoved into its exact place in the Legacy. The list had been running through her head all night, becoming etched on her brain while she loaded the car, and right beside the concern of leaving behind something she would need was the sister worry of whether she was forgetting to cover a track that would allow Victor to determine where she'd gone. She didn't think it was possible, but her imagination begged to differ, on edge with a thousand hunches that she'd blown her cover and would never know it.

The studio was empty, stripped down to the wallpaper. From the depth of emotion she'd experienced in front of her little stereo on the sill, she'd assumed that packing the brushes, tubes, jars, and canvases would've taken much longer, as though they too must have naturally become waterlogged with attachment. In its prime, the studio had been her portal to other worlds, ones that fell under the unchallenged control of her nimble fingertips, but now bare, the whole room felt more like a fleabag motel that a lost driver resorts to when surprised on the interstate by a storm. The only thing left was the comforter she had nailed down to the floor.

"You get in the car and drive away now," she said aloud to the part of her that felt pinned down to the couch.

On the floor next to the coffee table, Calvin picked his head up and licked his tongue against his whiskers. He and the rest of the dogs had been excited to follow her outside the first time she'd stamped through the living room with a basket of clothes to put in the car, but with trip after trip, they'd each settled into their favorite resting spots and dropped their faces between their paws. Behind their droopy eyes, they seemed to sense that she was going somewhere special and they weren't, intuitively deducing Davi's only major dilemma with Gladys' apartment: no pets.

She'd considered taking the gamble of sneaking them in with her, but the five of them had no chance of staying secret with Gladys living only fifty feet away. If they were discovered, both Davi and her boys could be put out on the street together, and what an awful backfire of her intentions that would be, needlessly exposing them all to disaster. Perhaps she could have managed to successfully smuggle in one or two, but the dogs were a pack and a family in their own right who depended on each other. Breaking them apart for the sake of what she wanted was repellant, but she didn't want to be a martyr either.

As Davi sat and quietly sniffled to herself, Calvin hoisted himself up and wandered over to her. He burrowed his head between her legs and into her hands, and as soon as the metal tag on his collar clinked against her apartment keys, heartache ripped through her chest. She could already feel that his precious memory was tainted inside her, that she would never again be able to think of him without a burning anchor plunging into her stomach and splashing acid up onto her tongue. All the worse, he would never understand why she'd had to leave them. He would never realize that he hadn't done anything wrong to cause her to go. He would never know that, if it could've only worked that way, she would have slit the throat of the entire world just so he would know how much she had loved him.

When she let him go, the fur on the top of his head was wet from her eyes, and he looked up in alarm. Propping himself up on the couch with his front legs, he licked her face over and over while Slick picked his head up and walked over to stand beside Calvin, his ears pointed backwards on his head and quivering at the tips. Curled on the couch, Monty hadn't eaten anything she'd put down for him around nine, and Zeke was lying outstretched in a sunbeam, periodically rolling over to catch up with its drift across the floor. Smokey stumbled in from the bedroom, and in the ground out back, Henry was still rotting away underneath the idyllic green.

Barging past Calvin and Slick, Davi got to her feet and plucked her keys off their hook by the door. She slid the Legacy key off the ring and threaded it onto its new one where it belonged. So close to the door, the tears ran out of her eyes even hotter, and she reached up to hang the house keys back in their place when a low, gruff bark from Calvin turned her head. She looked back at her hand, studying the keys and making them lightly tap together as she bounced them on her palm. Then, she walked over to Calvin and Slick, kissed them both between the eyes, and dropped the house keys on the center of the coffee table, dinging the wood finish.

The sound woke up Monty and Zeke, bringing them to their feet next to Calvin, Slick, and Smokey. Their five faces inspected hers, and beginning to feel nauseous, she hurried to the front door. As she reached for the doorknob, they bunched around the back of her legs and pressed their weight against them, attempting to squeeze out with her before she could close the door. She turned and knelt down in front of them.

"Take care of each other," she said, kissing them all on the whiskers where she always thought they felt it most. "I love you guys. I'll love you forever."

But she couldn't stand back up. Their blinking eyes would be gone to hers if she did. If she stood back up, the next motion would be to turn her back, and then they would be gone.

Leaving them was too much to ask. Their blameless faces deserved to have her in their lives. She owed them that much at least. How could she bear to let such a sizable debt go dishonored?

*   *   *

Amidst the laughing conversation in the living room, Davi sat on the edge of the bed and stared out the window. Victor had taken her stereo and plugged it in the outlet behind the recliner to play one of her Van Morrison CD's while the dogs were locked in the studio, safely put away before anyone had shown up. Slick had sunk his teeth into Victor's heel months ago during one of these gatherings, and Victor wasn't interested in seeing if the other dogs had it in them to do the same. Every now and then, one of their barks would be loud enough to mix in with the music, and Davi pretended they were there beside her when she heard them.

She could hear Victor and his friends pacing around the living room, taking turns around the small antique bookshelf to blow lines off the mirror resting on top of it. No sooner would she lose herself in 'Cleaning Windows' before a whooping snort and growl down the hall would stun her nerves back into spiking harmonics.

"Hey," Kyle said, poking his head through the doorway with a shortened straw raised in offering.

She smeared the wetness off her cheeks and nodded. When she came into the living room, Hank was cutting up two more, smacking the edge of a playing card against the mirror. He stepped back to give her some space, and Kyle handed her his straw. When she leaned over, her sunken reflection appeared in the mirror, just beyond the lines, and for a split second, her eyes couldn't resist gazing into themselves. She did one line and changed nostrils, snorting right over to the mirror's edge where the king of hearts was jamming his knife into the side of his head with a thin line of crystal white down one side of his card.

"Don't be rude," Hank said as Davi walked straight back into the bedroom without a word.

She sat down again on her side of the bed by the window. Her fingers rose up to her neck. Nothing on her skin there itched, but pulling and gripping it with her nails felt like relief, as though she was slowly letting the air out of an overfilled balloon rather than watch it continue to inflate and explode. The first time she'd dug deeply enough to turn her fingertips sticky red with blood had been surreal, but now she wouldn't stop until she saw it.

Carried by a flurry of footsteps, their glistening faces finally came into the bedroom. Paul looked at Victor, Victor looked back at him, and Paul came over to her side of the bed, standing her up in front of him. She tensed up at the smell of him, a pungent garlic odor that she knew would only get thicker and more oppressive. She closed the back of her nose as best she could and concentrated on breathing through her mouth. With any luck, her breath would be foul and disgust him just as much. Davi took one last look out the window, at the breeze sweeping over the lawn, and hoped to remember just how fine of a spring day it really was.

Paul buried his face in her neck, and her eyes were pushed up to the ceiling. Jangling belt buckles snapped open, and cotton rushed over itself, then stubble, then hair. She could feel her clothes being taken off, some lifted, some pulled hard enough to pop a few stitches. Their eight wild eyes traced exclamation points up and down her body, and the cells in her skin shrank in horror and huddled together. Her toes brushed the top of the carpet as she was lifted and tossed onto the bed. Paul dove between her legs while they were still flopping around from the drop, and Victor cemented his shin across her forearms, pinning them over her head. She let out a muffled howl of pain with his weight concentrated across her bones.

Something furious in the core of her body begged her to allow it to fight, but she knew it was useless. In fact, it was much worse than useless. Even if her muscles were all to triple in size right at that moment, she would never be able to shove them all away. Better to drop all resistance and play dead. They wouldn't enjoy that nearly as much. She fought to tap into the same part of her that would hear a drill in the dentist's office and immediately suck her consciousness into quiet retreat, knowing the pain was both inevitable and passing. The only defenses she couldn't control were her reflexes, which fired in her throat and thighs, and when they did, all four of them whooped in excitement.

The wildfire cutting through her forearms made them squirm to break free, but Victor pressed down harder, sending long, wispy trails of pastel colors through her sight. She could feel her brain beginning to shut down rather than endure the unsolvable, claustrophobic pain when, just then, Victor picked his leg off her arms and held them down with his hands instead. Paul pinched her face in his hand, and drops of garlicky sweat plopped onto her throat. He snarled in long guttural rips, and Hank cheered and passed him the cigarette he'd been smoking as he stood back up.

Hank came next with his hanging silver chain that raked across her face when he was on top of her. Her hips began to throb from being stretched open. The pain of the thrusts and the panic of smothering immobility forced some tears out of the outside corners of her eyes where they might have stayed if she could've just screamed or breathed or passed out. Instead, they turned loose down her temples, and Hank's oversized hand mixed them with Paul's sweat and rubbed them all over her squirming face.

The sight of the ceiling jerking back and forth made her dizzy, but she refused to close her eyes. Even with Hank's hand squeezing her throat and pushing them up towards the ceiling, they had to stay open. If her muscles were overmatched, her eyes were the only weapons she had left when they could be pointed in the right direction. She commanded her eyes to stare at all of them whenever they could, neither to intimidate nor to promise unflinching revenge but rather to deliver the message that she saw them, to spoil their fantasy by forcing them to see her eyes seeing them when they fancied themselves invisible.

Hank closed his eyes and moaned in ecstasy, and Kyle came over to the bed once he'd moved off. He and Victor flipped her over and buried her face in the mattress. She could still scarcely breathe, but at least the pressure of being stretched apart and compressed with weight had subsided. She whispered little things into the sheets just to hear her own voice instead of theirs. What she said didn't even make sense, merely familiar words to remind herself that she was still alive and that the real part of her was always safe from all their strength, buried in places they could never reach.

Her joints and muscles drooped with fatigue, and the pain in her hips was beginning to radiate through her lower back. Kyle slapped her on the rear and walked to the back of the bedroom with Hank. Victor was the only one left, but Paul jumped towards her again before he let her hands go. She rolled her head on the sheets towards Hank and Kyle. Luckily, their faces didn't seem as though they had another round in them. Instead, they were laced with sobering, abashed glances that avoided looking back at her, now turned inwards and lost in strange interludes of withdrawal.

Paul pulled her head back by her hair, and more tears leaked out from the tightened skin around her eyes. Victor put his face right in front of hers and smiled the same smile he did when he would make her stay and watch his videos and DVD's with him right after Seinfeld. "Look at that." He'd pinch her face in his hand and point it at the TV when he saw something that made him crazy. "Look at that." His smile stretched and warped when he went sideways with lust, and she hated when he said that to her. "Look at that."

Paul pulled up his underwear beside Hank and Kyle and jokingly pumped his arms like a marathon runner. Victor threw her on her back, and the blood rushed back into the side of her face that had been pressed against the mattress. A feeling like extreme hunger materialized in her stomach, and her muscles screamed to throw a fit to reclaim what was theirs. But she wouldn't let them. She had been here before. There was no escape, and she had known it as soon as he'd told her that he'd called them, falling to tears and begging him to call them back. At that moment, the conveyor belt had begun slowly taking her on a path that inextricably led through the grinders and choppers of their factory, and to resist now was to prolong it. To resist now would sound the same to their ears as the addictive and satisfying squeak of Calvin's chew toy did to his when he bit it.

With his pants back on, Paul lit a cigarette and made a joke to Hank about how he'd one day learn how to go twice when he got a bit older. Davi counted to a hundred and stared at the indifferent ceiling. She could breathe again, but the agony got worse with the oxygen flooding back. When she'd been struggling for little gasps, the searing pain must have had to take a backseat to the central emergency of catastrophic system collapse, but what she had escaped in the asphyxiation came back with a vengeance with every breath she took. Everything was raw and wiped out, and she could feel how torn she was on the inside.

Finally, Victor pressed his hand into her face as he got off and went to the bathroom. The others left for the living room to get in their cars and leave as soon as Victor came back out. Davi rolled her legs to the side of the bed, her body still humming kinetic even as it was finally still. She desperately wanted to wipe their stink off her face but couldn't stomach touching it with her hands. She would just wait for the water to wash it away instead, right down the drain, right into the sewer. After the toilet flushed, the bathroom door opened, and Victor pulled on his jeans.

"You need to shower. You smell disgusting," he said as he went into the hallway towards the living room.

"You're right. I smell like you slobs," she said.

The insides of her thighs felt weak and began to drip as she switched on the light. She turned on the shower and leaned over the sink to take the weight off her legs while the water got warm. The familiar hot sensation began to rise in her belly. Once it hit her diaphragm, she would gasp, and once it hit her throat, she would sob. She rubbed her thighs to make sure they weren't so sapped that they would collapse stepping into the shower. If they had to give out once she was under the water, she could live with that.

The ball of internal heat rose into her chest, and a stampede broke free inside her as she tried to catch her breath. When would it be that it would all happen again? How long did she have to make a plan? What would she do with it when it was done? How much longer could she stand their wood-vise hands and sandpaper tongues to touch her skin? The soap slipped out of her hand as she reached for her underarms and felt a twinge of pulled muscle in her rib cage.

Bending and standing back up slowly, she realized the pain couldn't beat her. If it could, it would have by now. It was the relentless anxiety spent anticipating having to brace for the pain that was tearing her apart. Even now, a pall of dread rolled back over her. What could be next? Would she just be left alone for the rest of today? And what of tomorrow? They might all come back tomorrow. They might strip her down and fuck her again tomorrow. Her face might be pushed down and smothered into aqua bed sheets tomorrow. They might drunkenly laugh and lick the tears from her eyes tomorrow—

*   *   *

But not today, she thought. The screen door slapped closed behind her.

15.

Davi planned to be holed up in the apartment well before three-thirty when Victor would get home and instantly know she'd run off as soon as he saw the Legacy missing from the driveway. Deep down, she had to admit she was relieved that Karen had seemed to ignore her advice. Having Victor occupied with someone else could only increase her margin for error, and she could already tell she would need it. The mere thought of walking into Kellerman's for training tomorrow morning made her palms clammy.

Suddenly, she remembered that she would need to call Mona and Mills to give each of them her new phone number once she'd gotten to the apartment. On the phone, they both would reiterate how they wanted to be told about any emergencies as they unfolded, and Davi would feign a promise, having no idea what would qualify other than a gut feeling that their bar was far lower than what she had come to know. She pulled out the jittery to-do list she'd written for herself that morning, flattened the crumpled paper on the steering wheel, and added the two phone calls to the bottom.

The Legacy's brakes brought the car to a stop with a reedy squeak. The frustration of the other drivers caught in lunchtime traffic seeped through the windows at the red light. In the car to her left, a kid with a backwards cap and blaring techno music snapped his cigarette out of his mouth and blew the smoke through his tight lips. A mom in the van behind her perked her chin up with a drawn-out exhale and pushed the hair away from her forehead. The bald man in the silver Mercedes in front was darting around all of his mirrors, apparently hatching a plan to somehow weave his way through the blockade.

The corner of Davi's mouth drew back slightly in a suppressed smile. She felt like a secret agent amidst a drone population that was poised to intercept her if her skills let her down for even an instant, but no one knew who she was or how to crack her case because keeping secrets was her trade. They would only ever know what she showed them, and even if she wanted to bolt or fall to pieces like all spies would when they had a flashlight shining in their faces, none of the strain would manifest on the surface. Even sympathetic journalists baiting her into telling tales in exchange for the spotlight would be met with anonymous cluelessness. The loudmouth hacks might have the luxury of making spectacles of themselves for the camera, but she wouldn't, not if she intended to blend back into the city's forgettable camouflage of chain link and neon like a proper professional.

On second thought, the kid, mom, and bald man were probably all spies too, given away by their ho-hum exteriors, and fate had brought the four of them together for a few ironic seconds of mutual underestimation while they hid sly grins in the muscles just below the ones connected to the skin on their faces. They were all alive out there and just hid it from each other. They were all spies, secret agents that hid their true intentions and affiliations unless it served the objective. Some had just been in deep cover for so long that they'd been doubled and thought they really were the people they'd once pretended to be, disastrously forgetting that even mirrors can lie.

She took a deep breath. Something had broken inside of her belly, filling her abdomen with honey-gold vibrations.

The Legacy's engine labored under the weight of her packed bags and boxed art supplies, but no failure indicators were lighting up the dashboard. None of the needles were out of position. Age and inertia had simply fatigued its works, and all the engine could manage at this point was reaching ramming speed for a kamikaze mission directly into the side of the great smugness that was betting its steel would quietly fall to weeds in a rotten junkyard somewhere, full of busted refrigerators and clock radios. Throwing a piston right through the block as the needles fluttered on the dash would be worth it if that was the way it had to go. As long as nothing was left on the table. As long as the stoic trees near the highway could look down on the smolder after the fact and think to themselves, *That was an engine.*

Nothing was going to go wrong. Her lungs were taking the air differently. Her eyes were hungry and precise. Her fingertips ate up every nook and groove in the steering wheel. She wanted to lick the brick wall outside Kellerman's when she walked back to the car. She wanted to roll around in the oil sheen in the parking lot from some truck's leaking undercarriage. Her atoms reached out for everything to rub all over themselves and wouldn't stop until they were drunk on kerosene and full as ticks who had feasted on particleboard.

Even the way the sun was shining overhead seemed subtly impossible, making both perfect and zero sense, and Davi began to suspect that perhaps this was all a terrible dream whose gorgeous rainbow skin was preparing to pop into droplets like a blown bubble. She couldn't rule it out. But even if her REM brain could fool itself into thinking that streetlights always had slimy millipedes pouring out of their lamps and to see anything otherwise would be insane, it had never slowed the world down around her like this. Maybe she was hitting just the right speed and angle on the earth to offset the sum total of forces acting on her to the edges of the universe, and against all odds, she was zeroed out and completely still. Too bad for the other drivers that they were just a shade off the sweet spot, but at least they'd never know what they were missing, to be floating like a feather in the eye of a galaxy twisting like a hurricane.

She slid her key into the lock and pulled it towards her as Gladys had said. The glass jars of paint rattled together in the shoebox in her arms.

This time, the whole apartment could be her studio. Nothing precluded the possibility. There was plenty of space at the foot of the bed for the easel, and she could move one of the night tables over for her brushes and paints. When she was done with the painting, she could smear her hands all over the wet canvas, wipe them down her face like a Sioux warrior, and fall down backwards asleep covered in bright yellow. Every option was on the table, and there was no sense in judging any of them. Her imagination deserved to run amok, free of the thankless security detail of constantly dreaming up worst-case scenarios that grinded down its will like a belt sander.

She could prop up a canvas in the sink and gaze out into the bleak branches that cut arterial patterns through the sky. The woods would be a lovely thing to study with a brush in her hand, full of trees ready to be loaded up with different personalities. The towering one to the right with the thick trunk was too majestic to be a bully, just a shade closer to elder statesman than mafia don. The simpering shrimp next to him would be smothered in vines by the summertime, like a weakened child with tuberculosis who was learning how the earth came to be through collisions and impact craters. A crack of lightning could bring either of them down without warning, and they would be helpless to avoid the storms when they came. They could only stand and ride them out where they always had in the hopes that sheer respect would save them from being detonated into toothpicks. Nevertheless, the sapling would know from its older neighbor that the lightning sometimes struck even still, and if it was one day forced to watch one of the bolts shred through its bark, there wouldn't be anything to apologize for or lament.

That could go on one of the blank canvases. A windblown forest with jagged electric streaks tearing through the sky in the distance overhead. She would leave it up to the viewer to determine whether the storm was on its way or had just passed. The image would have wonderful tension between light and dark, and by being meticulous with the shadows, she could layer depth into the foreground. If her hand was steady enough to deal in the microscopic, she could add a bullfrog, sheltering under the exposed root structure of an oak towards the back. No one would even know it was there, and if her hand could make a bullfrog that small, then surely it would be steady enough to sign her name across its fat, croaking back so they could both be invisible in the stormy woods together.

Then, there were the other three canvases to consider. Perhaps a show horse being taught how to prance on a lonely panorama in Kentucky around dusk. One of those dark brown ones with a black mane and the whole scene spilling over with all-American clichés of rising dirt and cut grass. A carnival sideshow with a man in a pinstripe suit shouting down to a small crowd of titillated couples about how his attractions were grotesque and renowned throughout the world, from Gibraltar to Helsinki. Something like that could take months with its huge potential for color and motion. For the last one, maybe she could retry the seascape from two years ago that she'd never gotten right with her new brushes and paints, retry her first framing of the waves in purple and nickel midnight.

Dropping the shower liner and bottles of cleaners on the table, she picked the cordless phone off its stand and dialed Mills' office.

She could even ride the bus around town for hours just to find someone with an interesting face. The green bus stop with the orange Hertz advertisement on the side was just around the corner on the main route. She'd bring a pad and pencil on with her, quickly sketching the features that caught her eye while the bus idled at stop signs, and if one face went cold, there would be others to cut apart and mix into the blank spots. Perhaps when she was done, the eyes of the uninspired commuters percolating through migraine lives would make surprising sense lashed together with a retiree's million-dollar smile, but if a portrait was on the menu, she could just as easily stand in the bathroom, render her own image in the mirror, and save the fare altogether.

But a self-portrait would sting, a total war between the face she imagined was still wrapped around her eyes and the one she could see in the mirror as the actual. The open pores, the deepening lines, the shocks of white in her hair were all familiar, but as a rule, she avoided mirrors. Perhaps that meant these truths weren't registering. In that case, she felt a rising appetite to stare right at them, to lay down new rover tracks in the red Martian dust and examine all the things it shared with Utahan rock landscapes, even if worlds apart. And if the damage turned out to be more than she expected, she could decide to be proud of it like beaming citizens were of soldiers who came home to purple in sedate jewelry boxes and ribbons over car dealerships.

If the scars couldn't change, then they belonged to her now as reminders that she had endured, and even if she'd been broken somewhere along the line, she hadn't stayed that way. The fresh-faced could never understand that survival was an art. They probably imagined that if the pressure was ever on them they could hold out forever because 'forever' was such a lovely word to say, but if it was their smashed faces held in front of mirrors to assassinate their spirit, they would cave. The ordeal wouldn't even reach the point where the jailer would have to level with them and whisper sweet sabotage in their ear like, "One way or the other, everyone eventually gives up."

She beeped the phone off, then back on. Her thumb typed in Mona's number next.

A wave of déjà vu swept over her as she waited for the line to connect, something about the way the sink looked below the kitchen window with just that amount of low winter sunlight glazing the branches outside. Maybe the wonderful feeling back in the car hadn't had anything to do with her stillness but rather with all the different versions of her in all the countless universes lining up together. Whatever storylines they had followed in their lives had still eventually led each of them to a little apartment just like this one, holding a phone to her ear just like she was now, looking over at the sink from the other room at just this angle, all funneled into the same bottleneck. How else could it be that nostalgia could mix with the unprecedented to create a feeling so oddly sublime?

If only she could trigger déjà vu without limit, how much lower the world's volume would be around her. To sense that she had somehow already been everywhere she was now going and to deduce that, no matter what happened along the way, she would survive as she had then. More than survive, she would never feel a trace of anxiety with every moment emptied of drama, lost among a vast ocean of cycling memories, and if she could somehow make that perspective permanent, panic would never again come. Fear of anything would be hard to understand. Even if she were to look over just then to see a shark's eye staring into hers, the threat would never occur to her. Threats would cease to exist, and she would smile into the shark's bear-trap jaws as she was smiling just then at the sunlight in the window, unsure of how it was all going to play out but placing beyond doubt the proposition that her life's loop circled much further than she could fairly appreciate from her little view into the woods.

Her chin pinned a pillow against her chest while she shook it down into its case and tossed it onto the bed.

From that same vista, nothing was personal. Merely springs and cogs twisting each other by design, keeping time by the tensions, and everything was perfectly predictable with the right statistics, just like baseball. Nothing was personal about managerial moves that sent players back down to the minors, ignoring what they might have earned if desire and work ethic had been the only salient metrics. The team might have just had twenty-some-odd players who happened to be better, and there wasn't anyone to blame for that. No one to blame and nowhere to escape from the dreadful, monorail conclusion that a person's best could still fail to be good enough, outmatched on a basic and indecent level.

Back down in the minors, a player could drive himself mad with recollections of college days when the crowds came to their feet for every plate appearance, when the sophomore girls cupped their hands over each other's ears to whisper mischief in the bleachers, when professional scouts squinted through binoculars with contracts folded up in their breast pockets, when the future was all spread open and waiting to be taken. He'd just never expected how difficult the competition would get. Only back down in the minors, in the batting cages, would it dawn on the player that there had been no starting gun and never would be, and he might have simply been unprepared, never expecting the franchises to throw him onto the scrap heap, never understanding how costly a practice it was to live today dreaming of tomorrow, stuck in yesterday way back when.

The brush scrubbed into the tiles in the shower, and a layer of grime melted away, revealing a much brighter blue.

The droplets of time always settled and congealed when they weren't shaken off. The scientists who thought of time as a dimension or a fabric or an illusion had it wrong. Time was a mist, building up on anything that stopped moving for long enough, and once the yesterdays had stuck, they would spoil into a tacky film no matter how sweet they once might have been, no matter how dearly one might have wanted to keep them. She'd never noticed the mist until she'd lost all her velocity, and day after day, the growing fog somehow made sense, as though she was disappearing into it like she deserved to. Somewhere along the line, easterly winds had come and blown enough of the mist away to the point where she could feel its insanity all over her and could no longer stand its watery smell in the back of her throat.

The mist had to stay fluid. That was the only way to make sense of any of it, and she had to shake it off before it caked up on her, had to aim her boat directly into the waves when she saw them arcing up on her starboard, had to race horseback down the shoreline through the blinding rain while firing a revolver into the clouds, had to dance around the lit firecrackers she happily dropped at her feet, had to sink her hands into the rancid stew up to her elbows, had to let go of the ripcord, had to unbuckle herself from the parachute altogether, had to shatter her teeth on belt leather while speeding fast enough for the droplets to strip off her and lift back up into the aerosol.

By rights, yesterdays could only sit on the sidelines and peddle their wares to sullen passersby who'd walk their fingers over the dust jackets on the off-chance that they'd find that one gem amidst the driftwood, and if they failed, well, at least they'd passed the time. Yesterdays were jealous things, covetous to come back to life and adhere to the present. They'd come back as long as she was in the mist. They'd come back and imply that she was nothing without them, and maybe they'd be right. But if she was nothing without them, then they were nothing without her. Ghosts and memories, hauntings and reverie. These yesterdays. These tomorrows. These nevers.

She threw open the shower liner, and the smell of new plastic flooded the bathroom. Her shoulders burned, reaching up to lace the rings through the holes.

She came back into the main room and tapped her nails on the tabletop. The numbered items on the list were all crossed off, and while she felt like she was forgetting something with how quickly everything had gotten done, she crumpled the paper up and tossed it in the new trash can in the kitchen. She put her hands on her hips and shrugged. All this time, life had seemed like it could never change, until somehow, one day, out of the blue, just like that, action.

16.

Kellerman's had changed their uniforms in the years since Davi had last worn them. The inside stitching felt itchy and cheap. She lifted the shirt off to see what was jabbing the skin on her shoulder blade, but there wasn't anything to cut away when she turned it inside out. The material was just a lesser quality and had characteristic stiffness, as though polygon edges had been inexplicably woven into the cloth. She wanted to buy some undershirts if her first paycheck allowed for it, but since she didn't remember the share that taxes would take out of her base pay, counting on finding extra money in the budget for comfort expenses seemed foolish.

The previous day's euphoria had wound down around midnight when turbocharged anxiety started pumping into her veins, and she'd spent the entire night sleepless, never approaching a calm that would permit her to drift off. Not having slept in two days would have been trying enough in the luxury of the usual rut, but with all of her routines having been flipped upside down, she didn't know what to expect from her body. Her ears already felt overactive, her eyes drifting and zoning out, and she knew she'd have to manage hallucinations throughout the day. As she picked her purse off the table, she just hoped that her energy wasn't so drained that she would have to contend with the awful word centrifuge powering back up in her brain and collapsing everything she heard into gibberish.

She reached for the deadbolt, and her calves tensed on their own, expecting to have to compensate for the pressure of five anxious dogs pushing against them to get outside with her. When she turned around and saw only the faint footpath discoloration in the carpeting, she slung her purse higher on her shoulder and opened the door. By the time she came home from work that evening, she hoped the exhaustion would turn in her favor and empty her reserves completely, leaving her to collapse asleep onto her pillow before she could think of the dogs again.

On her way to the car, the faces of her boys kept running through her head, and she shook them off as quickly as she could. Perhaps they had in fact been able to see how crazy everything had become and regretted in their own right that she was filled with tearful apologies, that they themselves couldn't make her understand how none of them blamed her for making a run for it. Even if it were so, she couldn't escape the stinging refrain that they had come to depend on her and that she'd let them down when they needed her most.

"Ah, good morning."

Davi's shoulders jerked from the sound, and her key carved a line of paint off the door.

"I didn't mean to startle you, dear," Gladys said from her rocking chair on the porch.

"I'm sorry, no. You didn't startle me," Davi said, walking around the front of the car and over to the porch steps. "Well, a little bit. I haven't heard anyone say 'Good morning' to me like that in a long time."

"Oh? Did I say it strange?" Gladys asked, her face suddenly awash with confusion.

"No. I think that was me."

"I see," Gladys said, putting her coffee cup back down on the table next to her rocking chair. "Excited for your first day?"

"I think so. Yes, I'm excited. Just wondering if I'm ready for it and all that," Davi said, the last couple of words getting partially lodged in the back of her throat. "You're not cold?"

"I've got a blanket on my legs, my good wool coat, and some hot coffee. As long as the wind doesn't decide to come up here, I think it's very fine."

Davi nodded and stuffed her chilled hands in her jacket pockets.

"Just kind of wakes you up," Gladys said.

Gladys' eyes drifted off towards the trees on the side of the house as she finished her thought, and Davi turned and walked back to the Legacy. At the car door, her eyes caught the squiggle of scratched paint by the keyhole, and a gauzy sense of social slight crawled up her spine. She trotted back to the base of the steps where Gladys could see her best.

"I've got to get going, Gladys. See you later," she said with a wave.

"Have a good day, dear."

Understanding how to end conversations shouldn't have been so evasive. Losing the skill at all seemed ludicrous, but here she was, having stumbled again in the fact of innocent decorum. As though concluding an interface with a dot matrix AIM screen, her body wanted to just wander away once the pertinent information for the interaction had been delivered and received, oblivious to the secondary currency of courtesy. She didn't know how to stop, other than to try to relax and slow down in order to give the old patterns a chance to resurface.

When Davi turned off the engine in the sprawling parking lot in front of Kellerman's, nausea bled across her belly and pushed drops of sweat onto the back of her neck. A handful of employees and trainees were strolling across the blacktop towards the store, and to her dismay, some seemed to already know each other, shaking hands midstride and nodding their heads hello. Overhead, two geese were flying by each other's side, honking loudly enough into the wind for Davi to hear. On another day, their distant honks might have been soothing, but right then as she smeared her clammy hands down her jacket, the peaceful sound was unwelcome, amounting to an alarming heartbeat in what was supposed to be dead morning air.

Her hand launched for the key in the ignition and turned it. Instantly, her pores closed up with the growl of the engine, stemming the tide of sweat that had beaded all over her forehead, and she burped and breathed a little easier with the honking drowned out by the sound. If she could just get the sweat off her, the nausea would calm down with it, and if she could stop both, maybe then she could focus on taking today's training step by step without losing control of the ultra-panic that was greasing up everything her brain wanted to touch, sending it flipping and flopping from one bad grip to the next.

Near the front doors to Kellerman's, two trainees turned their heads in her direction as she drove the Legacy out of its spot, wrapped around the perimeter of the entire lot, and landed nearly back where she'd started. This time, she parked in the next row over, right beside the big, yellow concrete base of a towering light pole. Relative to the dizzying expanse of the empty lot, the spot by the pole felt sturdier, had more potential than plain flatness. She pushed the emergency brake down to the floor and got out of the car before all the little sounds and sensations could get on top of her again.

When Davi came through the automatic doors, a reddish-blond man was tapping his clipboard on the clear plastic edge of the strawberry display as he passed, casually pacing with his hand on his hip and his index finger resting on the top edge of his belt. Six other trainees were milling around the produce section with him, and she could already tell that most of them were far younger than she. Even if they were in their late twenties, they still looked like kids.

"Dah-vee Wallace?" the reddish-blond man asked.

"Day-vee," she said.

"Gotcha," he said, writing on his clipboard. "Day-vee. Well, welcome. I'm Michael. I'll be doing the training with you guys today."

"What's your last name?" she asked.

He paused for a moment, a look of mild surprise ringing through his eyes.

"My last name's Bunkley. Michael Bunkley," he said.

"Okay," she said.

"You didn't bring a lunch with you?" he asked.

Her face lit up like a Christmas ornament. She'd forgotten all about preparing a lunch once she'd started cleaning the apartment and had just started to paint for hours once the place was set up.

"Um, no. I, um—"

"It's okay. Luckily, we work in a grocery store. Right, guys?" he said, directing his voice more to the trainees as a group than to her.

IIis joke didn't land with the crowd, except for one girl with freckles across the bridge of her nose. She let out a nervous chuckle and nodded. Davi pinched the corner of her eyes, squinting them shut. The ambient glow of fluorescent in the store was already getting to her.

"Okay, guys. Everyone, follow me, and let's get right into learning the system," Michael said, leading the group over to the nearest checkout lane.

"Hi, I'm Allison," the freckled girl said to Davi.

"Davi," she said, shaking her hand.

"I like your hair," Allison said, nodding at the white streaks through the sides of Davi's wavy mop.

"Are you being serious?"

"Yeah, totally. It gives me like a metal vibe," Allison said.

"Like the music?"

Allison nodded. She pushed up the sleeve of her long-sleeved t-shirt, and the jawbone of a tattooed skull emerged on the underside of her forearm.

"Hey, guys," Michael said to them over the shoulders of the other trainees. "Stay with me up here while the computer boots up, okay? I know the bar scanner seems like it'll do everything, but there are still a lot of things it won't know how to handle. The scanner itself could malfunction, maybe the sale price doesn't come up the way the customer saw it marked on the shelf, you'll get WIC program purchases—"

His list continued in fits and starts, and the light upturn in his lips betrayed a suppressed smile peeking through in delight with his answer to his own test question. Hopefully, he was a specialist from corporate who only came in for training sessions. She couldn't imagine how she could bear to be around someone so fruitlessly talkative any more than she could imagine standing smiling beside a jet engine on the tarmac as her eardrums exploded. Allison tapped her on the elbow and rolled her eyes in jest when Davi looked over.

When it came time for lunch, Davi lingered to the back of the group as they climbed the stairs to the break room. Her body drooped with each step. Time had screeched to a halt in the last hour of training on the register, and her body had begun to overheat and feel like its circuits were melting on the board. She hoped the microwaveable croissant sandwich she'd picked at random from the freezers would give her enough of a boost to carry through the rest of the day, but focusing her attention on Michael's instruction was taking more out of her than she'd expected.

Maybe she had slept more than she ever realized back at the house, or perhaps she'd become a master of autopilot, always operating in a mode ultimately designed for energy rationing. Either way, she didn't recognize this brand of fatigue that made her feel less like an exhausted muscled skeleton and rather more like a pool of sludge, inching along with favorable tilts and gradients in the ground.

The sumptuous smell of buttery sausage emanated from the microwave, and her eyes came back to life. With a few seconds left on the timer, she opened the microwave door, snatched the sandwich off the revolving plate, and headed to a table in the opposite corner of the room with the stack of napkins she'd gathered to take the oily shine off her face. She took one off the top and pressed it against her forehead. Just feeling its dryness against her skin bolstered her mood.

"Hey there," a young man said, sliding onto the seat across from her with his can of soda grazing the table top.

"Hello," Davi answered flatly, taking the napkin away and crumpling it up on the table.

"My name's Keith."

She took a big bite and nodded at him with her mouth full. Keith was one of the other trainees and had been sitting amongst the group's chatter while she was at the microwave. With him at the table, what had felt like a tiny nook just for her to steal a few minutes of quiet and regroup suddenly ballooned into a cavernous airplane hangar. She didn't want to participate in their conversation. That was the entire point of taking the table wedged into the corner. She wondered how that couldn't have been obvious.

"And you're Davi, right?"

"Yeah," she said, stopping her chewing. "How'd you know that?"

"You said it in front of everyone earlier," he said, pulling his phone out of his pants pocket. "When you came in."

The conversations across the room seemed to get louder as he spoke, like he'd brought their noise over with him, and the cold sweat began to condense again on the back of her neck. A neon bulb in the panel overhead was dimly flickering, pulsing shadows through her vision. She closed her eyes.

"What do you want?" she asked, snatching two more napkins and dabbing the back of her neck.

"I just wanted to get your number," he said before cutting himself off with a quick grin. "Not like that. I mean that a few of us are interested in getting together for some drinks at one of our places once training is over. Probably my place. So, I wanted your number to call you about that."

She didn't believe his smile. There was something affected about it, as though he'd rehearsed a charming misstep into awkwardness just to frame himself as more harmless than he really was.

"I don't give my phone number out," she said.

"Oh," he said, putting his phone away. "Well, one of us can just tell you like place and time on Friday then. That's cool too. The guy with the glasses over there is my buddy from school, Jack. He's my roommate. Really nice guy."

Davi twisted her head between her hands until the left side of her neck cracked, releasing some of the tension that was building up in her shoulders. Her heart was pounding harder, and she still couldn't believe that Keith had come right over and sat down like he owned the place.

"Okay," Davi said, breathing loud, impatient gusts through her nose.

Her fingers curled over and around to grip the edge of the tabletop. She was starving, but her appetite had disappeared. Her pressure gauges were all redlining, and she was running out of ways to cover the rolling boil of spattering panic and frustration.

"And the guy next to him is—"

"What the fuck do I care?" she snarled, sticking her head across the table. "Who asked you to come tell me any of this?"

Keith sat back in the chair while Davi held her red face over the table. Slowly, he slid out of his seat, all of his casualness evaporated into thin air.

"Sorry if I bothered you," he said. "I didn't mean to."

He walked across the room, and Davi kept her grip on the table, trying to keep from being swept away in the surge. Her other hand grabbed two more napkins as the tears welled up in her eyes, and she turned her face to the wall to dab them away. The chirpy laughter from the other side of the room dipped into murmurs as the legs of Keith's chair scraped over the floor. If she could have spared a moment to think straight, she might've been mortified at their little blow-dart whispers sticking into her skin, but they were easily ignored just then. Leaving her sandwich on its plastic wrapper, she shot out of her chair and out the door before anyone else decided to come over for a chat.

The tears kept flowing through her vision, and her hand insisted on clenching the pipe banister running down the stairs with the same force it would've used to rip it loose. Too frustrated to bear it, Davi stopped at the foot of the steps and pressed her last napkin directly against the whites of her eyes until they were dry and itchy. With the tears stopped, she headed towards the frozen food section to find something to bring her temperature down.

At the freezer, she threw open the door and grabbed the first two pints of ice cream she could reach. The cold blast through her palms forced everything to hit the brakes, especially her heart that had felt like it was promising to explode on each beat. She pressed the pint of vanilla against her forearm to take the heat out of her faster. As she moved away to pace in the aisle with her ice cream, the freezer door slid off her hip and slapped softly shut.

"No big deal," she muttered under her breath, pacing down the row of freezers. "Nobody noticed. Nobody noticed fucking anything. You left because you felt like it. That's why you walked out. You felt like leaving, so you did."

The bags of frozen spinach and corn looked contemptuous as she passed them, so nicely lined up in rows where they belonged. If it wouldn't have meant her job, she'd have opened up each of the freezer doors and swept all the bags off their shelves and racks, straight onto the floor for a few stomps. Instead, a woman pushing a cart with a little boy riding on the front of it turned down the aisle before she could toy any further with the idea, and Davi hurried to put her two pints back where she'd gotten them.

"Can't get one fucking second alone," she said to herself, the venom still simmering in her blood. "That's too much to ask, right?"

She looked over her shoulder at the woman studying the frozen pizzas. The little boy popped off the front of the cart and drove his finger against the glass at one in particular. The woman opened the door and threw two in her cart.

"Bitch," Davi said softly, catching the swinging door handle behind her and pushing it shut.

Davi headed out of the aisle towards the front of the store where the other trainees were already gathered back around the register with Michael. She must have spent longer than she thought pacing around the freezers, cursing the broccoli and TV dinners. One of the trainees must have noticed her as she hurried over because Michael suddenly turned his head her direction like he knew she was there all along.

"In your own time, Miss Wallace," Michael said across the store, opening his arms sarcastically.

As Davi came over to the group, Allison was standing towards the back. She held out her hand to give Davi what was left of her croissant sandwich, placed neatly back inside its plastic wrapper.

Coming home after the day was over, Davi slammed and locked the apartment door behind her, shook her hands like they were wet, pushed them against her face, and screamed. She whipped her purse onto the table, and something plastic cracked inside it. Then, she grabbed the edge of the tabletop and flung the whole thing onto its side, only getting a gentle thud into the matted-down carpeting when her ears had wanted a crash. When she kicked one of the upturned table legs and stubbed her toe, the rage finally broke and gave way to a gasp. Collapsing onto the couch, she held her foot on her lap and writhed around while the amputating pain dissipated.

As her head cleared, she remembered the easy relief her old pills had to offer, yearning for the power they had to paint the world over in anesthesia grains, and if she ever had a day like today, the solutions for it were only ever two inches away, down into translucent orange, far closer than some fool's errand into untold wrinkles of gray matter. She closed her eyes and imagined Mills being in the room, calmly righting a chair and sitting down across from her in it.

"So, what happened in here, Davi? ... I see. Well, why continue? Maybe there's no sense in putting yourself through anymore. ... Then tell me this: who are you doing this for, Davi? Do you even know? Who are you doing all this for?"

Davi got up and righted the table. Pulling a pen and a stack of sticky notes out of her purse, she saw that it was her compact that had been obliterated from the swinging impact against the wood. The inside flap had powdery foundation all over it, but she closed it back up and placed it on the chair beside her.

She wrote a little something on the first note, pulled it off, and stuck it to the tabletop. The second note went next to it, then the third, until the entire surface of the round table was plastered with a hundred yellow sticky notes. She folded her hands on her lap and watched them bob up and down in gentle, imperceptible air currents.

She had hoped her anxiety would grind away as it was confronted by new scenarios that were sanitized from danger, and perhaps they would in time. But the bouts of full-body chaos were too intense to accept, and she needed a new, supplemental plan for the sake of morale. If her emotions were going to put up such frightful resistance to change, then they needed to be seduced into accepting it instead.

Note 1: "Smile, Davi" – pressed onto the plastic face of the alarm clock, just far enough to the side to be out of the way of the digits.

Note 2: "Your hair looks great today" – pressed onto the bottom edge of the bathroom mirror, right down the center.

Note 3: "Tomorrow is going to be even better" – glued to the front edge of the bookshelf in the bedroom, on the second divider.

Note 4: "You're the fucking boss now, Davi" - stuck on the back of the front door for her to see whenever she headed out into the world.

She plucked a fifth note off the table, walked around to the next place that felt right, stuck it there, and came back for another. Over and over, she paced the apartment and redecorated in adhesive yellow until she only had one left to place. The lamp next to the bed would be the last thing she would see at night when she rolled over to turn off the light, but the glue for the last note wouldn't stick to the lampshade. So, she pressed it onto the base instead, its message reading: "This one's for me."

If Gladys were to come in there, she would think her to be out of her mind. To her eyes though, a new courtship had begun, and these cheap, flapping scraps of paper were the love letters to prove it.

17.

Davi leaned back against the driver's side of the Legacy and crossed her arms over her stomach. She'd woken up in such a good mood too. The temperature outside was edging upwards, and for the first time that morning, she'd been able to crack the apartment windows to clear out the winter stuffiness.

"So, what do you think?" she asked.

"We don't get many calls for vandalism. Just not that common," the cop said. "And you said that two windows were smashed last time?"

"Both of these," she said, knocking her knuckle against the window next to her.

"When was that?"

"Maybe three weeks ago. I could check my receipts if you had to know exactly."

"Anything left behind around the car that time? In the street, in the car, anything like that?"

"Not aside from the glass," she said flatly, staring off into the asphalt.

"I see," he said, reading over his notes and flipping his book closed. "Well, I think the first time on its own could have been anyone for any reason. But twice? In that short amount of time? People can run into bad luck every now and then, but you know."

She nodded and chewed her lip. The police weren't going to be sending the detectives to crack this one, and even if they were so inclined, there was nothing to investigate. One tire had been flattened, and almost certainly, no one had seen anything.

"Thanks for coming out," she said.

"If anything else comes up or if you find something later on, let us know, and maybe we can do better on this. For now, maybe think about parking under a streetlight or on a more trafficked street. I know that's not ideal, but it might protect the car if it's more visible," he said.

Davi shook his hand, and he walked back to the squad car. She didn't know why she'd called the police again when there was so little to discuss, but at least the cop had seemed to understand. When he pulled out and nodded at her grimly through the windshield, she could see in his eyes that he'd visited with people in her position before, with no choice but to take their chances in that unpoliceable space between probably hunted and definite prey.

She bounced up off the side of the car and kicked the flat tire. The car's weight must have been down on the rim for at least a few hours.

"You fuck," she muttered.

Tapping the insurance company to cover the cost of repair was useless. She couldn't imagine that the damage exceeded her deductible, and even if it did, she wouldn't be able to afford the higher premium. Better to eat the one-time payment and try to pick up extra hours at work whenever she could rather than endure a permanently raised charge, and while she didn't know where she would find the money, the Legacy was a necessity that was worth the strain.

She jumped behind the wheel and looked back over her shoulder to make sure the squad car was all the way gone. As long as she could make it down the road without the rim spraying sparks all over or breaking clean from the axle, she could drop the car at the mechanic's shop in the strip mall across from Kellerman's and work her shift while it was getting fixed. She switched on her hazard lights and pulled out, away from the main route where she'd never be able to match the speed of the bustling commuters. Instead, she turned as slowly as she could onto Hardwick and hoped the smaller residential road would afford her a snail's pace.

In her rear view mirror, a red pickup was gaining on her fast, and she pulled over to the curb, braking harder than she wanted. After the truck had passed and she'd turned back onto the street, the floppy flat tire felt more unstable, and she craned her neck all around her mirrors to see if pieces of it were being spit out onto the street behind her. The back left side of the car started to swivel like it had had enough and wasn't going to grip the road anymore, but when she brought her speed back down to a crawl, the control came back. At last, the Legacy dragged itself over the incline into the parking lot and hobbled through the empty spots, towards the mechanic in the corner of the shopping plaza.

"Hey!" she yelled through her window at a young man walking towards the shop with a baseball cap pulled down over his face. "You work there?"

"Yeah," he yelled back. "Let me get inside, and I'll raise the shudders."

Davi tapped her thumb against the steering wheel and looked over at Kellerman's on the opposite side of the lot. Between her and there, a large puddle had formed in some of the distant, inconvenient parking spots that were only ever taken around Christmas, and a handful of birds were wading through the water, shaking their wings. Her head snapped back to the right as a chain started to be wrenched in concerted pulls, ratcheting the metal shudders up. When the garage was finally open, he motioned for her to pull towards him and stop.

"So, how did that happen?" he said.

"What's it going to cost to fix?" she asked, slamming the car door behind her.

"Damn, looks like it's just gouged," he said, kneeling down and pulling at the tear in the rubber.

"Yep."

"You might need a new rim on this too, unless it just happened before you saw me."

"How much?"

He lightly bobbed his head side to side and clicked his tongue off the roof of his mouth.

"A hundred," he said. "If the rim's fine under there and all that."

"I'll pay seventy for it," Davi said, scoffing at his price. "The whole goddamn car probably isn't even worth a hundred bucks as it sits."

He looked up from the tire and smiled at her under the bill of his cap.

"Yeah, okay. Seventy bucks. But if I get in there and see other damage, that's going to go up," he said.

"It won't. The tire is all I need. And forget about the alignment. That's been fucked for years," she said.

She gathered her keys in her hand to separate the car key from the apartment key, but her fingernail kept missing the seam in the ring.

"You work over at Kellerman's?"

"What gave it away?" she asked sarcastically.

"The uniform," he said as a matter of fact.

Her eyes ached to roll right in front of him, but she made them close first.

"So, when will it be done?" she asked, handing over the key.

"When's your shift over?"

"When will you have it done?" she asked again, creeping impatience pinching the pitch of her voice.

"Hey, I'm not trying to wait on it. But if a rush job comes in, it doesn't make sense to get yours done first when it'll just sit for another three hours."

"I need it done by two," she said, working in a two-hour buffer before she actually got off work.

"Seventy bucks, done by two. Good deal," he said.

Back outside the mechanic's shop, Davi walked towards the giant birdbath puddle in the parking lot, grumbling under her breath. From a distance, the gulls took notice of her path in their direction, wading around less and less in the pool with each of her steps. Then, they began to waddle away from the course she was taking through the water. One took off into the air and landed again a few empty parking spots over.

"Hey! What're you doing over there?"

Davi looked up and saw Michelle leaning out of the window of her pickup all the way across the lot. She didn't feel like yelling back and just threw her hands in the air instead, as though she hadn't understood a word. Michelle turned back to the wheel and drove over.

"What did you say?" Davi asked, walking around the puddle to get to the truck.

"I asked what you were doing," Michelle said, leaning over to the passenger door and pushing it open.

"I had to take my car in," Davi said.

"Did it finally break down on you?"

"No. No, the car's fine. The engine and all that, I mean."

"So?"

Davi took a deep breath and shook her head with the frustration of someone filling out their tax forms in triplicate.

"So, I decided to splurge on a new paint job. Something sporty, you know? Maybe some flames on the hood and down the side panels. I think it could be a good look for me," she said.

"Absolutely," Michelle said, unbuckling her seat belt. "Put a big dragon head smack dab in the middle of the hood too. None of that could possibly backfire."

"I should have thought of the dragon," Davi said.

"Yeah, very funny," Michelle said. "Look, come upstairs with me before you clock in. Just for a few minutes."

"Anything wrong?"

"Just come upstairs with me please," she said, the automatic doors zipping open in front of them.

All of the errors and oversights Davi had made in her first few months of work came back to her, but none of them seemed big enough to fit. Maybe her tone in Michelle's pickup had come off more obnoxious than she'd intended.

"Close the door behind you please," Michelle said, dropping a paper bag on her desk and pulling out a rich-smelling egg and cheese sandwich on a bagel.

"What's up?" Davi asked.

"Not much, but good question," Michelle said, taking a bite. "That's all I really wanted to talk about is what's up with you."

"How do you mean?"

"In general. How is everything?"

Davi fell into one of the chairs in front of Michelle's desk and rubbed her eyes.

"Well, do you want the messed-up truth or the Hollywood-ending version?"

"Are those my only options?" Michelle wondered, biting into her bagel again.

Davi chuckled and tilted the chair onto its back legs.

"That's all that's springing to mind at the moment," she said.

"How about the version you'd tell a friend because you wouldn't want to upset her unless it was absolutely necessary?" Michelle asked.

Davi looked across the desk at Michelle who bit into her sandwich and stared back with a sleepy but serious gaze.

"Well, I'm fine. I really am. Things get tough every now and then. Stressful. But that's how it goes for everyone, you know? Stress. How has my work been anyway?"

"Oh, please," Michelle said with a dismissive wave of her hand, as though she'd found the question too trifling to leave without taking a smack at it. "You know that I don't ever mean to intrude."

"Don't be silly," Davi said.

Michelle wiped the crumbs off her hands and chewed up the last bits of egg and cheese. She nodded to herself in quiet reflection.

"I wonder, do you know why I got upset when I saw you that day you came in to ask for a job?" Michelle asked.

"Because I looked nothing like the person you once knew."

Michelle shook her head while sipping her coffee. Davi's face scrunched in confusion, and the front legs of her chair clapped back down onto the ground.

"You don't remember seeing each other at the mall, maybe two years ago? Or at the Chevron across from Wawa a few months after that?" Michelle asked.

Now that she mentioned it, Michelle's face did ring a bell somewhere in the fog, but Davi couldn't honestly say she recalled. Faces were so miscellaneous and disposable back then.

"We may very well have seen each other," Davi said with a sigh. "But it didn't register. Just blankness."

Her fingers slid over her closed eyelids, landing on and pinching the bridge of her nose. Never in her wildest dreams did she expect what the dredges constantly unearthed about her, to the point where each new story to cross her path felt like it belonged to someone else's life. The feeling of cringing, critical hindsight that accompanied them was the only way she knew they were hers.

"For your information, the reason I got upset when you first came in here for a job was because I had seen you during those times, and I thought that, whatever was wrong, there wasn't any coming back from it. So, imagine my surprise when all of a sudden you turn up in my office a couple years later. I couldn't believe it, and it wasn't because of how bad you'd gotten. It was about how far you'd come back."

As bad as the day had started, Davi couldn't resist cracking a smile. If only she'd been able to stick around a little longer in Michelle's office that day to hear her say that.

"Most of the time it feels like I haven't accomplished anything. A whole bunch of square-ones everywhere I look," Davi said.

"You ask a lot of yourself, and that's a good thing," Michelle said, balling up the wrapper and tossing it into the trash with a hook shot. "Just don't ask for too much, you know?"

"And how do you know when you're doing that?"

"I don't know. Maybe when everyone in your life is impressed with what you've done, and you're not."

Davi nodded and stood up. She had to get to work before the minutes off the clock kept adding up and ate their way through her lunch break.

"Thanks, Michelle."

"You got it. Punch me in too when you're down there, okay?" Michelle said, spinning her chair around to face the computer.

Downstairs, Davi took Michelle's card out of its slot first, let the clock thump the time down onto it, and slid it back. When she fed her time card into the clock, the 'Wallace' written at the top poked out from under her thumb and brought the Legacy back to the front of her mind. She crammed her card back into the gray slats and made for the front of the store.

At lane three, she powered up the computer in the register, and flicked the switch that illuminated the round, white bulb with a '3' on it. No customers were up at the registers yet, but it wouldn't be long now with the few early risers who were already strolling the aisles.

"Hey, Davi," Allison said from lane six. "Good morning."

"Good morning, Allie."

"How was your night last night?"

"Just painted and fell asleep early," Davi said, leaning back on the counter behind her. "How was the date you were supposed to have with what's-his-name? Or was that two nights ago?"

"I'll tell you about it during lunch. Not so hot," Allison said as groceries began to slide her way down the conveyor belt.

Until she got the Legacy off her mind, Davi said a little prayer for all of the customers to funnel into Allison's lane and give her a break to wallow without interruption for a few minutes. Just then, a woman in nurse's scrubs jogged through the automatic doors, and Davi instantly knew that she would be a problem: day job, probably already late, worried about traffic, stopped to get one thing, would prioritize the register by the exit.

The nurse disappeared around the side of the bread and cereal aisle, only to pop back out all the way down the other end of the store by the cosmetics and first aid. Davi crossed her arms and watched her hurry towards the registers.

"You're going to buy some hand cream for four bucks and pay with a check, aren't you?" Davi said to herself. "Then, when it takes a couple minutes longer to process the check, you'll get on my case and say how you're in this big rush—"

The conveyor belt next to her shook as an old man dropped a gallon of milk on it. He slowly reached down into his cart, turned back with a can of cashews, and placed it next to the milk.

"How are you?" he said in a thin, distant voice.

"I'm okay," Davi said, opening some brown paper bags and flipping the switch that brought the conveyor belt to life.

On her way home after work, Davi could feel the extra play in the steering wheel and a general loss of alignment to the left, but the Legacy was back on its feet. Coming off the main route, she passed her usual space and parked under a streetlight down the block where the houses were more frequent and closer together.

Gathering her grocery bag in the back seat, Davi looked over her shoulder to inspect the two men she'd passed in the driveway, standing around the propped silver hood of Gladys' Cadillac. She pulled her apartment key out of her purse and linked it back together with the car key on their ring, wondering if Gladys' car had been vandalized the previous night too. She hoisted the groceries into her arms and headed towards the apartment. As she got close, shifting the weight of the grocery bag made her drop her keys, and she stooped down to pick them up.

"Hey," he said.

She looked up and stopped in her tracks. Hank was standing ten feet in front of her, smiling on one side of his mouth. The other man was still tinkering away under the hood of Gladys' car behind him.

Hank opened his arms for a hug and took a few steps towards her. With apartment key in hand, Davi shifted her grocery bag back to the center of her body and wrapped her arms around it. She glared at his smile from behind the top edges of the brown paper, wondering how it could possibly be authentic.

"What, we're not friends anymore?" he asked.

"What are you doing here?"

His arms dropped back down to his side.

"This is my buddy's grandma's place," he said, throwing his thumb over his shoulder. "She wanted him to take a look at her car, and he asked me to help. What about you?"

"I live here," she said.

He nodded with mild surprise. The paper grain in the grocery bags was getting moist and flimsy where her palms were pressed.

"Small world," he said.

"So it would seem."

"Everything been going alright?" he asked.

Dumbfounded, she paused and looked his face all over.

"Yeah. Everything is great," she said, walking past him and towards the backyard.

"No reason to be rude," he said. "Good to see you again."

She rounded the corner of the house just as Hank and his friend broke into a low laugh that echoed louder under the hood. At the steps to the apartment, she whipped her head around quickly, but no one was there. The key danced along the face of the lock, circling the slot wildly as she felt steps coming up behind her. She popped her grocery bag up onto her arm to use her hands on the key together, but in getting it to the new position, the quart of orange juice flung out of the top and exploded with a wet splat on the ground. The key finally slid into the door, and she left the busted carton on the grass and hurried inside.

As soon as she closed and locked the door, her first impulse was to reach back and hurl the whole grocery bag at the wall across the room. Instead, she gritted her teeth and let out an impatient growl while placing the bag on the table. As she sat down on the couch, the burning inside flared up again, and she rocketed her keys into the kitchen where they ricocheted off the toaster and into the sink. Her head clunked back on the top of the couch. With the way the day had gone, they'd probably shot right down into the pipes.

She bounced back to her feet and paced in little circles in the living room. A strange pattern emerged in the room with each revolution. The whole place was top heavy. All of her yellow notes were stuck to things about the height of the main table or higher, and her paints and brushes were all crammed in together on the top shelf. She hadn't even noticed that she'd been doing it. When she had placed the notes and art supplies, they had simply felt good in their spots, and only now did she realize how odd everything looked up at that height, especially without insatiable dog noses running around to warrant the precaution.

"This is such goddamn bullshit," she said to herself, scooping her paints into her arms and shoveling them onto the bottom shelf.

She snatched each yellow note and brought it down a foot or two, even if she could no longer read its message without hunching over.

"They're gone. You left them, and they're gone. Do you understand that? Gone."

She ripped the grocery bag in half, sending the pretzels, bacon, eggs, lettuce, and the rest cascading all over the carpet. In the places where the food bunched up, she kicked the products off each other, spreading them evenly over the floor. Dropping back onto the couch, she reached and grabbed the cordless phone off its cradle. Now that she was seated and still, the bacon and its shiny plastic looked out of place on top of the carpet fabric. Her eyes closed.

"Oh, my God," she gasped, pressing her face against the phone. "What the fuck is wrong with me?"

izzzrohnngwethmee

The phone beeped under her thumb, and she dialed Mona's number. She hated that she was going to call her like this, even though Mona wouldn't have it any other way. She hummed to blot out any more words from cycling through her head while she waited for her to pick up.

"Hello?"

"Mona, it's me. I'm sorry. I just need to talk to you for a little bit please. You know, if you can," Davi said while her finger twirled in circles, searching out for the curly cord of the phone it remembered at the old house.

"Of course, of course. What's going on?"

"Nothing. I'm fine. Just know that first of all."

"You don't sound fine," Mona said.

"I'm— I don't know what I feel," she said, her vision going slightly blurry.

"Just tell me what you're thinking. What's going on?"

Davi sighed into the phone. Mona would say she understood and that dramatic, unannounced phone calls would never be a bother. Nevertheless, Davi worried that even Mona's patience had limits, and what a sour day it would be if she ever reached them.

"Well, I'm scared. I guess that's how I feel. Everything has been hitting me all at once in the last couple of hours, and I realize how much more I have to do just to be normal. Just to have a normal life. I'm not scared. That's not the way to put it. I'm exhausted. I'm all used up—"

"I don't blame you," Mona interjected, trying to get a word in edgewise.

"And I don't know how to get in front of all this," Davi said, getting up to see where her keys had wound up. "I've got to work this job and fight the urge to freak out in there every day just from being outside. Then, I've got to go through the divorce, meet with this lawyer, probably a court date, all while watching my ass and trying to not be so goddamn weird all the time, and I'm sorry to say that it's hard, way harder than you'd think. Way harder than I ever thought it would be. I mean, what the hell am I supposed to do? How many more mountains do I have to climb? How much longer does this go on?"

"It's going to go on forever," Mona said as a matter of fact.

In the sink, her keys were halfway down the drain but not disappeared. The key ring had caught on a fork from breakfast she hadn't cared to clean.

"It goes on forever, Davi. When you beat this, it'll be something else, and when you beat that, it'll be the next thing. And when everything about this awful ordeal is behind you, it's going to be something else. It's never going to stop."

18.

The gusts were picking up outside, whistling past the apartment, and the long, slender branch on the tree out front was getting blown against the living room siding to make its usual, irregular tapping. In the woods, a branch broke off one of the trees with a crack and tumbled down to the ground.

Davi opened the lock to the kitchen window and closed it again slowly, threading the curved metal into the base. She shook the window upwards a few times and felt that it still had a little play. She undid the lock, leaned her weight down on the top of the window frame until it was as far down as it would go, and slowly locked it again. She pulled the lace curtains closed, keeping her eyes peeled on the lock, and then threw them back apart to redo the steps all over again. When the lock finally felt just so, the kitchen light snapped off, and she headed for the bathroom.

There were two windows in the living room, one in the kitchen, one in the bathroom, two in the bedroom, one door, and eight locks altogether, and she could think of no worse disappointment than glancing back after having just finished the bathroom and seeing one of the blinds hanging cockeyed in the living room. Then, all the lights had to go back on, and the process started again with the front door. One, two, three. One, two, three.

Closing all the locks on the first try hadn't been a problem in the early days in the apartment, but quickly, she'd gravitated towards testing each of them in threes. If all the window corners refused to come flush or the blinds failed to zip exactly into position on take three, she would hurry through the next two tries just to get to the sixth where the next realistic chance of breaking the repetition would come. What felt best was nine, three sets of three, but with the agonizing scrutiny she invested in every point of entry, nine attempts apiece would burn a full two hours before bed.

Inside the tub, her fingers slid onto the gummed-up lock on the little bathroom window. In the middle of her second try at securing it, the beads of water still clinging to the tiles from her shower hours earlier caught the corner of her eye, and the muscles in her chest locked up. The walls suddenly felt like they were tilting over and stacking themselves right on top of her, and the tingling sensation of eyes behind her began, groping at her legs and feet. With a gasp, she stepped out of the tub and locked the bathroom door. Ever since she'd begun to kill off the jackhammer impulse to wipe every drop of water off the shower tiles when she got out, some nights were better than others at the bathroom window.

"That's a normal reaction to drops of water on a wall. Everyone reacts like that," she said to herself, fighting to take deeper breaths.

With the door locked, the bathroom somehow felt both more and less claustrophobic, and Davi closed her eyes to concentrate on drawing her breath in and out completely, emptying her mind of water and tiles and soap and anything that bore any connection to showers. When they did appear, the electrified ideas were jettisoned before they could stick, and the muscles in her rib cage unclenched.

She smiled and opened her eyes. Not so long ago, she would have run to the closet for a towel to smear down the shower tiles as soon as the iron fist grabbed and cinched her lungs shut, but there was only so much running she could stomach, having fled so many times before only to look back from the horizon and wonder what had sent her rocketing away in the first place. There was no sense in flight if she carried the danger with her, transporting it in the fibers of her clothes like contagion to infect and destroy the next place she happened upon that was good enough to call home.

Back in the tub, she began again, twisting the window lock open and closed, moving the window up and down. Finally, she made it to the third try in the third cycle, and the whole room felt crisp and secure, even with a gust from the windstorm outside slamming into the pane as she jammed the lock home. Turning her attention to the wall, she looked right at the blue tile next to her that had a few drops of water on it and made herself dip her fingertip into its filth, smearing it around. Tears pumped into her eyes, so she closed them and breathed into calmness again. She took her finger away from the droplets and washed her hands in the sink, satisfied with the extra defiance she'd been able to muster for good measure. She snapped the light off in the bathroom and closed the door.

Nearly asleep on her feet, Davi wrapped up the two windows in her bedroom, dropped the blinds, and collapsed onto the bed. Flopping onto the mattress popped her books into the air, sending them poking into her thigh and ribs. Even if she went weeks without opening them, she still slept easier with them resting beside her. She took one hand away from her stomach and laid it on the Torah next to her. The massive size of the book felt sturdy and permanent, and she began to feel like maybe sleep would come after all if she could just keep her hand on its cover through the night.

The light from the bedside lamp cast strange shadows on the stucco ceiling, revealing impish faces in its texture. One to the left had an intrepid look with closed eyes and chin lifted high. Another had arched eyebrows and seemed terribly surprised to be missing a nose. Another had a sinister moustache, all thin angles and jagged edges. She yawned, and her eyes lost focus, sending the outlines of the faces melting back into the random stucco splatters. She reached over and twisted the switch on the lamp, and then, it was dark.

Despite the exhaustion, renegade anxiety manifested in her belly and casually wandered up into her chest. She squirmed on her back and rubbed her heels back and forth against the sheets. The rhythmic whooshing sound they made against the bedspread felt wonderful, as though the problem with her nerves had only ever been as simple as an itch on her eardrum that was just missing being scratched by all the normal, common frequencies. Her jaws stretched open with another yawn, and a throaty engine rumbled in the distance, turned down the street, and cut off.

Davi closed her eyes and sighed, and when she opened them, the clock on the nightstand read three-fourteen in blinking digital numbers. The windstorm must have made the power flicker. She thumped her fist down on the mattress next to her, resenting how rolling over to reset the clock for the alarm would snap the whooshing hypnosis that made her feel as though she was floating on waves of her own creation. She was too relaxed to give it up right away and decided to risk falling asleep without the alarm to wake her up just to enjoy it a little longer.

The branch outside the living room started to slap the siding again, beating away amidst another series of swirling gusts. As the wind fell silent, the tapping continued into the quiet. Davi opened her eyes towards the ceiling and scrunched her face. There was a faint scraping interspersed among the taps.

She sat up onto her elbows, and her ears ratcheted up their sensitivity until her heartbeat banged inside them, blotting out the sounds outside. She turned her head to the side and dared the taps and scrapes to grow louder. The digital numbers on the alarm clock throbbed off and on, and she closed her eyes to focus on listening. Finally, the stronger winds came again and blew against the house, sending the branch knocking into the siding just like it was supposed to.

Frustrated, she spun her legs off the bed and turned the bedside lamp back on. The shutdown rituals had dragged on too long, and now she was hearing things from the exhaustion. She grabbed her pack off the nightstand and lit a cigarette. With a long exhale of smoke, she sat back against the wall and looked over at the sticky note on the Torah's cover. Forgetting how far she'd come in the past few months was easy to do, especially in the face of the river of anxiety that broke its banks whenever it pleased, but her notes had done their job well. There was at least one person who cared about her without qualification or judgment, and one would do.

The light scraping sound came again, this time on the bedroom wall to her right. She froze with her cigarette just a hair away from her lips and attempted to make out what it could be. A mouse in the walls? A piece of siding that had come loose? The windows all felt wide open, as though she hadn't spent hours ensuring that they were locked. With the blinds closed, the thought of having to spread them open even a centimeter to see what was causing the sound was pure vertigo.

Instead, she chose to sit and smoke in ultra-quiet, slowing all of her motion down to one-eighth speed. She should never have turned back on the lamp next to her. Its light made her feel exposed and vulnerable.

In a flash, Victor's snarling face appeared in her mind, and she gasped, stubbing her cigarette out in disgust. She drove her heels into the floor and stormed to the kitchen to get something to drink.

"Yeah, you've really got steel in your spine, girl," she whispered, filling a glass from the tap. "Turned to a big bowl of Jell-O over a goddamn twig in the breeze."

She began to pace around the kitchen in her tank top and shorts, drinking in thirsty gulps with her hand on her hip.

"Is this what you went to Mills for all that time?" she whispered to herself. "All that trouble and work and sneaking around, and for what? All the risk, and for what?! So you could keep being afraid of what was going to happen next? What a joke."

The glass rattled in the sink. She stamped back to bed and sneered at the closed blinds before snapping off the lamp's switch again.

"Why aren't you asleep?"

Her face went ice cold. Someone had whispered outside the window. She couldn't tell whose voice it was. Now, the wind seemed to calm down or stop altogether, and she clapped her hands over her mouth to smother the involuntary cry rising up inside of her throat. Her heartbeat pounded through the pin-drop silence as her eyes raced around the room, sizing up everything they could make out in the blackness for its fitness as a weapon.

Snatching the cordless phone from her mess of scattered books, she slid away from the window and off the foot of the

bed. Even with the apartment dark again, she couldn't make
out any figure through the blinds. The streetlight out front was
the only light source at this hour. It could be anyone. Victor.
Hank. Maybe even just a random prowler. Her mind churned
up a foam of panicked guesses, and in the midst of the paralysis,
she realized she had the phone in her hand.

Tiptoeing into the kitchen, she squatted down by the
kitchen sink and hit 'TALK'. The phone beeped loudly and
returned a dial tone. Smashing her palm against the noisy end
of the phone that did the beeping, Davi dialed 9-1-1 and cupped
her hand over her mouth and against the speaker. But nothing
seemed to happen. The line didn't connect.

"You son of a bitch! Come on."

She shook the phone and smacked it against her hip where
the sound of the impact would get muffled in her clothes. The
scraping sound came again behind the kitchen. Tears started to
boil out of her eyes. She reached up into the dish rack for her
chopping knife and grabbed it by the blade in the rush.
Instantly, her palm felt wet and sticky, but the pain never came,
somehow bypassed. All she had to know that the damage was
done was the slight slicing friction of the blade and the feeling
of something being beyond the normal depth of her skin, albeit
painlessly. She stared off towards the bookshelf in the living
room to avoid looking at it.

What was that scraping? It sounded so light, like whatever
it was couldn't be very big. Was he just dragging his keys along
the siding? Had he picked up a branch? Davi's eyes shot open.
It was a knife. She squeezed the handle of hers even tighter,
sending blood squishing through her fingers and down over her
knuckles.

Holding her cut hand to the side and away from where she
would see it, she tried dialing the phone again, pushing each

button slowly to make sure she got it right. This time, the phone's battery light flashed and died. She swore and tried to break it against her hip. Then, someone knocked on the front door three times.

"Oh, Jesus, fuck," she gasped.

Leaving the phone on the floor, she crept over to the wall to look at the door before heading down the hallway and back to the bedroom. The digital numbers of the alarm clock strobed the room with red light, blinking 3:14 over and over. She scurried to the bed and knelt next to it, at a loss to think of any better plan. She was beginning to feel cold and shaky like she might pass out, so her bloodied right hand passed its knife over to the left one and pulled the big, heavy Torah over on the bed to lean itself on it. The knocking had stopped, but she hadn't heard any footsteps back down the front steps. Whoever it was was still at the door.

The phone on the kitchen floor suddenly sprang to life and blared a recorded message from the phone company through its speaker.

"If you'd like to make a call—"

The front door shook from impact. Someone was throwing himself against it. Davi gasped, then screamed. She scared herself with the volume of her voice, ringing out into what had felt like years of silence. The wet knife handle squirted out of her grip, and both of her hands chased after it, frantic to snatch it back up.

"—please hang up and try again—"

Prayers paraded through her head. She opened her palm again on the cover of the Torah, and her gashed hand smeared blood all over it. The blinking of the digital numbers had gotten so bright it was taking her breath away. She turned to unplug it and saw the sticky note on her alarm clock that was the one that told her to smile. Now, it simply read 'Victor' in scrawling cursive. All the notes all over the room did.

"—if you need help—"

The front door banged again, and a tool of some kind was being driven into its jamb. Davi drifted all over the room in disbelieving horror to see each uplifting reminder now rewritten with 'Victor' in a flowing hand. The edges of her sight began to flicker and get dark.

"—hang up, and then dial your operator. Thank you."

The recording ended, and the line clicked over to a rapid alarm tone that echoed off the walls. The wood around the lock of the front door began to crunch under the tool being driven into it, and a man's voice out front bellowed in rage.

"DAVI!!"

The hammering through the door quickened. The alarm clock digits flashed over and over. The phone's tone rang through the apartment. The knife fell out of her hand as she leaned into the wall with her shoulder. Her senses felt like they could all explode at once. The world went black, and all she heard then was a splintering crack from the front door giving way and the phone relentlessly beeping its awful sound.

Davi shot up in bed and yelped. The alarm clock next to her was going off. It was quarter to seven.

She grabbed the waste basket next to her bed and threw up. Her sheets were soaked. At her first moment of reprieve from vomiting, she looked at her right hand and pressed it against her chest in relief that it was completely fine and not pouring blood, though all of the nerves inside it tingled, all of its muscles felt tender. She picked up the waste basket and walked to the front door with it. No one was there, and it was untouched. She threw up again on her feet. Her jaw was locking up from her having clenched her teeth in her sleep, and the sizzling pain of so much force on them to open while she was sick dropped her to a knee.

The nightmares had been getting worse lately, and Davi wasn't surprised. It wouldn't be long now before Victor got the divorce papers in the mail, and soon after that, the proceedings themselves would take place. She just couldn't foresee what he might be capable of doing once that happened, and the trepidation was leaking out in her sleep. At the very least, she'd been recovering faster from the terror in her dreams. Not so long ago, a nightmare like that would have sent her lunging for the phone, frantically dialing Mills or Mona just to hear the calmness of their voices in her ear.

Her drenched clothes got stripped off and thrown in the hamper while the hot steam from the shower filled the bathroom. She rubbed her palm on the smooth porcelain corner of the sink to make the tingling go away, but its muscles still felt weak like they would refuse to grasp or make a fist. The mirror fogged up while Davi slapped her hand against her thigh and shook it in the air. She reached for her towel on the rack and grabbed it as hard as she could, but again, the ticklish weakness appeared in her muscles and shorted them out. She forced her hand to squeeze again so hard that she laughed involuntarily from the quivering sensation. Then, she went over to the sink and smeared the fog into the corners of the mirror.

"Okay, here's the deal. Did you have a bad dream? No one cares. No one cares. Deal with it."

Her gaze burned into itself, and floating droplets of mist from the running shower all hovered through the room, in snapshot. Slowly, her lips spread into a satisfied grin.

"And as for you," she said as she looked at her noncompliant hand and squeezed it again, feeling the hangover effect subside even more. "Well, that goes double for you."

She slid back the shower curtain with her right hand that was finally all the way awake from the nightmare along with her. Throwing her leg in the tub, she yelped and jumped back. While she'd been occupied, the hot water had all run down the drain.

"I'm definitely not shaving today," she mused to herself, staring at the icy water. "Okay, let's do it."

She jumped in and started bouncing foot to foot, humming involuntarily and scrubbing. Splashing the cold water onto her face, she gasped. She swept her head under the stream and shrieked a little. Then, she put her whole face under the showerhead and held it there. She started to laugh.

19.

Davi dreaded the feeling around the courthouse, all creased faces and metal detectors. The inside promised to be a catacomb of echoing whispers, bouncing off hardwood banisters and impermeable marble, pooling back together in the open air as one, muffled shout, but this was where Mara's attorney friend had requested that she meet him instead of his office. With the divorce proceeding only a week away, she hadn't requested a new venue for their talk. She needed the practice.

As she got to the top of the front steps, two women with ID cards hanging from lanyards around their necks were smoking beside the courthouse doors. Taking her hand off the door handle, Davi tucked herself behind one of the pillars downwind of them to catch wafts of their smoke. Her appetite for cigarettes had abruptly disappeared since leaving Victor's house, perhaps for as simple a reason as no longer being able to afford them, and she had come to find their smell lightly repellant, like an old friend who never called anymore, dealing slights that added up to distance. But the sight of the massive courthouse in front of her had awoken the bond once more.

Passively smelling their smoke seemed a better alternative to asking the women outright if she could have one of her own, sparing herself the lightheadedness and upset stomach that would come after just a few drags. Davi stood and held her face up to catch the warm spring sun while the women's conversation moved away from meaningless chitchat and into some hubbub that had apparently happened with a Judge Walsh the previous day. Something about how a man had tried to cut his own throat with a razor blade in front of the bench in a fit of madness over threats of prison for failure to pay child support. The smoke started to make Davi feel queasy, and she opened the oversized door to the entrance.

"Hello, Davi," Carpenter said, getting up off a bench just on the other side of security.

"How are you?" she replied.

They shook hands, and he gestured for her to follow him away from the bustling center of the courthouse.

"So, you've got lots of business here today?" she asked.

"I've got a few matters to take care of but not full-on trials. Just negotiations, pre-trial motions, stuff like that."

"You do a lot of that?"

"Oh, yeah," he said with emphasis. "You want a coffee or bagel or something? There's a little cafeteria right around the corner here."

"No, thank you."

"Just want to get right to it?"

"I don't see any other way. My stomach is flipping out right now. I couldn't eat," she said.

"Gotcha. Not a problem," he said, holding open the door to a tiny conference room.

Davi took her seat and left her purse on her shoulder. She liked the feeling of her hands being up and at the ready like they were when they clutched the strap. Carpenter sat down across from her and pulled out a legal pad littered with notes, some with big arrows drawn near them to connect the thought to others. She caught her reflection in the sliver of vertical glass in the door and was surprised at how tense her body looked in her favorite position. She forced her hands to take the bag off and fold themselves together on the table in a way that made her reflection look more natural.

"So, the big day is coming up," he said. "You have any thoughts or concerns for me before I tell you what I think about everything? Anything at all."

Davi reflected for a moment and then shook her head.

"Nothing new springs to mind. I think we've already covered all of my concerns and what-not."

"Just making sure," he said before clearing his throat loudly. "Well, let's get the bad news out of the way up front. After reviewing what you've told me about your husband, I don't think it's in your best interests to press criminal charges here."

Her hands rubbed against one another before pulling back towards her stomach, smearing sweaty condensation on the tabletop beneath them.

"Why is that?"

"First, understand that this is an issue of evidence, not whether I believe you. I do believe everything you've told me. This is about the case that a jury would get to hear, and that case has serious problems."

"Like what?" Davi asked calmly.

"For starters, not everything you've told me is admissible. Much of it is hearsay, which means a jury wouldn't be allowed to hear most of it. That being said, if a lot of hearsay was the main problem here, I'd say go for it. A bigger problem is the lack of physical evidence with respect to—"

"My tooth," she said, quickly pulling her lip back. "I had to get an implant from him knocking this tooth out."

"Did that happen during a sexual assault?"

"No, we were eating dinner. It was just for no reason."

"Simple assault and battery isn't going to bring any meaningful prison time with his record. It's the rape counts that would do that. The tooth is good for establishing a violent temperament, maybe even a violent relationship, but rape is a far cry from that. The jury wouldn't have a bridge of evidence to take them from that general violent temperament into a sexual offender."

Davi nodded, her hands squirming against each other on her lap.

"So, is that it?"

"Not having physical evidence of sexual assault isn't the end of the world. Having witnesses would work too, but the witnesses here would be the accused, and that is often a problem in these cases. They can't be compelled to testify in a manner that would incriminate them, and they will have lawyers who will likely advise them to answer nothing whatsoever when it comes to those questions," Carpenter said.

"I'm a witness too," she said.

"Yes, you are. Your testimony as to what happened is really the only evidence to support any significant charges, but that brings me to the last problem that I see with the case. You were heavily medicated at the time, anti-depressants, anti-psychotics, mood stabilizers. Then, there was the recreational drug use."

Davi crossed her arms over her stomach and turned slightly red. Recreational drugs, as he called them, had seemed so natural when she was immersed in the culture and surrounded by people who did them with her, but reviewing it with a lawyer during business hours colored them with foreign, diagnosing words that felt simultaneously accurate and unfair, as though the square lexicon refused to accommodate them as anything other than the playthings of an underclass. As far as she was concerned, they had done more to keep her alive than the fancy ones with the embossed letters and numbers stamped on each pill.

"I don't mean that that makes you a bad person but rather that drug use goes to your credibility, specifically your ability to accurately and reliably perceive what was going on around you. Realistically, it also has to be said that an average juror may have his or her own personal prejudices around drug users, and that doesn't help. Bottom line? When your testimony is the only admissible evidence for the prosecution and you have credibility problems, well... It's a mess is what it is, and the defense attorney will be merciless with you on the stand. Truthfully, that is my main concern."

"That he'll run circles around me?"

"That he'll embarrass you and make you look crazy when you and I both know you're not," he said.

Davi nodded slowly.

"Only you can decide if the risk is worth it, and if you do, I'll contact the D.A. and set up a meeting with them to hear you out. They'll ultimately make the call on whether to prosecute after they review everything like I have," he said.

The picture was starting to come together. He had to say it his way with awful legal precision, but everything boiled down to the fact that there was only one of her and as many as four of them. Just like old times.

"So, they walk," she said with a little dip of her head.

"Yeah."

Carpenter looked back down at his pad and drew some sharp lines through a numbered item. He patted his breast pocket and grunted under his breath.

"What is it?" she asked.

"Just quit smoking. It's been eight days, but I'm still fidgety."

"Cold turkey?"

"I've got the gum," he said, pulling out a pack of nicotine gum and spinning it onto the table. "That helps, but well, you saw what I just did. I used to keep my pack right in there. The physical habits are just as bad as the chemical ones."

"Sounds like recreational drug addiction to me," Davi said with a wry smile.

"When the government says it's okay, it's not recreational drug use. Then, it's just a citizen enjoying his liberties and assuming the risk."

"I see," she said. "Funny how that works."

"Isn't it?" he said, his pen finishing another line.

Davi looked over at her purse slouched next to her and flipped the strap that was half-dangling over the edge of the table onto the top of the bag.

"I quit smoking recently too," she said.

"Oh? What did it for you?"

"Nothing really. Just kind of dropped it," she said.

"No, I meant why. For me, I was kicking the soccer ball around with my son, and my chest got so damn tight. Scared the hell out of me."

"You put on weight?"

"Not yet," he said.

"I don't think I have a reason, and sitting here now, I couldn't tell you why I started either. I guess there isn't a 'why' really, and if there was, I don't remember it."

"Well, you're better off either way," he said.

Her shoulders liked her hands being down. Muscles she didn't even know were tight began to unwind, changing her posture and loosening up her breathing.

"If it makes you feel any better, I don't think I would have cared to prosecute, but I appreciate the work you did there," she said.

Carpenter didn't look up, but his pen shot down to the bottom of the pad and wrote a new item. He underlined part of it.

"Have you had any problems with any of these people since you left?" he asked.

"Nothing I can't handle," she said as a matter of fact.

He sighed and leaned forward onto his elbow.

"See, that concerns me when you say something like that."

"I actually thought it would set your mind at ease," she said.

He nodded and waved his hand just above the surface of the table.

"I like your guts. Don't get me wrong there. But what you just said tells me that pressure is being applied, and if that is—"

"Pressure is being attempted, shall we say."

His eyebrows popped up, and he slowly spun his head towards the wall behind him then back to her.

"Well, jeez. If I hadn't just watched you pass through security, I'd be a little nervous right now."

Davi laughed bashfully and fidgeted in her chair. She wasn't sure what part of her had said that.

"I just feel that I know these people, and I know how they think. If you're worried that I'm backing off because they're getting to me, that's just not the case," she said.

He flicked his pen around in his fingers, seeming to want to pry deeper but stuck being torn as to how to phrase the question to his satisfaction.

"Your will is completely uninfluenced by anyone else at this time. That's what you're saying?"

"That's what I'm saying," she said.

"And you're sure?" he asked, unapologetically inspecting her body language for one last answer.

"One hundred percent."

His pen went to work again, and he seemed to accept that she was as comfortable and collected as she would have him believe.

"So," he began, looking back up. "Do you have any questions about what will happen in the divorce proceeding next week? Since everything has been expedited here due to our grounds of extreme cruelty, the judge may ask you to speak."

"And there won't be any cross-examination or—"

"No cross-examination, no jury, nothing like that. I'm not saying that it's going to happen or even that it's likely, but I just wanted you to know that it's a possibility."

"Okay," she said. "I'll just have to think about that."

"These things are all mainly formalities, I assure you," he said, looking back down. "How's Mara, by the way?"

"She's fine, I think," Davi said.

"I've never met her before, but my wife is going to ask."

"How's your wife?"

He looked up from his pad with a broad grin.

"She's good."

"Excellent," she said.

He flipped the top page over and wrapped it around the back of the pad. This one was blank.

"So, tell me some of the specific things you'd like to have from the house."

"I don't know. I think I took everything I needed when I left. Well, except the dogs, of course."

"So, the dogs then."

"No, don't write that down."

"But you just—"

"I don't have the space or money for them, and that's just all there is to it. Can't be done," she said with her voice cracking slightly.

"I see."

She reached into her purse quickly without looking to find anything in particular.

"Would you mind if I took a second outside?" she asked. "Maybe I will get a coffee after all."

"Of course. If you go right out the door, make your first right after that, and you'll run into the cafeteria."

"Okay, great," she said, lifting her purse off the table. "Want me to get you anything?"

"No. Thank you, though," he said.

She closed the door behind her and headed to the right. His natural assumption about her wanting the dogs had brought their faces drifting back into her mind. She passed the turn for the cafeteria and walked all the way back to the security checkpoint at the entrance. Her legs seemed to want to make a run for it, having led her to the exit of their own accord. Having to say aloud that she didn't want the dogs had shaken her, and she worried that if she had to say it over and over that eventually it might wind up turning into the truth.

She took a seat on the bench Carpenter had been sitting on when she'd arrived. Getting in the car and leaving didn't have any appeal right then, yet there she was anyway, moved along by muscles that were lost to habits that no longer applied. Back in the house, she'd never noticed that her legs were running when she would retreat into her studio and out of Victor's crucible. Now that she was venturing into bigger spaces, the distances her legs had to cover in order to escape were more noticeable, where she wound up more arbitrary.

At the metal detector, a white-haired man seemed to resent having to take off his tweed sports jacket to put on the conveyor belt. Once the security guard had waved him through, he gathered his briefcase, jacket, and bowl of metal objects and sat them down on the bench next to Davi. There was a deep, blotchy rash all over his forearms that shined as though freshly treated with ointment. Once he had his keys and loose coins back in his pocket, he stood up his briefcase and sighed. He'd probably spent all morning worried about the unsightly blotches and being able to hide them, only for the whole plan to come totally and predictably undone. Davi could sense that his face was red and averted her eyes from his direction.

"There's no goddamn decency anymore. What the hell kind of trouble do you expect from an old man?"

He was speaking in her direction, but his cadence didn't sound like he was looking for an answer or a conversation. She folded her arms across her stomach and watched him out of the corner of her eye. In his rush to put on his jacket, he accidentally swept the fabric the wrong way over his thinning hair, leaving the middle of it sticking up.

"I guess they have to treat everyone the same. Even still. Being safe isn't that goddamn important," he muttered.

Davi's heels clicked against the marble as she stood up and faced him. He seemed surprised to see her, as though he'd just assumed the bench was empty.

"May I?" she said, arching her eyebrows up towards his hair.

"Did I mess it up?"

She dabbed her fingertips on her tongue and pushed the out of place hairs back down.

"These things happen when you're in a hurry," she said. "That's better."

"Yes, they do," he said, running his own hand over his head to feel if it was all smoothed down. "Thank you."

"Sure," she said.

"Good luck with whatever it is that brings you here," he said, picking up his fatigued briefcase and nodding goodbye.

"You too," she said, turning to walk back down the hall.

As she passed the hallway leading to the cafeteria on her way to the conference room, she still didn't have her usual appetite for coffee and walked straight by the turn again.

"You didn't get anything?" Carpenter asked as she entered.

"No, I guess I was wrong about wanting a cup. I just walked around for a few minutes instead. Sorry about that," she said.

"Not to worry," he said, dropping his pen. "Frankly, we're pretty much done if you don't want anything specific or special from your soon-to-be-ex-husband. He has to give you some things under the law, of course. Those are automatic."

"Like what?"

"Basic rehabilitative alimony."

"And that's just to get me back on my feet?"

"That's correct. And if you're about to tell me that you don't want even that, then allow me to remind you that I would make an excellent charitable recipient for the money," he said with a smile.

"And there's no debating it? No negotiations?"

"Nope. In this state, it's determined according to a formula that takes into account your relative incomes, years married, things of that nature. No debate at all," he said.

"Okay, fine. That much will be fine. God knows how I've been squeaking by this whole time anyway."

She chuckled and slung her purse off her shoulder. Carpenter sat looking at a spot on the table, seemingly lost in thought.

"Is what I'm doing here unusual?" Davi asked.

Carpenter snapped out of his trance and sat up straighter in his chair.

"It is," he said. "Not that unusual is bad. These are your decisions. If my reactions are odd, it's because I'm used to people doing the same things. They want money, the special china, the house, the kids, the bullshit Renoir print they picked out for the foyer two Christmases ago that reminds them of Florence, whatever. Whatever they want, I try to get it. If you happen to want very little, so be it. It's not a problem. I just want you to understand you won't be able to change your mind about this after a certain point. So, I want to know that you're sure."

With a different attorney, Davi might have jumped to the conclusion that he was dismayed by a decision of hers that could potentially shrink his pay on the case, but he genuinely seemed too odd to care. She liked him more for that.

"I'm sure," she said.

He scribbled on his pad again, and Davi smiled to herself. Seeing his tie wobble back and forth with his arm writing frantically reminded her of sitting across from Mills for the first time a year earlier.

"Can I ask you something?" he wondered.

"Of course."

"We started everything off with some pretty bad news with respect to the potential for criminal charges in all of this, and while I know you said you didn't care to press charges and I believe that, you're telling me now that you don't want any more than the minimum amount of money your husband must give you by law in a divorce. I guess I'm just wondering why."

"Why?" she asked.

"Yes."

"Well, that's just all I want," she said, leaving her mouth open to say something else but shaking her head instead. "I guess I don't understand what you mean."

He folded his hands behind his head and leaned back, making the springs in his chair creak under him.

"After everything you've told me about what happened, I don't understand why that's all you want. This isn't a legal thing. I'm just curious."

Davi had been seeing a lot of this question lately, almost always left silently implied by befuddled looks and checked gasps. She didn't understand why she'd had to explain it over and over, especially to Mona. Davi had just assumed that Mona's usual understanding had been blocked by guilt over not intervening or the simple opinion that her big sister had been through enough. Carpenter didn't have that same emotional connection with her, yet his face still wore the identical concern that Mona's had over lunch the previous week. She began to realize that they thought she was just handing over all this currency, instead of buying something for her money.

"For almost the whole time I lived in that house, I was a dog. I was not human. I did the things I wanted to do until he needed something, and then everything that I wanted had to stop instantly. I stayed awake all night and slept when he was at work. He sucked all the time that I had out of me and made it his own. I've been married to him for seven years. Seven years out of my thirty-five. That's plenty. You want to know why I don't want more from him? The answer is so obvious to me that I barely understand the question. It's because I've given him all the time in my life that I'm willing to give, and I won't give him even a second more."

Carpenter rocked back in his chair and pushed a piece of nicotine gum through the foil seal.

"I want my name back. I want my identity back. I want my dignity back. Those are the things I'm willing to fight for here. Those things I can't live without. People seem to think I should want revenge, and they can go and get it for themselves if they're ever in my shoes. It makes no difference to me. All I know is that I'm finished doing what anyone else demands that I do. Not him, you, or anyone else. What I value is my time in this skin as a person with a mind of her own. Not a dog. And every second that I spend taking revenge on him only amounts to another second that he takes from me."

He chewed his gum silently. Then, he sat forward and turned the pages of his legal pad back over to the beginning.

"You have a strange attitude," he said, closing his file and squaring it on the conference table. "But an interesting one, Davi Ross."

20.

The courtroom doors swung closed behind the four men, and briefly, their voices shouted at each other outside, until finally calming down and becoming unintelligible. The hush that had fallen over the gallery broke, and the plodding conversations discussing car titles and custody agreements renewed between the other lawyers and their clients. Davi smoothed the lapels of her black suit jacket with the palm of her hand.

"The bailiffs have guns," Carpenter said to her in a low voice. "They're taking him out there to calm him down. It's not uncommon, okay? The bailiffs are used to doing this."

Davi shook her head in disbelief. She couldn't remember the last time anyone else had seen Victor act that way, if ever. Even after six months away from his tantrums, they still felt like a dirty secret that she kept, as though a part of her could always pretend they'd only ever been in her head if no one else became privy to them. But the whole gallery of strangers had witnessed his outburst too, and she didn't quite know how to feel about that through the flashes of surreal embarrassment.

"Hey," Carpenter said, lightly shaking her shoulder.

"Hm?" Davi said, snapping back to the present.

"You okay?"

"Yeah, I'm fine," she said, running her palm down her suit jacket's lapels again. "What do you think his lawyer was telling him to make him freak out like that?"

"Must have been that he was going to have to pay your attorney's fees. Everything else was pretty well settled as of last week," Carpenter said.

"Jesus Christ," she said in amazement. "What the hell is wrong with him?"

"He's not that crazy," Carpenter said, clicking the end of his pen and crossing his legs. "He shut up long enough to walk out on his own before the bailiffs decided to pick him up and carry him out."

Davi pulled out her compact and zipped her eyes around the mirror. She was sure that she was fine but wanted to have a look at the outside for herself. As she'd hoped, the quickened heartbeat in her chest was invisible on her face. She breathed a slow exhale through her mouth.

"So, listen," he said. "Ours will be the first case heard. Don't say anything unless I tell you to. Just relax, sit quietly, and we should be out of here in about fifteen minutes," Carpenter said.

"And then?"

"And then, you just sort of walk out the door and continue your life," he said with a shrug. "Just like that."

"Just like that," Davi said with a smile, closing her compact.

"Magic, right?"

The door behind the judge's bench opened, and the third bailiff who'd stayed behind in the courtroom shouted "All rise" to the gallery.

"Be seated," the judge said, pulling his high-backed seat under him.

While the judge organized the files on his desk, the bailiff went over to the front of the bench and whispered a few comments over the gold nameplate. The judge nodded without looking up, his reading glasses resting on the tip of his nose.

"Go see if they're ready please," the judge said in a low voice to the bailiff. "No matter what's happening, make sure Mister Rosica comes back in to speak with me."

"Yes, Judge," the bailiff said.

"Mister Carpenter, Missus Wallace?" the judge asked the room while he kept reading.

"Yes, Judge," Carpenter said, getting to his feet and gesturing for Davi to do the same.

"Come on up please," he said.

Before heading to the back of the courtroom, the bailiff stopped and held open the waist-high gallery doors for them. Carpenter pointed the way to the table to their right and pulled out her chair. Glancing over her shoulder as she took her seat, she was sure that every single eye in the gallery was staring directly into the back of her head, incredulous that she was the one who'd brought the furious man into their midst. Then again, they had no reason to stare for more than a couple rubbernecked seconds before their thoughts had to cycle back to their own problems and grievances. Davi plucked a few tissues out of the box on the table and wadded them up in her palms to dry up the sweat.

The courtroom doors swung open, and a cluster of men's footsteps clapped down the aisle with the bailiffs at the front, all jangling something metallic on their belts as they walked. Somewhere behind their jangling, he was there, blending into the other sounds. Even with her face forward and fixed on the judge's bench, she could feel him, her own personal nuclear reactor's core, melting his way through the amateur gazes of the other soon-to-be-divorcees waiting in the gallery. Whether her eyes looked over or not, her skin still remembered what his presence felt like.

The bailiff who'd gone out to get the four of them passed in front of her and back over to his post on the side of the room. Davi's neck tingled heat below her left ear, and she concentrated on the tissues in her hands. The thought of looking away when she could feel him staring became disgusting, like a bite of her favorite tenderloin turning to spoiled milk on her tongue, so she put her arm on the back of the chair and spun around, only to see Victor's lawyer wholly blocking any view between them. They turned left through the gallery doors, and one of the bailiffs remained standing in the aisle between them, keeping his back to her and Carpenter.

"I apologize for the delay, Judge," Rosica said.

"Everything alright?" the judge asked, looking up.

"Yes, Your Honor."

"And have the parties reached an agreement on the marital property?"

"We have," Rosica said.

"And that would be this?" the judge asked, holding up a packet of paper. "This is a settlement agreement you filed on June sixth of this year, dated June second."

"That's correct."

The judge peeked over the top of his reading glasses in Carpenter's direction.

"Yes, sir. That's the one," Carpenter said, getting halfway to his feet to speak then sitting back down.

The judge licked his thumb and began to leaf through the document as Rosica recited the key details aloud.

"...agreed to a fifty-percent split on the present balance of the Visa card..."

"What's the judge's name?" Davi whispered in Carpenter's ear.

"Suarez."

"...no further contact with or control over my client's property..."

"Interesting," Davi said.

"Why?" Carpenter asked.

She thought for a moment.

"I don't know," she said bashfully.

"...checks to be delivered no later than the first of each month to the post office box provided..."

"Just relax. Only a few more minutes," Carpenter said, resting his hand on the top of hers for a moment.

Rosica concluded his summary, but the judge continued to pore over the agreement.

"Missus Wallace?" he eventually said.

"Stand up," Carpenter whispered to her.

She moved all her tissues into her left hand and got to her feet along with Carpenter. The bailiffs to the side of the room in front of her kept their eyes trained on Victor's table.

"Are you comfortable with the terms of this agreement, Missus Wallace?" he asked.

"Yes, I am, Judge."

"I have to say, I don't think you're getting what you are entitled to. The agreed-upon alimony payments do not put you up at the quality of life to which you had been accustomed during your marriage to Mister Wallace. I don't see how they even approach hitting that mark."

Davi looked over at Carpenter and shrugged slightly. His playful eyes became rarely serious.

"This is your opportunity to get everything on record. Let him know why this is what you're settling for," he whispered.

"I do have a job now," she began.

"From what I see in the calculations section on page seven here, your job pays just above minimum wage. Even adding in the alimony payments, that's not getting you anywhere near the standard of living you're used to," he said, finally looking up from the settlement agreement. "Do you understand my concern?"

"I do," she said.

"Well then? Why would you accept so little?"

So little. As though cash covered any bill. As though stacks of hundreds were worth more than a single soiled cocktail napkin with "Divorce Decree" printed at the top and a notary's seal embossed across the bottom. As though the food she might have bought with his money would have had any chance of staying down in her stomach. As though seven years could be written off as some sort of grotesque tax deduction. As though money meant anything at all to someone who had so recently and reasonably assumed she was just about out of time, "—and I won't miss that standard of living," Davi said, taking her seat.

Suarez looked down solemnly and nodded, uneasy concern spreading through his lips. Maybe it was that salt-and-pepper hair of his, having been through acres of divorces and having grown tired of martyrs and ideals and anything that didn't add up in dollars and cents. Whatever practical advisories were twitching away behind his bushy eyebrows would have to just get swallowed back down until the next case came up from the gallery. The terms of the settlement had been running through her mind for months, and she'd never second-guessed what she wanted even once.

"Very well," Suarez said.

"Your Honor," Rosica said, getting back to his feet. "While it is memorialized in the settlement agreement itself, I'd like the court to confirm for the record that Missus Wallace agrees that she will be unable to return to her former house to recover anything else whatsoever once the settlement has been accepted."

Suarez looked over at Carpenter.

"That clause has been read, understood, and agreed to," Carpenter said, lifting himself up again.

Drawn by the movement, Davi looked over at Carpenter, and behind his head, Karen was reaching over the railing and rubbing Victor's back. She was wearing more makeup than the woman Davi remembered meeting in the kitchen, having switched from flats and jeans to heels and a tight skirt. Davi turned back to face the judge's bench and shook her head disappointedly, knowing that Karen's makeup would only get thicker, her heels higher, the demands harsher and more frequent, until everything collapsed and she no longer wanted to go out at all, just to avoid the hassle of what she'd have to look like to get past the front door.

"Okay," Suarez said, clipping his file together and handing it down to a clerk in front of the bench. "I accept the agreement between the parties as it sits in the filing. If anything else comes up, you know what to do."

"And that's it," Carpenter said to her with a casual smirk. "Congratulations, Davi."

She shook his hand as the two bailiffs walked into the gallery, towards the courtroom doors. The third stayed at the side of Victor's table, between him and Davi.

"Thank you, Jeff," she said. "Thank you so much for everything."

"Don't mention it," Carpenter said, picking up his briefcase. "Besides, this was the most fun I've ever had in a divorce proceeding. So, thank you."

Carpenter held open the waist-high door to the gallery, almost touching shoulders with the bailiff. Davi turned down the aisle.

"You're welcome," she said. "I'm glad you said that. Surprised you said it really."

"I didn't mean I was calling Parker Brothers tomorrow to try to sell this as a board game," he said.

Davi laughed aloud and then covered her mouth until she could make it through the doors the bailiffs were holding open for them at the exit. She and Carpenter stopped in the hallway outside while she let the last few laughs out, and the two bailiffs smiled at her and clapped. Five other people from the gallery who happened to be scattered around outside the courtroom started to clap with them. Her face blushed in surprise, but she was proud that she at least remembered to smile back. The bailiffs went back inside, closing the doors behind them.

"Oh, they must've thought I was laughing because I was so happy for it to be done," she said to Carpenter.

"Well, aren't you?" he asked, pulling his nicotine gum out of his coat pocket. "Happy, I mean."

"Of course," she said, her eyes lighting back up.

Carpenter reached out and shook her hand again.

"Miss Ross. Pleasure to meet you," he said.

She smiled and dipped down in a curtsy, catching her heel on the way back up. Rosica came through the courtroom doors while she and Carpenter chuckled over the stumble.

"Excuse me," Rosica said to Davi. "I wanted to let you know that the first check will arrive on the first of August, not July. It's just a question of being realistic about timing and how quickly this whole thing has taken place."

Davi looked over at Carpenter whose smile had bent into a look of distaste. She'd only briefly met Rosica a few times before, but his face was already on her nerves, always tucking a plausibly deniable smirk into the corner of his mouth.

"I expect every term of the settlement to be followed," Davi said casually. "If they're not, if those checks are even a day late, I'm coming back here. You can take your chances then on getting a better deal than the one you got today."

Rosica's smirk melted away, and he blushed slightly.

"I understand," he said.

He turned and walked back into the courtroom, and Davi and Carpenter made for the elevator bank. Carpenter slid his sleeve back to check the time.

"He shouldn't be doing that, should he?" Davi asked.

"No, for many reasons," he said.

Davi went silent as they crossed into the empty elevator, and Carpenter cleared his throat loudly.

"If you think you're insulted, think about me. Floating something like that in front of your lawyer, like that's going to fly," he said.

"Prick," she said.

"Him? Or lawyers, in general?" he asked.

Davi turned, grabbed him by the shoulders, and shook him playfully.

"Everyone, Jeff! Everyone!"

The elevator slowed to a stop, and the doors rolled open with an automated ding. Carpenter straightened his tie and headed through the bustling crowd waiting to take the elevator back up.

"You heading out to celebrate, or is it straight to work for you?" he asked.

"Eh, I need the hours at work. I guess I could ask Allison to hang out afterwards. I've just been so nervous thinking about today that celebrating never occurred to me."

"I'd have a beer with you, but I'm stuck here until at least three."

"I don't drink," she said.

"Then, you're really out of luck," he said, pointing towards the men's room where he was headed. "I'll give you a call on Monday."

The restroom door swung closed behind him, and Davi continued down the corridor toward the front exit, past the security lines, finally stepping out into the sun.

Her stomach grumbled as the Legacy wound its way down the levels of the parking garage. She burped under her breath. Suddenly, making a beeline straight to work made less and less sense if she would have to stay off the clock to eat lunch as soon as she got there. She could feel the anxious adrenaline of the morning draining from her system, and the sharp pangs of hunger that were coming in its wake made up her mind that she would pull into the next restaurant that she remembered liking.

That was Graziano's, the white building with the lime green tiles all over its roof, probably fashioned to look like some caricature of a postcard from Tuscany. Davi hadn't eaten there in years, not since Victor used to take her there for dinner from time to time, but she hoped the ownership and menu was still the same.

Inside, the interior color design still had the black chairs and white tabletops that matched her memory. The servers still wore black slacks and button-down shirts. The only difference seemed to be the floor. What had once been carpet was now lustrous hardwood, and with the handsome gleam coming off the panels, she couldn't remember what color the carpet used to be. Davi folded her hands in front of her as a smiling waiter walked over.

"Hello," he said. "Just one for lunch?"

"Yes, but I have to get back to work soon," Davi said.

"No problem. The kitchen sends the food out really fast for business lunches, and you're here before the rush too."

The waiter turned to head into the other dining room with his menu.

"Wait," she said. "Could I have this table over here?"

He turned and looked at the empty section where she was pointing.

"Oh, sure," he said, escorting her over.

She pulled the seat under her and placed her purse on the floor next to her feet. The waiter handed her the menu.

"I'll give you a minute to look over—"

"No, I'm all set right now," she said.

"Fantastic," the waiter said, pulling out his pad. "Then, you'll really make it out of here fast."

"I'll have the chicken parmesan. No salad, soup, or anything extra. And please switch out whatever pasta it comes on for cappellini."

"Very good. That's not a lunch special, though. Just so you know," he said.

"No problem," she said.

"Okay, I'll put that in right now," he said, drifting towards the kitchen. "Something to drink?"

"Diet Coke with no lemon, please."

Glancing to her left, she saw the little blond boy in his booth shyly smiling at her while his parents talked about tedious grown-up things. He kicked his feet around excitedly when she smiled back. Behind her, the phlegmatic cough of a gruff, withered fellow crawled up her spine and chipped away at her appetite. Across from her, Victor casually reached out his hand and rested it on the white tabletop, palm up, asking for hers in return. He smiled and crossed his legs to the side.

"Diet Coke, no lemon," the waiter said, placing the glass on the table. "Chicken parm should be up in just a few minutes."

"Thank you. Would you take this other place setting away as well?"

"Oh, sorry about that. Just rushing too much," the waiter said, scooping up the plate, silverware, napkin, and glass.

"Not at all. Thank you very much," she said.

She reached down for her purse, grabbed it, thought twice, and placed it back down on the floor. Her palms rubbed together on her lap, and slowly, she could feel herself relax in the empty section of the restaurant. The bright sunlight coming through the window and bouncing off the black booth cushion made the little blond boy's face begin to feel grainy and disintegrated.

The waiter came back around the corner with a steaming plate, and Davi pushed her silverware to the side to make space.

"Pretty quick, right?" he said as he served the plate.

"Very fast. Thank the cooks for me," she said.

"Sure thing. Enjoy."

The salty butter in the steam drifted up her nose. She picked up her knife and fork and looked across the table at the empty chair and blank tabletop. Then, she spun her fork around in the bed of pasta, cut the chicken, and ate them both down at once. She sat back and grunted with delight. It was even better than she'd remembered. Her knife hurried to cut another piece as the hideous coughing behind her was gradually scrubbed out by a conversation at the front door between a waitress and two businessmen in suits who had been waiting to be seated.

Through the window, she could see the traffic building on the main route and waved at the waiter to get his attention. He raised his hand and nodded as he ran back into the kitchen from the other room. She was getting full anyway, and the rest would be good to heat up for dinner at home.

"Would you like a box for the rest?"

"Mm," Davi said, chewing down a mouthful. "Please. And the check. I'm just cutting it too close with getting back to work, you know?"

"I completely understand," he said, dropping the bill on the table. "I hope you enjoyed everything."

Back at Kellerman's, Davi strolled through the automatic doors and waved to Allison at the register. Allison paused her scanning and raised her eyebrows at her, and Davi smiled and nodded, pointing to the back of the store. Allison nodded excitedly, beaming up at the customer in front of her.

At the clock, Davi pulled her timecard from its gray metal slot on the wall. 'Davi Ross Wallace' was the name she'd written at the top, as she had since her first day. She reached for a blank card and picked up the pen in front of the clock. She wrote 'Davi Ross' across the top of the new one, but the words came out scrunched together, leaving conspicuously unused space at the end of the line. She ripped the new card in half, then quarters, and grabbed another replacement. This time, she controlled her strokes to make sure 'Davi Ross' filled the entire line and stamped the Friday slot with twelve twenty-one PM. She stapled the top of her new card, fastening it in front of the one she'd been using all week, and slid them both back into their spot on the wall.

21.

The humidity was getting thicker in the air with each July day, transforming every breath into sticky flypaper in her lungs. Wearing small summer clothes and feeling the sensation of air currents sweeping over her bare skin still felt bizarre, as though she was too exposed, even downright nude, but with the news having predicted a high of ninety-five by mid-afternoon, she'd given in and opted for khaki shorts and a white tank top to avoid melting into the asphalt as soon as she stepped out of the car.

On her way to Mills' office, she passed the turn that would have led to Victor's house, casually glancing down the innocent, shaded street before looking back at the road in front of her. She wondered how she had ever managed to muster the energy to clean that place every day from top to bottom. She wondered how Calvin, Monty, Zeke, Smokey, and Slick were and whether Victor and Karen were taking care of them. She wondered if they ever wondered about her.

A convection-oven blast of sauna air shot into the car, and Davi stepped out and closed the door.

"Oh, my poor hair," she said, feeling the humidity already digging into her curls and puffing them all up.

As soon as she passed inside, the office building's air conditioning cut through the smothering humidity, overcompensating with a chill, and Davi gratefully slipped on her long-sleeved knit cardigan as she walked towards the receptionist's desk where Janice was.   Having become accustomed to meeting with Mills at the end of the day when most of the office had gone home, Davi had forgotten about her altogether.

"Hey, Janice," Davi said, sliding up to the counter and resting her hip against it. "Long time, no see. I'm here for my two-thirty appointment with Doctor Mills."

Mills' office door was open, and Davi could hear him push his chair back to get up.

"Never mind, he—"

She turned her head back towards the counter, and Janice suddenly cupped her hands over her mouth and nose, her eyes glassy with tears.   Mills popped through the doorway with a smile that vanished when he saw Janice. He drew some tissues out of the box on the waiting room table and waved Davi into his office. She took a seat, and he came back in, closing the door behind him.

"Hey, I didn't say hardly anything to her," Davi explained. "I just told her we had an appointment."

"She hasn't seen you since your first few visits here, right?"

"Yeah."

"Suffice it to say you didn't leave a great impression on her at the time.   I don't think she can believe how much you've changed. Hell, sometimes I can't."

"Still seems odd.   We'd only ever even seen each other a few times," she said, dropping her purse next to her.

"Davi, not everyone does what you've done. Not everyone can."

She nodded in quiet reflection, and slowly, a mischievous smile crept across her face.

"You once told me you didn't think I had the guts for this sort of therapy," she said.

"Well, it worked, didn't it?"

"It made me mad," she admitted.

"Then, it worked," he said.

Davi smirked. Those gladiator days seemed long ago, Mills' office feeling so much bigger then. Rubbing her hand on the arm rest now, she felt like the room had shrunk or that she had grown in size, taking up more space than she remembered.

"So, I found a therapist who specializes in recovering from sexual abuse and trauma, and I like her. Mallory Heifet. Not sure if you know her," she said.

"I don't, but I'm sure she'll do fine. The main thing is that you're comfortable with her. That's an excellent start, I think."

She nodded and exhaled concertedly through her mouth, a new trick she'd recently discovered that somehow helped her eyes reabsorb budding tears.

"We're going to talk about some very heavy stuff, me and her. Things that I hid from you in here. Things I've never told anyone."

"How does that make you feel?" Mills asked.

"Pretty terrified."

"I think that's normal. You haven't—"

"But I know I have to do it," Davi interjected.

Mills opened his hands over his ink blotter, gesturing for her to explain.

"When something happened to me in that house, I used to tell myself that I wasn't my body, I was my mind, and I survived like that. But it's as true out here as it was in there, and my mind still isn't right. I can feel it. And if I don't get it right and understand what happened and what went wrong as best I can, then my body made it out but my mind didn't, and if my mind didn't make it out, then I never left."

Mills took a deep breath and cleared his throat.

"I'm glad Janice wasn't around to hear that," he said, rubbing the inside corners of his eyes with his index fingers.

"You're going soft on me, Doc," she said, unwrapping a stick of gum.

"Doc? What happened to 'Millsy'?"

She shrugged and popped up her eyebrows, offering the pack of gum his way. He reached over and took a piece, and Davi popped herself up in her seat and put her purse back on her lap.

"I want to thank you, Mills. I know that you do this for a living and that some other nutcase is going to walk in here starting from scratch as soon as I leave, but you made a difference in my life. I wanted you to know that."

"You made the difference, Davi. Nothing I did could ever have worked without your effort."

"Thank you anyway."

"You're welcome," he said.

Davi got to her feet and lifted her purse strap back onto her shoulder.

"Jesus, you're a pain in the ass. Just take the compliment next time," she said.

Mills laughed and got up to follow her out the door.

"Bye, Janice," Davi whispered, trying to avoid distracting her on the phone.

Janice smiled broadly and waved back.

"By the way, Mills, the art you have hanging around here is just awful. You should buy some of my pieces. I'll give you a call, and we'll make a deal."

Mills wandered out of the doorway to his office and into the waiting room to get a better look at them.

"They're not that bad, right? I've never even noticed them," he said.

"Exactly," Davi said, waving and walking back out into the safari heat.

She started the car and turned the knob for the air conditioner all the way up, letting the cold air roar into her face and flood the sweltering car. Before she backed out, she dug a tissue out of her purse and blotted the bottoms of her eyes gently. Things had started to go a little blurry when the office door had closed behind her, and she couldn't risk showing up to lunch with runny mascara. Mona would eat her alive.

She reclined the driver's seat a couple of notches and gripped the steering wheel towards the bottom, grunting and writhing her shoulders forward. If only she had gotten better sleep the previous night. She had come to expect a smattering of four hours of sleep throughout any given night, but the previous night felt more like two. As a result, the dull, nagging ache was alive in her upper back, attaching a little spike of pain to the end of every breath she took. She shallowed out her breathing as best she could to avoid the big inhales that would stretch her chest and force the tight spot to expand.

At a red light, she squirmed in her seat and arched her lower back forward, finally finding some relief. Ever since Victor's ambush at that party way back when, the little scorpion's tail had been there in her back, right between her shoulder blade and spine, always stinging worse when she could least afford the extra strain. Whatever he'd done that night, the pain seemed chronic, maybe nerve damage or a cracked bone that hadn't healed correctly. She grunted and found another position, stretching her head to the side in a way that felt like it was releasing the strain. When the light turned green, her foot went back on the gas, and she sat all the way back against the seat.

Davi parked and hurried into Desmond's, forgetting her cardigan on the passenger seat. If Mona had gotten there early as she had the last time, she might've been waiting twenty minutes already.

"Excuse me," Davi said to a waitress who crossed her path as soon as she stepped inside. "I'm meeting someone here. She kind of looks like me, except dorkier and less attractive."

"I think I know who you mean," the waitress said with a chuckle. "Right this way."

Just a few booths away, Mona was leafing through the menu, sipping her Sprite through a straw.

"Hey!" Davi said.

"Hey! Sit down, sit down. Good timing. I only got here a few minutes ago."

"Oh, fantastic. I thought I was late for sure."

"Could I get you something to drink?" the waitress asked Davi.

"What's your name, doll?" Davi asked while she placed her purse on the seat next to her.

"My name's Nancie."

"Okay, Nancie. I'll have a Diet Coke with no lemon please, and how do you like the corned beef sandwich?"

"I haven't had it myself, but it's very popular."

"I'll have that on seedless rye please," Davi said, raising her eyebrows at Mona.

Mona sat back and scrunched her face at the menu.

"And I thought I had a good ten more minutes to make up my mind with how you study these things," she said.

"I could give you some more time," Nancie said.

"No, it's fine," Mona said, closing the menu and handing it over. "I'll have the same thing."

"I've heard really good things about the corned beef sandwich here is why I was so sure. Very exciting," Davi said, clapping her hands quickly.

"So, tell me how you are," Mona said.

"Yeah, everything's been good. I feel really good too."

"I've got some clothes for you in the trunk. Don't let me leave without taking them because I'll turn around and drive all the way back. You know I will."

"I'll remember. And thank you. Really."

"Of course."

Nancie came back and placed Davi's Diet Coke on the table.

"Heard much from Mom and Dad lately?" Davi asked, taking the paper wrapping off her straw.

"Not since the wedding. I worry about how much Daddy drinks now, though. I don't think he's as in control of it as he pretends to be. I don't know why they don't just go to treatment. I mean, of course I understand why they don't, but I've known people who've gone through it. Seems like there's something to it."

Davi sipped her drink, imagining burned rubber tracks and twisted steel on the highway. Crashes were always linear and predictable in the forensics lab after the fact, but inside the cars at impact, drivers surely never saw them coming.

"I'm sure all of you sat around and wondered what the hell was wrong with me just this same way."

"Of course, we did," Mona said.

Davi nodded and unfolded her napkin onto her lap.

"It's not like I didn't know I looked insane way back when, you know. Of course, I knew, and if I had just woken up one morning like that out of nowhere, I'd have freaked out. You wind up there exactly because it doesn't happen all at once, and you don't think to stop it because you're too busy spending all of your time dreading what else you'll lose today. And that's how you die if you're not careful. In small bites."

"That's how my sandwich is gonna die in a few minutes, I can tell you that much," Mona said.

"Have you eaten anything today?"

"Not yet," Mona said, craning her head over the back of the booth to see the door to the kitchen. "And if Nancie comes back over here without at least a dinner roll, I'll chew her hand clean off."

"What about Declan?"

"He still has both of his hands."

"I'm asking how your married life has been," Davi said, smiling.

"Better than yours," Mona said with a wink.

Davi smacked the table and laughed. The silverware and glasses all clinked, and the bartender in the other room turned his head towards the noise.

"Like that's something to brag about," she said.

"No, everything's the same as it was. There's no difference from when we were just living together and not married. The wedding was this big party in the middle of it all, and then we came back to the same lives we'd left."

"And?"

"And nothing. It's wonderful. What can I say? I love that moron."

Davi smiled a little just before her lips caught the straw in her soda. For only having danced with Declan the one time at the wedding, she felt strangely proud of him.

"How's divorced life?" Mona asked.

"Just as fabulous in the opposite direction," Davi said.

Nancie came out of the kitchen carrying two identical plates and placed them on the table in front of Davi and Mona along with some extra napkins. Mona reached for the mustard.

"I can't wait. It looks amazing," Mona said.

"It really does."

Suddenly, she started to feel slightly short of breath, and a light, cold sweat was coming through on the back of her neck.

"You need the mustard?" Mona asked, gesturing with the bottle.

"Please."

Davi took the toothpicks out of each end of the sandwich and pulled the bread off. The rising panic tingled its way into her chest as she picked up the mustard bottle. She was asking a lot of herself with these two appointments in only a tank top and shorts. She scooted forward until the bare backs of her thighs were no longer touching the vinyl seat.

"Fuck me. It's awesome," Mona said, chewing a bite.

"That's what I've heard."

"You saving yours or something?"

"Just for a second," Davi said.

Mona took another ravenous bite and concentrated on her sandwich. Davi was grateful for Mona's silence, quietly leaving her to handle whatever she needed to do. Once they'd discovered that she was in the midst of a panic attack, most would have wanted to help solve it, as though her marionette strings were in their hands instead of hers.

"Have you been painting?" Mona asked.

"I have actually," Davi said, delighted by the subject change into something non-frivolous.

"What's the latest one you did?"

"It's not done yet, but I love it so far. The sky is gray in the background, and the scene is all through the top of this massive tree, above where the trunk stops. Everything's bare, and right in this tangled nest of branches is this cardinal minding his own business."

"So, the color is all gray and brown—"

"And dreary. Except for this little red cardinal in the corner who's just sort of hanging out by himself," Davi said.

"I bet the color really pops. From the contrast."

"It does. Catches the eye, I think," Davi said while she put the mustard bottle back down and closed up both halves of her sandwich.

"How do you come up with what you want to put on a canvas anyway?"

"Sometimes, you get lucky, and the whole image comes to you at once. More often, you're focusing on one color you want to use or a certain vibe you want it to have, and you slowly build up all the detail around that."

The sweat on the back of her neck was drying, and she was back to being hungry. Hearing her voice speak aloud was helping, as though her brain had given up the panic simply because it couldn't do both things at once. She picked up a half of the sandwich and tucked some of the loose shreds of corned beef back between the rye.

"Damn," she said after a bite.

"Right?"

"Mm-hm."

"I love when the meat is cut this thin. Attention to detail," Mona said, raising her index finger. "That's the sign of a quality establishment."

Nancie looked over at their table with a platter of dishes resting on her shoulder. Davi held up her hand to say that everything was fine.

"You know, I've been thinking," Davi said.

"Yeah? What about?"

"Just about everything that happened with Victor in order to have some things ready to discuss with Doctor Heifet—"

"When do you see her again?"

"Next Tuesday."

Mona nodded as she chewed.

"Anyway, when I've been thinking things over, I don't understand why people keep saying that I wasn't responsible for what happened to me. Everyone keeps saying that. 'It wasn't your fault.' 'You were an innocent victim.' Everyone keeps saying that to me."

"What about it?"

"I don't understand why my being made a victim can't be my fault. Saying that makes it feel like I never had a chance against these big, scary men, that I was just some weak woman by nature," Davi said.

"I don't think that's what they're saying," Mona said.

"Maybe not, but they're implying it. Wasn't my fault? Wasn't my fault?!" she half-yelled before collecting herself. "I married this guy willingly and stayed with him for seven years. How much more at fault can I be when I let someone like that in my life?"

"Yeah, but you didn't know he was that way," Mona said.

"I found out. I think knowing who he was before he got that close to me was also my responsibility, but regardless, I found out. And I still let things go wrong for years."

"Okay," Mona said, staring at the last bits of her sandwich.

"So, what the hell?"

Mona sighed through her nose and shrugged.

"It's touchy, Davi. Most of the time, people don't know what to say if this subject comes up, just in general. No one wants to think about these things or these sorts of people."

Davi waved her hand at Mona in frustration and picked up her napkin.

"I'm sick of it. It's making me feel crazy," she said.

"Why are you so keen on taking responsibility here anyway?"

"How am I supposed to make sense of what went wrong otherwise? Without that, this whole thing becomes about Victor and his buddies and their actions, and I don't want this part of my life to read that way. It's not about them. This is about me. Even if it's about me at my worst, it's about me."

"What about their behavior?" Mona asked.

"They made their choices too. They had their own responsibilities. I think they all knew that they were hurting me, and they did it anyway. They've got their own garbage to root through."

Mona poked at the sliced pickle on her plate with one of the toothpicks from her sandwich.

"As long as you don't think that you deserved it."

Davi placed her sandwich down and rubbed her eyes, feigning that she had something in one of them that was bothering her. She wanted to be frustrated but also knew that Mona would never intentionally misunderstand her.

"Do you really think that that's what I'm saying?" Davi asked calmly. "No one deserves what I went through."

"I didn't think that's what you were saying, but I just wanted to make sure," Mona said.

"I didn't deserve any of it. But I did let someone into my life that wound up hurting me, and I can blame anyone for that. I can blame Victor and the rest of them. I can blame Mom and Dad. I can blame whoever. But how does that help me? I'm still left with me, and blame doesn't help unless it shows me how to avoid this ever happening again. Otherwise, blame is just a total waste of my time. I think I've thrown enough of that away already, don't you?"

Mona dropped her napkin on the plate and sipped her drink.

"I wasn't some bystander watching everything happen to me, by the way. I felt like I was, but I wasn't. Now, I realize that was a big reason I went off the rails in the first place. I didn't feel responsible for what was happening to me, and so, I didn't feel empowered to do anything to help myself. I'm not going back in the box for these people who think they're helping. Not even if this 'not responsible' thing supposedly suits me now," Davi said.

Mona didn't respond, but the stormy, suspicious look that had spread over her face a few minutes earlier was gone.

"I know I'm just dumping all this on you, but you're the only person I can talk to this way. Thank you for letting me get it out," Davi said.

"It's fine. I'm curious, though. You take these things on your shoulders in the way that you're saying, and what's the payoff for it? What's the reward?"

Davi chewed a bite down and scrunched her face in ecstasy.

"This is the best sandwich I've ever had."

"Yeah, mine was definitely really good too," Mona said, pushing her plate away from her a little.

"No," Davi said, looking up. "I mean this is the greatest thing I've ever fucking tasted, and it's got nothing to do with how thin they cut the meat. Today is the reward. Sitting here with you right now is the reward. Getting to live again when I thought I was dead. That's the reward. What's going to be better than that? What more could I possibly want?"

Mona leaned forward onto her elbows and reflected. Her eyes snapped back onto Davi's.

"Feel like some dessert?"

Davi smiled and dropped her chin to her chest. The kitchen doors behind Mona flew open, and out came Nancie who paused in front of the doorway for a moment, seemed to remember something, then went back inside.

"Yes," she said.

E.

Davi grabbed her cartoon bumblebee mug out of the coffee machine and fanned her face with her hand.

Christ, it's barely sunup, she thought.

The apartment wasn't cooling down at night, and the summer heat was totaling up in there in a way that left her feeling sapped all day long. Pulling her little fan over to the table and plugging it in, she tried to cool off from the shower by putting the cold milk carton against her forehead.

She leafed through the flyers and junk mail she'd left on the table the night before, casually trying her luck on running into a good deal on an air conditioning unit, when suddenly the phone rang next to her coffee mug. The hour of the call made her wonder.

"Hello?"

The caller didn't respond. Gurgling, watery sounds came through the receiver instead. Whoever it was, they sounded like they'd been sobbing.

"Who is this?"

"Me."

"Victor?"

"Yeah."

He was barely choking out single syllables before a spasm would cut him off.

"How did you get this number?" she asked, incredulous.

Now, she was going to have to change her unlisted number again, call everyone she knew, and make them take down another one. She shook her head in frustration.

"Well, what is it then? What's the matter?"

"I just— I just—," he managed to get out between heaving gasps for air.

His despair began to make her feel ill. That the emotion was capable of growing to that size made her head spin.

"Just take some deep breaths, and tell me what's going on."

Victor fought to breathe deeply and blew his nose.

"I just— I need you to forgive me," he said, still sounding quivery and congested.

Davi slid her coffee away from the whirring fan so it wouldn't get cold while it waited.

"Is that what this is about? You need me to forgive you?"

"I don't know if I can take it, unless you forgive me, just— for everything."

She sighed and shook her head.

"Victor, I've already forgiven you. I forgave you even before I walked out the door for the last time. Don't you understand that?"

The other end of the line fell silent, even the sniffling, and she knew he didn't understand.

"You need to forgive yourself for what's happened between us. It doesn't have anything to do with me, Victor. I doubt it ever did."

Davi was sure he hadn't slept. It didn't seem natural for a person to wake up at that hour just to be instantly consumed by a torrent of remorse. This was the sort of anguish that needed time awake to develop, cut off from the comforting escape of nightmares.

"You're probably right," he finally said.

"And maybe things don't have to go that way with Karen. Maybe you can be different with her," she said.

She could hear him searching for something to say, but nothing came as he exhaled into the phone. In the corner of her eye, the clock on the wall was just a few ticks away from quarter to eight.

"Are you okay?" she asked.

"Yeah, I think I'll be alright."

"Well, I've got to go. My coffee is getting cold, and I've got to get to work."

"Yeah, alright. I'm sorry," he said weakly.

"I believe you," she said. "Take care."

She hung up and slid the phone onto the kitchen table. The towel she had around her body was making her sweaty. She let it drop onto the chair as she stood up, and her fan blew the apartment's swamp air all over her.

Her coffee mug was still hot to the touch. Droplets of water tumbled down her spine and shoulders as she unwrapped the towel she had tied around her head. Sliding the mug over the surface of the wood, she arched her foot and cracked her toes against the carpet. Then, she poured the milk.

About the Author

Christopher Krzeminski is 33 years old at the time of this book's publication. He holds a B.A. in Mathematics from Duke University in Durham, NC and a J.D. from The University of Alabama School of Law in Tuscaloosa, AL. He currently resides in New Jersey.

Christopher may be contacted for questions or comments by email at chris.krzeminski1@gmail.com or on Twitter @CEKBooks.

www.ingramcontent.com/pod-product-compliance
Lightning Source LLC
LaVergne TN
LVHW041211080426
835508LV00011B/906